POLICING THE CITY

BOSTON 1822–1885

*A Publication of the Center for the Study of the
History of Liberty in America*

Harvard University

Policing the City

Boston 1822-1885

Roger Lane

HARVARD UNIVERSITY PRESS

Cambridge, Massachusetts

1967

*The Center for the Study of the History of Liberty in America
is aided by a grant from the Carnegie Corporation of New York*

To My Wife

Foreword

By Oscar Handlin

The growth of the nineteenth-century city created a painful dilemma for Americans who clung to republican views of power. Attitudes shaped by the intimate experience of small towns and rural counties were inappropriate to the great metropolitan centers that grew rapidly in population after 1830. The adjustment was difficult and slow.

The history of their colonial past had taught Americans that paid bodies of government officers were threats to popular liberty. Revolutionary rhetoric had warned the patriots about the dangers of professional placemen; people who held office for its own sake were open to corruption and acquired an unhealthy lust for power. The only safe course in a republic was to retain power where it belonged, in the hands of the citizens themselves. All necessary public functions could be performed by men temporarily designated to do so for a limited term by their fellows.

Faith in rotation in office had been adequate so long as the problems of order were simple and manageable. Each individual was his own best defender. Violations of the law could be controlled by the citizens' own instruments of detection and punishment—the sheriff's posse, the constable, and the grand jury.

The problem changed when the community increased in size to the point at which the old means of control were inadequate. Order in cities which numbered their population in the hundreds of thousands called for the services of men who devoted full time to their task, were therefore paid, and were selected for their expertise. Yet to bring into being a professional police force was to create precisely the kind of hireling body considered dangerous by conventional political theory. The result was a significant interplay of social, political, and intellectual forces that endowed American cities with a distinctive type of police force, quasi-military, professional, yet subject to civilian political control.

This evolution followed a particularly interesting course in Boston. That community at the opening of the nineteenth century was still relatively homogeneous, small, and able to govern itself by the traditional town meeting. After 1820, it grew in area, population, and complexity, and it was transformed by immigration and industrialization. Its effort to cope with the problem of the police illuminates a significant facet of American development which historians have hitherto neglected.

Contents

POLICING THE CITY

BOSTON 1822–1885

Introduction

The words "police" and "politics" are both derived from the Greek noun meaning "city." In the United States, the close association among the three terms provides a special challenge to the historian. This book was originally conceived as a study of the effect of police on civil liberties. It soon became clear, however, that the very character of police work made it undesirable to abstract any such single issue. During the formative years of the nineteenth century the business of an urban police department covered so great a range of politically sensitive local affairs that its development was inextricably part of the wider history of the city.

This study is intended then as a contribution to the already considerable literature on the history of Boston. But it is intended equally to suggest some more general conclusions. The important particularities of American municipal police systems do not obscure the basically similar pattern of their development. The precise terminal dates 1822 and 1885 have a uniquely local significance, but the period encompassed is of equal importance in all the major eastern cities. Each, at the beginning, had several kinds of officials serving various police functions, all of them haphazardly inherited from the British and colonial past. These agents were gradually drawn into better defined and more coherent organizations. At the same time, the exchange of information and ideas led to an increasing standardization among cities, symbolized by the almost universal adoption of uniform blue. By the end of the period, the era of flux and experiment was over, and the functions of the police had acquired a familiar and settled character not only in New York, Philadelphia, Brooklyn, Baltimore, and Boston, but in the newer cities all over the country which followed their example.

As increasing communication and imitation were the means, common experience was the most important factor in the resemblance among cities. Immigration, interdependence, new economic functions and social standards were all aspects of the most fundamental com-

1

mon experience, the process of growth. In Boston and elsewhere, the struggle to deal with the complex manifestations of growth was the theme which united all others.

The rapid increase in population called for continual expansion of such basic police functions as patrol and inspection. New municipal services were demanded as the tasks of government grew not merely larger but more complicated; changing behavior accompanied the rise in numbers. Cities were frightening places to many contemporaries. Rootless visitors and residents freed from the old restraints required new and sometimes harsh methods of control. The same people, on the other hand, were markedly dependent upon authority, inclined to turn to law and government in situations which had earlier been handled informally. And the availability of police called forth by these conditions helped create another, intellectual, dimension to growth. As the actual physical power of government increased, many citizens caught glimpses of an even greater potential. In combining older ideas of the authority of the state with a nineteenth-century faith in progress, they enlarged their expectations and hoped to use the law not merely to control behavior but forcibly to improve it.

Whatever their form, the problems of police were all subject to the political process. Some were settled without public attention, either because of indifference or because of general agreement. Other matters were discussed prosaically in terms of costs, efficiency, and relative need. But even at the most routine levels, there were reminders that the business of police was unusually sensitive. The men were everywhere, the most visible and widely used agents of government. And while force was properly only an instrument of authority, it had the capacity to affect ends as well. In some areas, involving powerful emotions and interests on both sides, the men who made the decisions were acutely conscious of their importance, and debated in fundamental terms of right and liberty, the proper scope of government, and the purpose of the law in a democracy. This study is the record of the way in which the decisions were made and the uses of force defined in Boston.

CHAPTER ONE

From Town to City:
The Police in 1822

On the twenty-third of February, 1822, the General Court of Massachusetts hesitantly approved an act to incorporate the municipality of Boston. The final decision was left to the voters, whose ratification would make the act law and the town a city. Legislators and citizens were both aware of the heavy weight of tradition. The town meeting had served their predecessors from colonial times through revolution and into the commonwealth period. The state had never chartered a "city"; the corporate municipality was widely suspect as of English origin, the nursery of monopolists and aristocrats. But it was clear to many residents that the familiar system had become archaic. The incorporation movement had been debated continually for nearly forty years. And Boston had finally to decide upon the need for "alterations in the present government of the police."[1]

This demand for improvement in the "police of the town" was at once inclusive and particular. In late federalist New England, the dual lines of descent toward the modern uses of the word "police" were already apparent. To Noah Webster, in 1828, the term was synonymous with the entire "government of a city or town," "the corporation or body of men governing a city." At the same time it was used increasingly in the less general sense, "the administration of the laws and regulations of a city . . . as the police of Boston," or "officer entrusted with the execution of the laws of a city." And in both senses, the need for change was evident.[2]

But the change was difficult to face. Bostonians had already several times rejected the movement to abandon their traditional system of direct democracy. The town meeting, however awkward, was the scene and symbol of revolutionary glory, and was symbolic also of a valued pattern of government. Since the seventeenth century there had

3

been marked changes in the nature and extent of the community controls exercised by church and class, family and education; the meeting had itself abandoned old functions and taken on new ones. But the forms were still familiar. And the relation between citizens and local authority remained both constant and intimate.[3]

Throughout the eighteenth century Boston probably enjoyed the most vital local government in the English-speaking world. Consent and cooperation were assured through the meeting, in which suffrage requirements based on taxation were widely met. All the town's officials—selectmen, constables, and fenceviewers—were elected there annually, a fact which enabled them to work effectively with a minimum of the means of coercion. The selectmen were recognized representatives of the social and financial elite and commanded respect with an authority wider than their office. Hogreeves and hay-weighers, in a town which in 1800 still numbered less than twenty-five thousand, were familiar to those with whom they dealt. The process of rotation, of part-time, amateur employment, made a reality of the concept of public service. And where officials did not reach, the citizens themselves, through the machinery of petition, complaint, and information, acted continuously as agents of administration.[4]

But this system, depending upon community relationships increasingly upset by changes in the nature as well as the size of the population, was not infinitely adaptable. Signs of strain were evident by the 1780's. Attendance at meetings, which at mid-century had varied usually between 250 and 400, became in later years erratic. Only a handful of officials and citizens appeared on ordinary occasions, while shouting crowds made the procedure difficult when more controversial matters were scheduled. By 1799, growth and shifting residential patterns made it necessary, in order to preserve the sense of intimacy, to bypass the meeting and elect certain officers by wards. Others, in the succeeding decades, became appointive. Local leaders complained that the increasing number of strangers and immigrants weakened the former sense of community. As the town spread out, distance contributed to indifference, while the varying sources of authority complicated the business of administration.[5]

Lapses in the conduct of the police, as more narrowly defined, added to the growing discontent with the system as a whole. Bostonians recognized two branches to the police, one concerned with matters of public health and the other with public order. And both were sensitive to the disturbing changes affecting the government as a whole.

Since the seventeenth century the town and colony had been concerned with protecting the public health. In dealing with some problems, Boston followed traditional principles inherited from late Tudor legislation. Methods of quarantining vessels and visitors developed through experience, with little dissent. Other issues were political, and the regulation of butchery, inoculation, and street-cleaning procedures all generated heated debates in the meeting. The selectmen, as in other matters, were the chief agents of execution, occasionally acting on the advice of physicians.[6]

But this system proved inadequate during a yellow fever epidemic in 1798; the next year the legislature provided for a board of health, elected by wards, to give continuous attention to the sanitary and medical problems only intermittently treated by the selectmen. The new board proved valuable both in improving the execution of older regulations and in developing new ones. Smallpox, the most feared of epidemic diseases, was controlled finally under its direction. The board administered quarantine equitably and well. And with a concern for the cleanliness of cellars, yards, and privies, as well as for the public streets and markets, it showed the way for new standards of sanitation. Boston's bills of mortality reflected its success; between 1812 and 1821 deaths averaged some twenty-two per thousand, relatively low for American cities in this period.[7]

But despite conscientious efforts, there was no real diminution in this death rate between 1799 and 1822. In part this was the result of the Augean nature of the task. As the population grew from less than twenty-five to nearly fifty thousand, living space in the central city grew proportionately more scarce. In 1795 Boston had been the first large American city to build an aqueduct, but backyard wells, increasingly contaminated, remained a more important source of water. Poor fire laws encouraged the spread of crowded wooden buildings, often breeding grounds for infection. Privies, "house dirt," and street refuse multiplied; sewers, still privately maintained, overflowed into the thoroughfares.[8]

The problem of growth was more than physical. The device of election by wards was not an adequate substitute for the intimacy of the eighteenth-century community. The board of health, while extending the range of its concern to include conditions in private houses, was not able correspondingly to extend its authority. In cases of extreme nuisance it had considerable formal powers of coercion. But board members, still part-time amateurs, found it difficult in practice to enforce regulations. There were no regular agents, no sanitary police, to take the initiative in searching out violations. The old process of complaint followed by investigation was especially unworkable in the most crowded sections of the town, where the inhabitants, living together in equally squalid conditions, found no reason to inform on each other.[9]

However well protected from epidemic disease, Boston smelled worse than ever before. This condition, together with controversy over the medical theories it propounded, involved the board of health in the debates surrounding the incorporation movement. Opponents of the town meeting found ready evidence in the air that the problems of health police could not be met under existing arrangements.[10]

Similar criticisms were leveled at the official agencies for the control of disorderly and criminal behavior. Here also change had made endemic problems increasingly obvious to the senses. Boston in 1822 contained no real class of professional criminals. Nor was it troubled by serious riots. The total number of criminal court cases, averaging about two thousand a year, was not rising markedly. The nearly fifty annual felony convictions, while relatively high as compared with later decades, were not cause for public concern.[11]

And yet the state of the public peace was disturbing to many. Two-thirds of criminal convictions were obtained in four categories, all involving highly visible offenses: common drunkenness, vagabondage, assault and battery, lewd and lascivious behavior. Boston was especially sensitive to unruly conduct. Within the narrow limits of the old peninsula it was more difficult than in other cities to isolate or ignore the areas in which vice and disorder reigned. Few could any longer maintain the walled protection of the country estate within the town. Neighborhoods were not clearly separated, and new construction made it more than ever difficult to draw the lines of privacy. The most notorious district, "Nigger Hill," was just behind Beacon Hill in the increasingly fashionable West End. And leading citizens complained that they witnessed unpleasant scenes while they passed the Common on social errands or through the North End on business.[12]

The same process which made disorder less tolerable also undermined the traditional means of dealing with it. The formal agencies

of control, the justices of the peace, sheriffs, constables, and watchmen, were all derived from the English, pre-urban past. Their effectiveness, in Massachusetts, depended upon the same conditions which
made the town meeting workable. Through the eighteenth century the
use of legal force was ordinarily a direct response to the demands of
private citizens for help. The victim of robbery or assault called a
watchman, if available, and afterward applied to a justice for a
warrant and a constable to make or aid in the arrest. The business of
detection was largely a private matter, with initiative encouraged
through a system of rewards and fines paid to informers. Neither state
nor town made any provision for the identification or pursuit of the
unknown offender, except through the coroner's inquest.[13]

By 1822 the kind of cooperation and consensus required under
such a loosely organized system was largely lacking. The number of
convictions for felony demonstrated that citizens deeply injured by
the desperate or hasty acts which accounted for most serious crime
could still find means of apprehending the guilty. But casual violence,
petty larceny, and especially vice, which injured no individual in
particular, posed a different set of problems. Under existing practice
justice could not be applied where it was not sought. In districts
inhabited by new arrivals and transients, the vicious, intimidated, or
uncomprehending, the agents of law were only occasional visitors,
controlling little and simply exciting resentment. The various peace
officers, without unified direction, were inadequate to the task of
police.[14]

The most distinguished of these officials, and for police purposes
the least useful, was the sheriff of Suffolk County. His office, introduced into Massachusetts in 1692, had in the succeeding one hundred
and thirty years already assumed its modern outlines. The sheriff,
assisted by his deputies, was charged with the execution of all warrants
directed to him, civil and criminal. Under the common law, reinforced
by the statutes of the commonwealth, he shared with other peace
officers special powers of arrest without warrant. He had in addition
certain legal duties in case of riot. But the structure of his interests did
not make him an important agent in the detection or prevention of
crime.[15]

A county officer, appointed by the governor, the sheriff maintained
his independence of the town authorities charged with the superintendence of police. Operating essentially as a free agent, he enjoyed

both security and opportunity. In practice, during the early nineteenth century, the appointment was for life. And in an address to the bar delivered in 1829, Sheriff Charles P. Sumner noted that while his English counterpart held a merely honorary position, his own was "one of profit and of honor." Even the job of deputy would be worthy of "a lawyer in the middle rank," and was "often filled by gentlemen of high rank in the militia and in the legislature of our commonwealth." The attractions were liberal enough. The basic income, in addition to jailer's fees, was three dollars a day for attendance at court. And to this was added a schedule of fees and expenses for over a dozen different kinds of service.[16]

This schedule mapped the road to profit, with directions clearly marked. The biggest gains lay in serving personal civil actions; the sheriff collected 4 per cent of damages and costs in judgments of up to one hundred dollars, 2 per cent between one and two hundred, and 1 per cent of all over two hundred dollars. The fee for the service of criminal warrants, just thirty cents, was no more than those for several kinds of routine civil writs, and less than some. The official charge to private parties for "Sheriff's aid in criminal cases, to each person for every twelve hours attendance, and in proportion for a greater or less time" was only one dollar. Such a schedule did not encourage arrests on the sheriff's own initiative without warrant, which could be financially as well as physically hazardous. Working always in an atmosphere of litigation, Sumner was ever conscious that "the loss of an hour may outweigh the profits of years." A series of decisions had affirmed the indivisibility of his office; responsible for the actions of all of his deputies, in cases of assault, escape, false arrest, and negligence, the successful sheriff had to be prudent. Any case involved the calculation of risks. And when the possible reward weighed only thirty cents, or perhaps eight and one-half cents an hour, the pursuit of profit was easily distinguished from the pursuit of crime. Sheriff Sumner's own attitude was demonstrated in his twenty-two-page address on the duties of his office, in which he found it only once necessary to use the word "criminal." The routine business of police simply did not occupy or concern him.[17]

Some of the conditions which limited the sheriff's interest in police work also applied to the several constables of the city. In Massachusetts, unlike Great Britain, these officials were empowered to serve civil as well as criminal processes; they were "little sheriffs," acting on the town or parish rather than the county level. The statutes defining the two offices were similar, and the schedule of fees nearly identical. But in Boston the difference involved more than scale. While limited by law and custom, the constables could make some adjustment to new conditions and perform certain useful police services.[18]

The office, in Massachusetts, was coeval with local government and essential to it. The constable acted as the messenger and symbol of authority not only as an arresting officer but as part of the machinery of town meetings and elections. During the eighteenth century, and in smaller towns even later, the job was as unpopular as it was important, and the first four sections of the basic statute dealt with the difficult business of catching a constable. But in Boston, constabulary duty was a busy and desirable occupation in itself, rather than a part-time drain on some other means of livelihood. In 1802 it was one of the first of the traditional town offices to be made appointive. The number of constables was left to the selectmen, who chose them at will, often annually. Thus, while the constables usually acted on their own, or as servants of the courts, they were ultimately responsible to the town authorities, who were concerned not with civil suits but with the performance of police duty.[19]

Constables were sometimes employed directly, "in the service of the town," for protection on potentially riotous occasions. They also served regularly as officers of the watch. In their remaining time, they were less tempted than the sheriff to neglect police for civil business. The constables received no jailer's fees, and only two dollars a day for attendance at court. More important, they were limited to personal civil actions involving less than seventy dollars. As heirs of the largely defunct office of tythingman, they were specifically charged with instituting complaints involving gambling, swearing, and violation of the Lord's Day. With standard witness fees ranging from fifty cents to one dollar, duty sometimes joined with interest to make criminal business a relatively important source of income.[20]

Some of this income was obtained in a manner unrecognized in law. Boston's twenty-four constables, with one exception, had all been drawn from the ranks of small business and the skilled trades. But by 1822, they were no longer expected to rotate in office, and were in fact becoming professionals, reappointed from year to year. As officers of the watch and of the courts, all acquired some sense of the customs and appearance of habitual criminal offenders. And over a quarter of them, before appointment, had been "grocers" or liquor dealers, men unusually familiar with criminal associations and sources of information. The total of the official income open to constables was not enough to assure all of them a proper livelihood; in 1821-22 the twenty-four received $3,694.90 from the county in the form of legal and court fees, and $792.00 from the town for police service. The need to supplement this income pool complemented the need, in what was increasingly a city of strangers, for some kind of detective service. A system at the least of private tips and rewards could fulfill both functions, quite substantially in the case of constables like George Reed, recalled by a later reporter as the greatest thief-taker of the 1820's. "The secret of his wonderful success, so it was said, was in his having in his employ parties who were in his power, whose liberty and in some cases, it was intimated, their permission to ply their vocation, depended upon the value of the information they were able to furnish him." While such practices remained extralegal, they were important and capable of expansion.[21]

Service on the nightly watch, meanwhile, remained the most important police function that the town regularly required of its constables. Men of experience and discretion, familiar with the law, were needed to supervise the "jaded stevedore, journeyman, and mechanic" who patrolled the streets at night. The watch in Boston, dating from 1634, was as old as the constabulary, and the association of the two was traditional. Both offices shared a reputation for unpleasantness; in the case of watchmen, as of constables, the statutes indicated that recruitment was normally a kind of draft. All males over eighteen were liable, with the exception of justices of the peace, selectmen, ministers, and sheriffs; those refusing to serve were required to furnish suitable substitutes. The responsibilities were simple but onerous. The basic act, still in most essentials applicable to modern policemen, required the men to "see that all disturbances and disorders in the night shall be prevented and suppressed." For that purpose, the watch had "authority to examine all persons, whom they have reason to suspect of any unlawful design, and to demand of them their business abroad at such time, and whither they are going; to enter any house of ill-fame for the purpose of suppressing any riot or disturbance." All persons so arrested were to be secured and taken the next morning before "one of the nearest justices of the peace, to be examined and proceeded against according to the nature of their offenses." The watchmen were to "walk the rounds in and about the streets, wharves, lanes, and principal inhabited parts, within each town, to prevent any danger by fire, and to see that good order is kept, taking particular observation and inspection of all houses and families of evil fame." In Boston, one further duty was added to this list; the head constable, or captain of the watch, was also customarily appointed superintendent of lamps, and a number of the men were charged with lighting and caring for these.[22]

Boston's size and the character of its population gave the problem of recruitment a special character. Only Boston, by a statute of 1801, was required to keep the watch continuously. Elsewhere the law was only permissive, and in smaller places the patrol was regarded as an emergency, almost military, arrangement. Boston, since it paid for the service, had no difficulty finding applicants. If the wage was low, fifty cents for a night's work, its regularity made it attractive as a supplement or even substitute for daytime income. But the men thus recruited were often a source of complaint. Watch duty in practice was a routine job, not an occasional public duty, and was especially inviting to the insecure and casually employed. The aged or sleepy watchman had been a stock joke since Shakespeare and before, and the danger in low standards was evident. To ensure responsibility the commonwealth required that at least one householder be included in each watch, and Boston's regulations provided further that all must be married taxpayers and voters. But at the existing pay rates these regulations often failed, and the personnel problem remained.[23]

Fiscal conservatism held down the numbers as well as the pay of watchmen. About eighty were appointed each year. Thirty-six worked each night, in two shifts, so that no more than eighteen went out at once. These were distributed in four stations, in order to get a fair geographical coverage of the central city, so that four men at a time patrolled the north and south divisions and five the east and west. The patrol lasted from 10:00 or 10:30 P.M. until sunup; while one half went on active duty, the others were in theory able to sleep. In practice, as the men on patrol were supposed to cover their beats every hour, they might shortly return with prisoners, whom their fellows had to guard, and to endure, until the constable in charge chose to take them to the jail on Leverett Street. South Boston, separated by water from the main peninsula, was not provided with watchmen, in part because it lacked jail facilities. The watch was often assaulted, and an attempt at night to transport prisoners by boat or bridge would leave them open to ambush by rescue parties.[24]

Many merchants supplemented this skeletal force out of their own resources. The town routinely granted warrants to privately paid watchmen, who exercised full powers over limited areas, reporting each morning to the captain of the watch. Store owners occasionally joined together to hire full private patrols. But for the majority, the public watch had to suffice. Armed with rattles for summoning help, and largely useless billhooks for collaring offenders, the men were simply "to report any thing out of order," and to respond to appeals for help. Only minimal services could be provided in practice, with the emphasis first on the protection of property from fire, and only second on the protection of persons from violence.[25]

But the watch had other interests which were not so widely approved. The members, like constables and other citizens, were entitled to witness fees when they appeared to testify in court. Such payment, designed to compensate for loss of time, equalled or exceeded their official wages, and was especially open to abuse when they lacked well-paid employment in the daytime. While the sheriff was reluctant to institute criminal complaints, the watch might be, in minor cases, too eager. Thus the agents of police, not only inefficient and limited in aim, were often an irritant to the problems they were in part designed to control. Josiah Quincy, Boston's most popular politician, complained that the helpless knew "justice chiefly in the hands of men, whom experience teaches them to consider as on the watch after opportunities of gain, from their vices; as making profit out of their passions, and as interested to enhance their losses and miseries."[26]

There was a deeply rooted problem expressed in Sheriff Sumner's complaint that the peace officers of Boston no longer dared to exercise their right to call upon the citizens for aid in making arrests. This complaint, in turn, was the symptom of an even deeper difficulty, one not confined to the agencies of police. The town's firewards, also, by 1822, were finding it difficult to organize bystanders into the traditional bucket brigades. The justices of the peace, once essential to local government, had been shown in a series of votes to have lost the respect and confidence of the majority. Many community leaders, upset by recent political embarrassments, were concerned about the practice of direct democracy.[27]

Problems of this order indicated that whatever its title, Boston was no longer a town in the old sense, governed by natural leaders and administered by recognized householders and neighbors. The debate over incorporation often centered about specific points, smells and costs and sidewalks, the desirability of taking over the functions of Suffolk County. Both sides talked of factions and demagogues; nostalgia for the revolutionary past was matched with visions of progress. But in a fundamental if inchoate way the debate was in fact about the changing nature of the community, and the relevance of the assumptions under which it was governed.[28]

On March 4 the voters finally ratified the act of incorporation, 2,797 to 1,881. Acceptance in itself solved few specific problems. While eliminating the board of health and many of the separate county agencies, the new charter was primarily concerned not with substance but with form. It provided for a mayor, eight aldermen elected at large, and forty-eight common councillors elected by wards. Beyond this it promised no new powers, except insofar as the administrative duties of the county justices of the peace were absorbed. The new title, the replacement of "town" with "city," was as important as anything else in the act. While it was not fully clear what this meant, the achievement of municipal status was in itself a challenge and a stimulus to experiment in the police of Boston.[29]

CHAPTER TWO

Change and Conservatism:
The City Marshal and the
Great Mayor, 1822-1829

The years immediately after the incorporation of Boston were marked by vigorous growth, as the population increased from approximately forty-nine thousand in 1822 to nearly sixty thousand in 1829. This rate of expansion, maintained since the end of the eighteenth century, continued to create problems for the police. These problems had already contributed to the movement for the new charter. But the charter itself had been opposed by a strong minority. Further innovation in "the government of the police" was resisted. As a result, important changes were made only because of a powerfully assertive leadership of a familiar and traditional kind.

The dispute over the adoption of the city charter was reflected again in Boston's first municipal election, in April of 1822. The leading candidates for the mayoralty, Josiah Quincy and Harrison Grey Otis, were both well-known Federalists, men of strong views, one a former opponent of the change in government and the other a supporter. When neither won the required majority, both followed custom and withdrew. But, while the indecision revealed in this deadlock was real, it was not so deep as to paralyze for long the political development of the city.[1]

The immediate impasse was easily solved, as both factions united on a third Federalist, John Phillips, who was elected overwhelmingly. Phillips was obviously an interim mayor, and his administration was correspondingly conservative. Meanwhile the hopes of those who wanted more of the new city government centered increasingly around the more popular figure of Josiah Quincy.[2]

As a congressman, state senator, speaker of the Massachusetts

14

House of Representatives, and finally a judge, Quincy had a long record of stubborn devotion to the interests of Boston. Bitterly Federalist, he was sometimes an embarrassment to the leaders of his own party. But while occasionally forced to act as a maverick, he had never lost his following. Thoroughly an aristocrat, Quincy was also a reformer, a critic especially of the state penal code and of criminal justice. In local politics he had been for years an advocate of the town meeting, sometimes a popular champion, and often a kind of humanitarian tribune. Attractive both to conservatives and to the proponents of change, he was approached, in the spring of 1822, by a nonpartisan committee which urged him, in that important period of transition, to take office and get things done. When Phillips declined renomination, Quincy became the party choice, this time winning narrowly and bringing with him an entire new slate of aldermen.[3]

The incoming mayor began his term under certain formal handicaps, since the new charter was not designed to encourage forceful executive action. Adhering as closely to old forms as possible, the framers had simply substituted representative for direct democracy. The mayor presided over the board of aldermen, but had no special voice or vote. The aldermen collectively replaced the selectmen by serving, through committees, as executive agents. Together the two branches of the city council replaced the town meeting in passing by-laws and taxes and appointing the many lesser officials. And provision was carefully made for the voters, assembled in wards, to issue resolutions and recommendations for action.[4]

But whatever the terms of the charter, Quincy was able to make it work. His victory in 1823 was the first of six; in the period from 1823 to 1829 he fully earned a reputation as "The Great Mayor" of Boston. His own strength, his position as a genuine leader of the community, and his insistence on serving as ex officio chairman of all important committees, enabled him to dominate the government. Much of the legacy of Quincy's six years was physically visible: a new public market, a city wharf, school buildings, land acquisitions. But at least equally important was the reorganization of several executive departments. Here, while moving toward a more specialized and professional system of administration, Quincy was able at the same time to maintain the traditions of aristocratic democracy and of citizens' responsibility.[5]

The new mayor's handling of the police problem was character-
istic of a method which combined limited innovation with personal
energy in the use of existing institutions. The first important act of
his administration was intended to improve the police system through
the establishment of the office of "Marshal of the City." This was a
new title, and a new job, but one derived from traditional sources.[6]

The term "peace officer" in Massachusetts ordinarily applied only
to sheriffs and constables, and sometimes to watchmen, but the special
powers implied were not limited to these officials. The statutes sometimes granted the right of arrest without warrant also to the selectmen
of the towns. And by an ordinance of 1801, the first selectman of
Boston, and later the mayor, was appointed "Superintendent of
Police," after 1811 assisted by a "Police Officer." The superintendent's
title confirmed his role as chief executive officer of the town; he was
expected to make trips through the streets, supervising the work of
the departments and when necessary enforcing the ordinance by
complaint or arrest. For the mayor of a city of fifty thousand these
responsibilities were overwhelming as well as redundant, and the
ordinance creating the city marshal also abolished the office of superintendent. "Police" duty, more narrowly defined, became a full-time
activity.[7]

There were significant advantages in the fact that the marshal was
the creature of the city rather than the state. The mayor and council,
under the charter, had wide power to delegate authority, and the
marshal's responsibilities, bound neither by statute nor tradition, were
capable of expansion at will. The original ordinance was simple and
flexible. The marshal, appointed annually by the mayor and aldermen,
was given the powers of a constable after posting a one-thousand-
dollar bond for faithful performance; his function was to enforce the
bylaws and ordinances. For this purpose he was given precedence
over all other constables when these were employed by the city, and
was required both to receive complaints during stated hours and to
walk the streets, at least once each week, in order personally to uncover violations.[8]

On June 16, 1823, Benjamin Pollard, Esq., was approved the first
marshal of the city, an office he filled until his death in 1836. The
character of the appointment was significant. Pollard, a Harvard
graduate and lawyer, had served as clerk of the Massachusetts House
during 1811-1815. He had some disappointed ambitions as a poet,

but his minor literary talents were outweighed by his major social qualifications. A man of presence, he was capable both of quelling a riot and of delivering the annual Fourth of July Oration, one of the most treasured honors granted by the city. His personal distinction was an addition to the inherent powers of his job, and contributed to the recognition by the common council that this was "not exceeded in importance by any other under the city government."[9]

During the 1820's and early 1830's, the key to this importance was the marshal's role as a health officer. The charter had abolished the old board of health, but the city council had merely substituted a new one, elected no longer by the citizens but by itself. The new board remained too independent for Mayor Quincy, and immediately after his second election, in May 1824, the council abolished it, providing:

1. That the police of the City of Boston, so far as regards its execution, be vested in three departments, to wit: That of internal police, that of external police, and that for the interment of the dead.

2. That the department of internal police be placed under the superintendence of the City Marshal. And that to this department shall belong, the care of the streets, the care of the common sewers, and the care of the vaults, and whatever else affects the health, security, and comfort of the city, from cause or means arising or existing within the limits thereof.

Only the quarantining of vessels and visitors, and the care of burial grounds, remained with other agencies.[10]

This left enormous power to the marshal. The ordinances provided only the outlines of a code of health; Pollard filled them in after consultation with a group of physicians. The marshal had to pass on all plans for the disposal of waste water by means other than the common sewers; he issued permits for the emptying of vaults, or had them emptied himself; as heir of the old board he was permitted to enter any house, between sunrise and sunset, in order to destroy a nuisance. With all of the sanitary provisions of city and commonwealth his to interpret, Pollard was in a real sense a legislator. He was also an arresting officer, and since the city solicitor or county attorney appeared only in important suits, he was ordinarily the prosecutor of those cases he chose to bring to court. He was the supervisor not only of the constables on city duty and his own deputies, but also of the whole body of teamsters and cartmen which the city employed to remove dirt from the streets. His authority was at first subject to close review by the council, but by the later 1820's the phrase "referred to the city marshal" had become the stock answer to most health questions raised in the board of aldermen.[11]

The marshal's office was used for an even greater variety of purposes when growth presented the city with new problems for which there were no traditional solutions. Despite the charter, Boston remained a town in more than sentiment. The city still clung to its fenceviewers, hayweighers, and hogreeves. Since much of its administrative machinery was archaic and limited by long custom, the flexibility of the marshal's office was especially useful. With the increase in population it became necessary to investigate more closely applicants for several kinds of licenses; the job was given to the marshal. The city began to license dogs in 1825, and to forbid the use of firearms within its limits; the marshal was charged with shooting strays and arresting poachers on the Common. The mayor feared that the loss of the former community sense prompted looting and disorder at fires; the marshal was required to attend. The marshal helped to plan processions, executed condemnation proceedings, assisted the clerks of the markets. His tours of the city enabled him to report to the council on new construction and similar matters. In all, the generalized nature of his duties allowed him to encompass both those traditional functions formerly exercised in person by the selectmen, and the new ones for which no other machinery had been as yet devised.[12]

There was some concern, in the 1820's, about the widening scope of the marshal's activities, and the common council tried repeatedly to obtain a voice in his appointment. But there was no serious complaint about an abuse of power. Pollard made no full or regular reports to the council, but he answered questions respectfully, and demonstrated a fine sense of subordination by occasionally referring the most minor matters to judgment by the aldermen. The marshal measured his own effectiveness by the number of nuisances and violations corrected; these were counted in some cases by the hundreds, even thousands. But Pollard was equally proud of the fact that he had seldom to resort to prosecution. Informal warnings, followed if necessary by official notice, were ordinarily enough. It was well known that the inhabitants with few exceptions were "most desirous of an equal and judicious enforcement of our prudential laws" and were "perfectly willing to submit themselves to the salutary restraints imposed upon them."[13]

An even greater check to the excessive use of the marshal's authority was imposed by his limited resources. For certain purposes he was able to employ or supervise a number of manual laborers, and for others, sometimes, the constables. But ordinarily, to assist in covering his responsibilities, the city provided Pollard with only one or two deputies and a horse. Clearly not all functions could be exercised equally and at once; it was necessary to establish priorities.[14]

Evidence of these priorities appeared in Pollard's one formal annual report, for the year 1834. His job, he wrote, was divided into two branches: "The first is the *health* division and the second is the division of *general police*." The former was treated first and at greater length. The most impressive statistics were afforded by the streets and privies: 1,500 loads of dirt removed, 3,120 vaults emptied. The superintendence of drains and sewers required the most paper work, involving blueprints, permits, and preliminary assessments. And the threat of Asiatic Cholera, in the hot months, required *daily* visits, by "agents of the city," to every house in Boston.[15]

The work of general police was more various and less amenable to sustained, routine effort:

The second division of the municipal police comprises the misdemeanors and irregularities affecting the safety, the peace, and convenience and comfort of the community. In this branch may be included the violation of the license laws, the infraction of the several ordinances, regulating the streets, trucks, carts, carriages and horses, dogs, exhibitions and public shows trespasses and offenses on the common and malls—the sale and stands of wood and bark—woodsawyers—unauthorized fire works—danger from lighted pipes and cigars—firing of loaded arms—unlawful games and plays —paving of streets and footwalks—dirt and rubbish—erecting of buildings —repairs of steps and cellar doors—projection on steps; signs, balconies and awnings—merchandise, snow and ice on sidewalks—coursing on sleds in the highways—swimming in exposed places—and various other subjects.[16]

This catalogue, while full enough for three men and a horse, contained some significant omissions. No felonious or moral offenses were included, and the report as a whole did not refer to "crime" or "criminals." The original ordinance of 1823, in creating the office of marshal, had stressed his role in administering the city's own regulations; the word "laws" was mentioned only once, almost as an after-thought. Whether through necessity or intent, what was an emphasis became in practice an exclusion. The commonwealth created the statutes, and the city would not accept responsibility for their enforcement. The marshal would do so much and no more.[17]

The unwillingness of the city to extend its responsibility for the control of crime did not indicate any indifference on the part of the mayor. Few problems, in fact, concerned Josiah Quincy more. While serving as a judge, in 1822, he had expressed his interest in the problems of "poverty, vice and crime" which he considered "little else than modifications of each other." Still earlier, as a member of the General Court, Quincy had moved a notable investigation of the causes of poverty and crime. His conclusions were published in 1820; their insistence on the transcendent causal importance of drink, on the evils of unsystematic outdoor relief, and on the need for a flexible and reformatory penal system was later echoed by three generations of Massachusetts reformers.[18]

Many of Quincy's recommendations were adopted, at least in part. One of his reasons for coming eventually to support the incorporation movement was that the new city charter eliminated the justices of the peace, with their iniquitous fee system, in favor of a municipal police court. As mayor he moved against conditions in Boston's crowded Leverett Street jail and almshouse, where the poor, insane, and vicious were carelessly detained together. One of the last acts of the town, under Quincy's prodding, was to authorize the building of a separate House of Industry for the unfortunate poor. It was built in 1822. A House of Correction for misdemeanants followed the next year. And in 1826 a portion of the latter building was set aside as a House of Reformation for Juvenile Offenders, in accord with the general plan of separating the public charges and trying to improve each class by the methods most appropriate.[19]

But reform stopped with the courts and penal institutions. Quincy did not share with later humanitarians the faith that progress would dramatically improve the state of public morals. Indeed, anticipating Henry George, he believed that an increase in poverty, vice, and crime was an inevitable consequence of the material improvements which Bostonians so eagerly sought. With his suspicion of the fee system, he had in particular no faith in the reforming ability of the agents of police, "those instruments which society employs in its lower departments for the . . . execution of the laws." The invention of the marshal's office, which gave the city a salaried, fully responsible police of its own, was enough to satisfy him. To the extent that the control of crime was in practice police or even public business, the responsibility remained as before with the constables and watch.[20]

Nor was any other authority concerned with revision of the traditional institutions of criminal police. Boston was still governed by the recognized social elite, some of whom, like Quincy, had a paternally humanitarian interest in criminality. But few in the 1820's felt seriously threatened by it, or unable to deal with it in traditional fashion.

The administration was especially conservative in handling the watch, whose members continued to work in the shadows, largely ignored. The watchmen were for ritual purposes "good and faithful" servants, but no more than servants; their names were not dignified by listing with those of other city employees. And despite the fact that the men on patrol were in a favorable position to gather signatures on their frequent petitions for raises in pay, and that requests from several wards suggested the need for an increase in number, the council and Quincy held firm on both counts. Thirty-six men at fifty cents a night remained the standard, and the budgets for the watch, out of a total city and county expenditure averaging around three hundred thousand dollars, remained at about eight thousand dollars a year. Individuals were still expected to furnish their own protection. Warrants for private watchmen continued to be granted to merchants and storekeepers, and Quincy also favored issuing these to volunteers in residential streets.[21]

The mayor's conservative attitude toward the watch, however, was balanced by his energy in personally commanding the police. While he had abandoned the title, he still retained the functions of superintendent. An old friend, years later, recalled Quincy's daily tours of inspection: "He was on his horse at five o'clock in the morning, and used to bow to me, for I was up at that time, and he used to say to me, 'If there is any stench around your house let me know.' "

Similar devotion was expected in the subordinate officers, who were in various ways made to feel the authority of the chief executive. The constables, ordinarily reappointed almost automatically, were subjected to a close review; the city council formally studied the manner of their selection, and three were fired outright in the summer of 1823. Quincy supported the captain of the watch both in a demand for a pay raise and in a series of disciplinary actions. Marshal Pollard, a personal friend, owed the mayor both his office and his appointment.[22]

Efficient agents, responsible to him, were essential to a proper police; and Quincy recognized other needs also. Shameless vice and a tendency toward mob disorder were both, he thought, consequences of population growth. His own attitudes were ambivalent, for while a champion of progress, he was also a conservative and even a fatalist. He had, in either case, a real sense of the changes occurring in Boston; and he did not hesitate, either through institutional reform or through a vigorous reassertion of older methods, to wage an often dramatic battle to preserve the public peace.

One of his most important acts was the reform of the fire companies, in which the transition from town to city had had especially disturbing consequences. In Boston as elsewhere, volunteer fire companies were politically powerful; in the early 1820's, when municipal elections brought out three or four thousand voters, several hundred were enrolled as firemen. Granted exemptions from jury and militia duty, the companies were also given cash prizes for being first or second to answer an alarm. Firefighting was for young men a rugged and even vicious form of sport: "To be first, nearest, and most conspicuous at fires was their greatest ambition." The rewards sometimes included loot as well as prizes, and the rivalry between companies was always a potential source of riot. During Quincy's first administration neither the government, the watchful insurance companies, nor the firemen themselves were satisfied with existing arrangements.[23]

Members of the city council and the mayor believed that the growth of insurance protection had enervated the citizens, and that a changing population made it impossible to rely any longer upon mutual cooperation. The old system of bucket brigades was still used to feed the engines, but the elective firewards were unable in practice to coerce the inhabitants into forming the lines, and large fires were scenes not of community solidarity but of turbulence and fights. New York and Philadelphia had adopted systems in which the engines fed each other through hoses, from wells especially adapted for the purpose, and Quincy urged that Boston follow their example.[24]

The firemen were unwilling to abandon the dramatic competition of the scramble for the tamer role of supplying rival companies with water. They had other grievances as well. New legislation had robbed their exemptions of advantage, and an improved militia competed for recruits. The sixteen companies were understaffed, with only 371 enrolled out of a full complement of 430. The council offered only to raise the prize money to fifteen dollars, and to grant each company an annual banquet allowance of twenty-five dollars. The firemen wanted fifty, and one foreman insisted that "forty-nine dollars and ninety-nine cents will not do."[25]

Despite the fact that "in the opinion of many citizens, the companies were composed of a class . . . whose claims it was unsafe to deny," Quincy and the council refused to make the "permanent safety of a city . . . dependent on the capricious estimate of their own importance by any set of men." No concessions were made, and on December 1 the captains of all companies resigned. The mayor immediately turned their engines over to the aldermen, and called for volunteers to fill the missing places. The response was heartening, and he was able that night to assure the council "that the fire department was in its usual state of efficiency."[26]

In 1825, after a two-year battle, Quincy finally began an entire reorganization of the department, on the basis of tightly regulated hose companies, supervised no longer by elective firewards but by engineers under a professional chief. Several thousand dollars was spent on wells, headquarters, and equipment; and the new companies, larger than the old, were also better disciplined. Neither Quincy nor Chief Engineer Samuel Harris was afraid to dismiss captains or even to disband whole companies for careless or unruly behavior, while the marshal and constables helped to enforce regulations at the scene. Increased protection from fire was measured by a 20 per cent drop in insurance rates. No less important was increased protection from firemen. Despite disorders "before and during a later period," during the later 1820's "all . . . worked together in entire harmony with each other."[27]

Another important source of trouble, in the West End, was brought even more dramatically under control. In 1823 twelve or fourteen "houses of infamous character were kept, without concealment and without shame." There were dances there almost every night and the whole street was "in a blaze of light from their windows." To put them down, without a military force, seemed impossible. "A man's life would not be safe who should attempt it." The company consisted of "highbinders, jailbirds, known thieves, and miscreants, with women of the worst description." Murders were committed there, and more were suspected; some officials thought that "vice and villainy were too strong for the police." But the mayor determined that "there shall at least be a struggle for the supremacy of the laws."[28]

Quincy immediately revoked all liquor licenses in the district, and organized "a strong police," or posse, which he personally led through a series of raids in the defiant neighborhood. A number of arrests for fiddling, dancing, and operating without licenses soon quieted the nuisance. "These measures did not originate in any theories, or visions of ideal purity . . . but in a single sense of duty and respect for the character of the city; proceeding upon the principle that if in great cities the existence of vice is inevitable, that its course should be in secret, like other filth, in drains, and in darkness; not obtrusive, not powerful, not prowling publicly in the streets."[29]

The reduction of liquor licenses was a permanent measure; the total, despite the population increase, was cut from 697 in 1822 to 554 in 1829. And police pressure in the "Nigger Hill" vicinity was also maintained. The city nearly doubled the expense for constables, in 1823-24, with half the money, $747.00, going to "special services at West Boston." Thereafter at least one man was constantly on duty in the West End. In 1827, another was detailed to patrol Ann Street, of similar reputation, to the north.[30]

But the mayor's was not the only campaign directed against the haunts of vice. In the summer of 1825, the *Columbian Centinel* noted that "For some nights past the peace and proverbial good order of the city have been disturbed by disgraceful and unmanly proceedings in attacking the houses inhabited by the frail sisterhood, in North Morgan, Prince, and Ann Streets." Mob activity continued sporadically for a week, July 22 to July 29, reaching a height with the destruction of a notorious building known as "The Beehive." Although the participants insisted that they were only venting an outraged sense of virtue, Quincy moved, after the first night, to stop them. "The police" were "vigilant and active," and the mayor, again at their head, enlisted the aid of forty truckmen in arresting twelve ringleaders and dispersing the rest.[31]

But doubts remained despite this success. The disorder had been quelled only through the exercise of the mayor's individual authority, his ability, in the old manner, to rally and lead a personal following from among the bystanders. And he was unwilling a second time to risk his prestige. When a few months later another riot followed the appearance of Edmund Kean at the National Theatre, Quincy refused to act, claiming that as mayor he lacked the needed authority. His job was only to take care that *"all laws for the government of the city are executed,"* and riot was an offense against the *state*. His next inaugural address contained an appeal, which went unanswered, for revision of the commonwealth's cumbersome riot act.[32]

But with this significant exception the mayor, upon reviewing his accomplishments in 1829, was fully satisfied with his own efforts on behalf of the police. A "systematic cleansing of the city," first carried out in 1823 and since policed by the marshal, had contributed to a drop in the death rate. From 23 per 1,000, during 1812-1823, this had declined to 20, between 1824 and 1827, and below 18 in the period 1826-1828. And the work of criminal police was equally gratifying. The timid might walk any street at any hour. And "where, in a city of equal population, are there fewer instances of those crimes, to which all populous places are subject?" The mayor was especially proud to note that, except for the marshal, "Not one man has been added to the ancient arm of police."[33]

Quincy's summary did not fully measure the accomplishments of his administration, notably the change symbolized by his own conversion from opponent of municipal government to "Great Mayor." The transition, bitterly debated a short time before, had not in fact proved radical. Some of the new building activity, such as the Quincy Market, had been inspired not by new conceptions of the role of the city but by the most ancient. Additions to the school system, the police court, the new penal institutions were all realizations of action begun under the town. And the new problems arising from size and increasing impersonality had been handled without violence to tradition. The introduction of professionalism into the fire department did not destroy its largely volunteer character. And the advent of a professional, specialized police officer, the marshal of the city, was softened by both the methods and the character of the appointee. The new vigor in government was the product largely of energy and political courage: "And these means, faithfully applied, are better than armies of constables and watchmen."[34]

CHAPTER THREE

Riots and A New Police, 1829-1838

The administrations of Josiah Quincy set standards in dealing with the police which were admired for years afterwards. But it was significant that the city's "Great Mayor" was for most purposes its first. His successors lacked not only his *élan* but also his arrogant sense of dominance over the city and its affairs. Quincy had himself noted the erosion of the older set of community controls which had governed the town. As population grew and the process continued, his own highly personal tactics became increasingly obsolete.

Complaints about the inadequacy of patrol protection, during the early 1830's, forced the government to strengthen "the ancient arm of police." It did so at first simply by expanding the existing body of constables and watchmen. But the problem of mob violence, which had already troubled Mayor Quincy, soon compelled the municipality to take a more significant step, to create a new class of permanent professional officers, with new standards of performance.

The need for a change was not immediately apparent when Josiah Quincy left office in 1829. The mayor retired to the presidency of Harvard College only after two successive elections in which he led but lacked a majority. His successor, General Harrison Grey Otis, was not an innovator. An aristocrat, little interested in the details of managing the city, the general chose to interpret his election simply as a belated referendum on the Hartford Convention. If Quincy represented the humanitarian element in Boston's aristocracy, Otis represented the conservative.[1]

The two men in fact had much in common and belonged to a continuing tradition. They were members of an upper class which shared the view that the city must be a place to stimulate pride in its inhabitants and admiration in its visitors. It was at the same time primarily a place of business, a port, a market and financial capital. To Otis, a large landholder and operator in real estate, the tax rate was of great but not transcendent importance. Expenditures designed either to enhance the city's magnificence or to increase its business were willingly met as the price of progress. Public institutions were frequently objects of private benevolence; individual gifts contributed to the charitable institutions in the 1820's, and would build schools in the 1830's and the library in the 1840's and 1850's. And during his three years as mayor Otis freely proposed such capital projects as a water supply, a new court house, and a railroad to the Hudson.[2]

Differences arose rather over the ordinary expenses for services less important to the upper classes than to others. When commercial depression prevented Otis from realizing his more ambitious plans, he was especially unwilling to pay for current items. Public demand made it necessary to continue Marshal Pollard's street-cleaning operations, although the mayor thought that these were "practiced to a needless and pernicious extreme." The marshal's salary was cut from one thousand to eight hundred dollars, however. Men like Otis, living on well-drained Beacon Hill, saw little purpose in the expansion of the sewer system, and this was also cut back. The same was true of the watch and constabulary. Secure behind the high brick walls which surrounded his own house, furnished with a number of servants and coachmen, the mayor was unresponsive to demands for an increase in the quality and extent of public protection.[3]

One of the first acts of the Otis administration was to remove the constables stationed in Ann Street and the West End, despite an increase in the number of liquor licenses. In the face of a continuing stream of petitions, no addition was made either to the pay or the numbers of the watch. While the population had grown from the forty-nine thousand in 1822 to about sixty-five thousand, the city in 1832 employed no more than the twenty-four constables and eighty watchmen inherited from the time of incorporation. This force, already overburdened, was unable to keep pace with a notable rise in violence.[4]

The city did not prepare to deal with this problem until 1832. When General Otis declined renomination in 1831, the city's Jacksonians nominated the Honorable Theodore Lyman, like Otis a silk-stocking former Federalist. The National Republican caucus, in a mild revolt, produced as his opponent Alderman Charles Wells, a master carpenter. The press had misgivings about this selection. But the voters decided, with the *Advertiser*, that a plain man from the dominant party was preferable to a gentleman of the minority. Wells was elected in December to the first of two terms.[5]

This choice was in part "a sort of protest from the middle classes against the magnificent way of doing things inaugurated by Quincy and Otis, and against any further increase in the city debt." In fact, with the return of prosperity, neither the aldermen nor the common council were eager for retrenchment, and the city's expenses rose considerably during 1832 and 1833. The recommendations of Mayor Wells proved little different from those of Mayor Otis except in two particulars: there was no mention of a railroad, and there was an increased sensitivity to the demands of individuals and neighborhoods suffering from the lack of police.[6]

The city marshal's salary was restored in 1832, and the appropriation for the department of internal health greatly increased, largely to battle an outbreak of cholera. More constables were appointed, including one to patrol "The Northern District," wards one to three, "for the purpose of arresting vagabonds and common drunkards." Wells noted a petition "praying that some measures may be taken to suppress the dangerous riots, routs, and tumultuous assemblies in and about Broad Street," and in July the aldermen "ordered, that the committee on the city watch be instructed to consider the expediency of providing a more extensive city watch than now exists, and by paying them more wages get a more efficient class of men."[7]

When the committee issued no report after six months, the mayor gave the problem special attention in his inaugural for 1833. He was disturbed not only by the persistent problems of pay and numbers, but by the hours, urging that the watch serve longer each night, from one hour after sunset to one hour before sunrise at least. With such changes, he argued, "great additional security would be rendered to the city, and if once adopted would receive the approbation of the citizens, notwithstanding the increase of expense."[8]

The watch committee finally reported in June, with a plan largely following the mayor's recommendations. During the winter months, it submitted, the watch should be set at 8:00 P.M., during the summer at 9:00. Four more men should be added at each of the four stations, raising the total from thirty-six to fifty-two, and the effective patrol by half as much. Two pay raises within the month boosted the scale to one dollar for officers of the watch and ninety cents for the men.[9]

These changes, together, nearly doubled the amount annually spent on the watch, the figures rising from $11,350.90 one year to $19,913.39 the next. Two years of pressure from Mayor Wells had in effect restored the ratio of watchmen to population to approximately the level existing at the time of incorporation.[10]

Complaints from unprotected neighborhoods and citizens could apparently produce no more. In the dozen years since 1822, only one individual, watchman Jonathan Houghton, shot while on duty, had been reported murdered. The increase in "riots, routs, and tumultuous assemblies" was not cause for excessive concern. The city had never fully abandoned responsibility for the conduct and even the morality of all of its inhabitants. No group or class in Boston was treated as beyond the pale of law enforcement, at least not since Quincy's raids in the West End. The drayman guilty of drunken assault on his fellows was subject, if caught or complained against, to the costly process of arrest, trial, and imprisonment. But the aimless brawls of Ann Street were dangerous largely to the participants, and not to those who governed the community. Small riots were often regarded as sporting events, as when, in 1832, the members of various fire companies and their critics scheduled a meeting at the National Theatre, to follow the regular minstrel performance by "Jumping Jim Crow" Rice. A certain degree of disorder was endemic, even traditional, and tolerated accordingly.[11]

The needs of urban living, together with changing standards of personal conduct, were already beginning to erode this tolerance by the middle 1830's. But this was a slow process, without dramatic impetus, until August of 1834 and the famed burning of the Charlestown Convent, an incident whose repercussions were felt for years.

The storm which eventually burst over the little school for girls on Mount Benedict had been gathering for some time during the hot weeks of July and early August. The "Boston Truckmen" were known to be hostile toward the convent, at once Irish, Romish, and aristocratic, and the Charlestown selectmen made some effort to allay their resentment. But the precise time of the attack, on August 11, was not known beforehand, and no preparations were made for it. That night a mob soon numbering several thousand surrounded the school. No harm was intended to the nuns; with the exception of their fiery superior, they simply scattered in the dark, seeking refuge in nearby houses, while their charges were "freed." The militia was not called, and except for one selectman, easily cowed, no one in authority appeared at the scene. No local peace officers were present, officially, and those from Boston were not requested. When the main building was finally set ablaze, a few Boston fire companies drove up, but they made no attempt to stop the destruction and were later accused of contributing to it.[12]

In Boston, next day, preparations were more complete. The mother superior had reportedly warned attackers that Bishop Fenwick would retaliate with "twenty thousand Irishmen," and members of the mob were expected to be looking for trouble. Harvard students armed themselves to protect the college. The city council spent over $1,500 on special constables, ordinarily a full year's appropriation, and Mayor Lyman arranged for both the *posse comitatus* and the militia. These actions, together with the bishop's warning to his own flock, prevented any further disturbance.[13]

But nothing could lessen the damage and the shock already experienced. The motives involved in firing the convent were complex; as complex as, and perhaps similar to, those involved in the destruction of the Beehive, nearly ten years before. But however the case appeared to the rioters, the reaction of official Boston was profoundly different. The most Protestant of the city's newspapers joined in denunciation of the Mount Benedict Outrage. On August 12 Mayor Lyman called an indignation meeting at Faneuil Hall, where Josiah Quincy and Harrison Grey Otis spoke passionately about this "base and cowardly" blot upon their city's reputation. Less than twenty-four hours after its occurrence the riot had already begun to pass into legend.[14]

It was not simply that this mob had acted more outrageously than others, or that it had more clearly indicated the vulnerability of the agencies of control. The burning of the convent had touched a nerve which previous incidents had not. This was riot with social, even political, implications. In the middle 1830's, the city's leadership, fully informed of developments in England and the Continent, were aware of the potential in political riot. They were further reminded on the Fourth of every July. Not only fear but a genuine conviction convinced them that history could not be allowed to repeat itself in contemporary Boston. The principle was best expressed three years later by Samuel A. Eliot: "Whatever may be the case in other countries, it is manifestly impossible that any sufficient or justifying cause for popular violence exists in this, where republican institutions secure to every individual his just share in the government of the whole."[15]

The General Court responded to the threat with a revision of the state's riot act. Last revised in 1786, the year of Shays' Rebellion, the existing law was largely copied from England's, and designed to deal with a slowly gathering rural uprising, not with a mercurial urban mob. A sheriff or justice of the peace might warn any group of twelve armed or thirty unarmed men to disperse, and after an hour's wait proceed to order arrests. The new law gave mayors and aldermen the authority to read the riot act, made it their duty to proceed at once to the scene, and eliminated the waiting period.[16]

Boston's own board of aldermen, at the regular meeting after the fire, "ordered that the mayor be authorized to establish in addition to the usual watch a strong and efficient body of patrol and stationary police, for the preservation of good order during the night . . . and to establish such rules and regulations respecting the same as may be deemed expedient." But unlike state legislation the board's order involved an additional expense to the city, and created a new class of officers; it failed to take effect. The total expended for constables and watch in 1835, as the memory of the fire faded, increased by about 3 per cent, to $31,887.75, while total expenditures rose about 9 per cent, to $701,611.22.[17]

The next major disturbance in the city, the assault on William Lloyd Garrison, in October 1835, was to Mayor Lyman "the most important event which occured [sic] while in office." As chief executive of an often turbulent city, he was continually concerned about the weaknesses of its police. That summer and autumn especially, he sensed that the public was in "a very heated, irritable state." And he made it a point, when controversial religious or antislavery meetings were scheduled, to request that they be called off. While affirming his duty to protect them, he warned that he might not be able to do so, and persuaded some societies to change their plans.[18]

These worries were well founded. Lyman's position was in fact difficult when, on the afternoon of October 21, he first noticed the crowd near the *Liberator* offices. He had no authority to call on the militia, and the watch would not be available until after dark. At first he sent over the aging Benjamin Pollard with his two deputies, Charles A. Wells, the marshal's sewer expert, and "Father" Hezekiah Earle, chief assistant in matters of health. These three gathered the few constables available, and Lyman followed, in accordance with law and duty. While Deputy Sheriff Parkman ultimately appeared, apparently toward the end of the trouble, he was not subject to orders from the mayor.[19]

Lyman did attempt, in the Quincy manner, to exercise his personal authority in dealing with the mob; Wendell Phillips later recalled him, "cap in hand, almost on his knees, entreating the men who were his social companions to have the kindness to obey the laws." But his presence had little effect. The crowd surged freely through streets and buildings, and at one time the abolitionist was roped and dragged along with it. The mayor himself was roughly handled, and his office in City Hall was stormed. The mob was neither beaten nor cowed, and Garrison was lodged safely in jail only through a series of luckily timed subterfuges.[20]

In the aftermath, few agreed with Phillips' criticism: "The city was mine as well as his, and I hung my head, ashamed of it and him." Aside from some letters in the *Liberator,* and a mild editorial in the evangelical Boston *Recorder,* the public press, while condemning both the riot and the abolitionists, praised the courage of the mayor. It was widely agreed that the crowd, while animated by basically patriotic motives, had gotten beyond control, but this was due not to individual failure but to a lamentable lack of police resources.[21]

This consensus, however, did not extend to the city government. Members of the council, on the afternoon of the riot, had not appeared to help the mayor, although the aldermen at least were enjoined by law to do so. Many, perhaps most, were fundamentally in sympathy with the "Broadcloth Mob" of State Street. Samuel Turrell Armstrong, president of the Tremont Bank, was elected mayor a few weeks after the riot; and he was not eager to air the police problems which it had revealed. Armstrong's inaugural address, in January, was a perfect expression of the merchant conservatives' view of municipal government: "Whatever is done for ourselves alone is done for the day that is passing; while that which is done for our city is to endure for generations." Total expenses for 1836, with an increase in capital projects, rose more than one hundred thousand dollars; the watch and constables were cut five thousand. The council was not persuaded to take stronger action for another year and a half, until after the city's third major riot in three years.[22]

The Broad Street Riot of June 11, 1837, broke out when some volunteer firemen, returning from an alarm, clashed with an Irish funeral procession. While the Irish had at first the advantage of numbers, more fire companies were summoned, and they were followed by others with grievances against the immigrants. It was a Sunday, few men were at work, and residents of the Irish tenements all along the street were driven out and beaten by a mob eventually estimated at fifteen thousand, more than one-sixth of the city's population. It was nearly two hours before Mayor Samuel Eliot was able to get help from a cavalry regiment of militia and restore order at the head of eight hundred horsemen.[23]

No one was killed, but large numbers were badly injured, and property damage amounted to several thousand dollars. The outbreak had not come in Charlestown, where Boston's responsibility was indirect, but in the heart of the city, with much of the blame belonging to men who represented it. The militia had been called out for the first time in its history; and now there was no sympathy, in official Boston, for the motives of the rioters. The council's formal report criticized the Irish for "retaining their national ways" but concluded that there was no room for hostility to immigrants in a free nation with high wages and a chronic shortage of labor. Something had to be done. Prompted by Mayor Eliot, the city government determined that it was necessary both to reorganize the fire department and to provide a stronger police.[24]

The movement for reform of the fire companies was an old one. After the brief period of relatively quiet behavior during the Quincy administration, the volunteers had again been a menace to the police of the city, participants not only in the Broad Street and perhaps Charlestown riots but in a number of smaller ones. Members of the department itself had joined the underwriters and other critics of the system. Willard Sears, a friend of Mayor Quincy, had in 1828 formed a company, number eight, whose recruits not only maintained strict discipline but took the pledge of temperance. Generally in better shape and more alert than their competitors, they proved not only superior at fighting fires but, in various intradepartmental feuds, at fighting firemen. Both through example and as a kind of lobby the men of number eight had kept the reform issue before the government for several years.[25]

The central problem was that the fire fighters considered themselves members of voluntary social organizations, who were doing the city a favor and were not therefore subject to official discipline. The usual proposal was to pay them in regular fashion, both to reduce the hectic pursuit of reward money and to provide a disciplinary lever. The council adopted this view in the summer of 1837, and in July provided for a severe reduction in the number of men, and for annual salaries ranging from sixty-five dollars up.[26]

With this accomplished, Mayor Eliot turned to the police. In a vigorous address to the council, on September 18, he called for the creation of a new class of officers. Citing the "spirit of violence abroad," he pointed out that the danger from "the incendiary, burglar, and the lawlessly violent" was "increasing at a ratio faster than that of population." The criminal, "no republican," was "guilty of treason against the constitution of his country." And it was necessary to take the strong measures appropriate to Boston's metropolitan standing: "The police of this city has hitherto consisted of a small number of constables, and is rather adapted to circumstances as they were half a century ago."[27]

The mayor recognized that money was the principal problem. But there was no alternative. The citizens would not or could not protect themselves. And the use of armed militia was dangerous as well as slow; "the prevention of an evil is far easier than the application of a remedy." The taxpayers must either "give their active personal exertions or . . . contribute a part of their substance to secure the value of the rest."[28]

The committee formed to consider Eliot's recommendation reported unanimously in favor. "It is intended to imitate, as far as may be, the system of London, were [sic] a similar patrol is established, and is found to be of advantage in various ways besides the enforcement of laws." While the mayor thought that the new men might specialize in dealing with crime, the committee was concerned also with the traditional business of the marshal's office, with ordinances, fires, accidents, and vagrant children. It suggested tentatively that the city be divided into four districts, each patrolled by eight men and a captain under the marshal. At the same time the members called for an increase of thirty watchmen, so that never less than forty would be on call during the night, and that an experienced reserve would be available when the threat of riot made it necessary to create special constables.[29]

The committee was not entirely clear about the nature of the officers it proposed to create. Few Americans were in fact acquainted with "the system of London." But some things were understood. The new officers would not have the official and civil functions of the constables, and would be "a special city police" under municipal control. Again unlike the constables, they would not be expected to pay for themselves through fees and other concessions but would be given regular wages, at the rate of two dollars a day. Unlike the watch, they would work in the daytime, full time. And most important, although less clear, they would be a "preventive" force.[30]

Mayor Eliot had stressed prevention in his original address. The same word was used in connection with similar movements in the same period, in Philadelphia and New York. The concept of prevention did not, in the 1830's, refer to the use of police as agents of social reform. But it did establish an important shift in emphasis or initiative. The new peace officers were expected to be professionals in the fullest sense. They would not, like the watch, be confined by custom to watching for fires and fights and other overt disturbances. They would not, like sheriffs and constables, rely largely upon the complaints of the injured. The police would prevent trouble by actively seeking it out on their own, before it had time to reach serious proportions.[31]

No real objection to any of these principles was offered in 1837, although the earlier reformation of the fire department had raised a storm. Most of the companies had resigned en masse, issuing proclamations and even establishing a newspaper to publish their complaints. For some time voluntary fire patrols were needed while new companies were organized; and the ex-firemen remained an important factor in local politics for several years. But the reformation of the police raised no such problems; once the fiscal conservatism of the council was overcome, its proposals passed smoothly on to the General Court for the necessary legislation.[32]

In Massachusetts, during the 1830's, no vocal group was concerned with the kind of liberties a vigorous police might violate. The sheriff and constables had been only tangentially involved in the issue of imprisonment for debt. And as the minimal activities of the other peace officers were seldom noticed, they provoked no controversy.

In part because it dealt with a neglected class, the watch was still little regarded. The captain, unlike many other city officers, held a notably insensitive position; only three men held the job between the incorporation of the city and 1854, the year in which the watch was abolished. Lack of attention was further reflected in confusion not only about the actual functions of watchmen but about their statutory powers and duties.[33]

The most important of these powers, the right of arrest, was not tested judicially until 1853, and then only at the police court level. The citizens did have legal recourse in case of abuses, but in practice suits for false or improper arrest were rare, and successful suits even more so. The city first faced the problem, apparently, in 1828, when it furnished counsel to a watchman summoned to court. The council did not consider this action a precedent, but it was willing to hear petitions from all employees so summoned who wanted compensation for legal costs. In the entire period 1822-1837, only one such petition appeared. When on scattered occasions citizens complained about rough handling directly to the council, they were uniformly dismissed. In one such case, involving both a beating and the refusal of bail, the committee commented simply that "it may happen that the complainants belong to a class not often exposed to the treatment they are likely to meet with in a watch house or jail." The formal devices of litigation and petition did not often occur to those so exposed. The usual response was more immediate; prosecutions for assaults on officers were numbered each year in the dozens.[34]

Confusion was not unique to the watch and the matter of brutality. In 1837, the statutory powers of all peace officers were defined in unclear and often contradictory fashion. The definitive right of arrest without warrant was the one most open to abuse; and the basic statute, covering the ordinary use of this right, was hedged with restrictions. Sheriffs, constables, and watchmen might seize those guilty of a long list of offenses against public morality, but only in public places, on the highways, and at night. Several exceptions to this general rule, such as the riot act or the statute authorizing arrests in case of disorder in court, covered emergency situations. But the legislature was not especially jealous of these restrictions. Random additions were made to the subject list of offenses, such as selling charcoal in boxes of unsuitable or misrepresented dimensions. Until the 1850's there were no specific statutory penalties attached either to failure to state the reason for arrest or to making an illegal arrest without warrant.[35]

The omissions and inconsistencies of legislation were in part remedied by the judiciary, drawing on the common law. But few relevant cases arose; the Supreme Judicial Court was not called to rule upon the inherent powers of police officers until 1845. And the common law, imperfectly understood, was never a firm guide to the laity.[36]

The essential reason for legislative carelessness was not confidence in the courts but indifference to the problems of criminal police. Of purely local importance, dealing in limited fashion with society's cripples, these were no threat to liberty in a republican society. The citizens of Boston were no more concerned. The chief complaint about the watch and constables was not their obtrusiveness but their inadequacy. The marshal's office, under which the new men were to operate, was associated largely with street cleaning. Since few license laws were enforced, the typical artisan or businessman had rarely any dealings with police.

By 1837 the concept of professionalism, also, was not in controversy. Even in 1822 the citizens had been no longer much involved in the administration of police, and under the charter this tradition had slipped further. In many criminal cases involving fines, private informers could collect half the amount imposed. In several years no such money at all was given out, and in few did the total approach one hundred dollars. The city several times offered special rewards for the detection of offenders, usually incendiaries, sometimes rioters, once a murderer; the only applicants were watchmen, constables, and their relatives. Not since Mayor Quincy had there been serious thought of a voluntary neighborhood watch. Mayor Eliot's offer of a choice between more "active personal exertions" and a professional police force was entirely rhetorical.[37]

On April 15, 1838, without notice in the press, the General Court passed the necessary bill allowing the City of Boston to appoint policemen with all but the civil powers of constables. Six were appointed in May, three more in July, all assigned to the marshal for whatever duties he and the council might require.[38]

The creation of a new police during the 1830's was a natural continuation of the process which had led the town to become the City of Boston. Professionalism had already been adopted in several departments as the citizens came to rely upon the government directly for services that they could not meet through private effort. The constables in practice had been appointive professionals for more than thirty years. So had the watch. The marshal had been a full-time specialist from the first. The next step, to a regular corps of salaried officers, was resisted not in principle but only through inertia and the fear of expense. No members of the government, in 1837, voiced Josiah Quincy's confidence that energy, and the older social authority, might serve as substitutes for a strong police. And none of them voiced his suspicion of police as possible oppressors. The new officers supplemented but did not replace the familiar system of constables and watchmen. They were created to deal with the immediate problem of riot. Aside from this, no untried objects were intended. The new "preventive" method was only tactical; the men were expected to do what had always been done, only better.

CHAPTER FOUR

Opportunities and Problems, 1838-1845

In 1839, Mayor Samuel A. Eliot announced to the city council that "The public peace has been . . . uninterrupted during the past year, and . . . the reputation of the city has suffered no such blow as was inflicted on it the previous years." The new police were working well. And the greatly increased expenditure for the watch and constables, which had tripled in six years to reach nearly forty-five thousand dollars, was making itself felt. "Great pains have been taken," Eliot noted, "to prevent the violation of the laws and ordinances, especially those the violation of which has a tendency to the breach of the peace." This was what the new men had been designed to accomplish, and the mayor could count upon a general approval of their objects and operations.[1]

But the existence of a strengthened instrument of police created demands for its exercise. And during the 1830's and 1840's changes in public attitudes and habits, as well as the needs of a growing city, suggested new uses for the force as well as new reactions to old uses. As responsibilities were added, controversy developed. In the years immediately following, increase in both the actual and potential power of police put a growing strain upon the general approval of 1838.

The first source of trouble between police and public grew out of an important shift of emphasis within the temperance movement. The creation of the new officers in 1838 was followed by the passage of the "Fifteen-Gallon Law," the first legislation intended seriously to restrict the private use of alcohol. Chapter 157 of the Acts of 1838 limited the sale of spirits to quantities of fifteen gallons or more, in order to deny their use as liquor especially to the poor and improvident. No special provisions were made for enforcement, but the various peace officers of the commonwealth were responsible.[2]

The sale of drink had always been subject to some restrictions. The first settlements both at Plymouth and at Massachusetts Bay had followed early medieval precedents in limiting retail sales through licenses. The purpose of these grants was threefold. The fees were sometimes a source of revenue. The recipients were given a valuable limited monopoly. And the authorities, in turn, required that strangers on the road be accommodated, and that certain prudential regulations be honored. While liquors were regarded as among the goods or even necessaries of life, it was recognized that their abuse in public places could produce disorder. The principle established by English precedent was mirrored in all colonial legislation; the right to sell by the glass was limited to genuine taverners, who were supposed to provide the full range of hospitality, room, board, and stabling as well as drink. Nontravelers might drink at home, but the congregation of local idlers could lead to neglect of work and family as well as disturbance of the peace.[3]

In 1786, under the new state constitution, the General Court passed a license law, based on earlier acts, which served the commonwealth for forty-five years. No liquor might be sold without license in quantities less than twenty-eight gallons. Licenses were granted, for one year only, by the court of general sessions upon the recommendations of the selectmen, who certified the number "necessary for the public good." The law required that "all public houses shall be on or near the high streets and places of great resort," allowed no credit over ten shillings, no sales to servants or minors without permission, and no sales at all to reputed common drunkards, whose names the selectmen were to post on the premises. The tythingmen were charged with the duty of inspection and complaint.[4]

These were stringent regulations, properly enforceable only in communities which were both willing and closely knit. Several interests in the larger towns were concerned with either violating or modifying the law. The connection between liquor and politics was traditional, and John Adams as early as 1761 had noted that "these houses are become, in many places, the nurseries of our legislators. An artful man may . . . multiply taverns and dramshops and thereby secure the votes of taverner, and retailer, and of all. . . ." Sellers were interested in making licenses less liable to forfeiture, and the wholesalers, merchants, and distillers were interested in multiplying retail outlets. These had power, and numbers were added by the numerous class of small retailers, "grocers" and "confectioners," who did not qualify as "taverners" or "common victuallers" under the law and who sold illegally if at all.[5]

Recognition was granted to the grocers of Boston by a special law of 1816, which granted licenses in that town to applicants who did not provide lodging or stables. In legal recognition of a *de facto* situation, the number of annual permits rose quickly from about fifty to over six hundred. When the city charter transferred the licensing power exclusively to the mayor and aldermen, Josiah Quincy was able for a time to decrease the total, but the number never fell below five hundred for a full year, and in his own opinion the effort to reduce it helped to cost him re-election. Throughout the period the "grocers" were among the several groups which held annual meetings or caucuses to endorse candidates for local office, and their power was respected.[6]

In 1832 the basic liquor law was considerably relaxed. Public houses no longer had to be located in "places of great repute." Ten rather than twenty-eight gallons became the minimum salable without license; the names of common drunkards were no longer posted; servants and minors might be served unless expressly forbidden. Fees were reduced, and in order to accommodate aliens, licensees were no longer required to take an oath of allegiance to the commonwealth.[7]

The older law, even with the modifications of 1816, had not been enforced, at least in Boston. About a quarter of the constables had themselves been grocers at some time, and since 1816 there had not been a single violation punished with forfeiture of bond. In 1830 the attorney general reported that, despite the fact that 690 liquor dealers were operating legally, roughly 300 more were selling without permits. About that time, the illegal sellers adopted a new "free rum" ideology, based on the concept that any license was a form of monopoly and that monopoly was odious.[8]

But the new law was challenged largely from another direction. The majority of legislators had always been conscious of the abuses of drink. Josiah Quincy's earlier conclusions were endorsed in 1834, when a poll of the physicians, prosecutors, judges, and correctional officers of Boston revealed that those most concerned believed that about three-quarters of all criminal offenses originated in drink.

Despite changes in the law, "free rum" remained an epithet to most, and liquor was widely recognized as a serious problem.[9]

A minority was even more deeply concerned. The Massachusetts Society for the Suppression of Intemperance had been founded in 1816. When this group weakened, the more militant American Society for the Promotion of Temperance was organized ten years later, after the Reverend Lyman Beecher's revival in Boston. In full accord with contemporary reform sentiment, the new society grew rapidly and helped to inspire similar groups throughout the nation. The temperance men of the commonwealth were in turn spurred on by their own pride in leadership: "It was in this state, and in this city, that men were first awakened." Failure could not be allowed in the birthplace of the movement.[10]

In the early 1830's, the antiliquor forces in both state and nation were increasingly divided over a series of related issues, the treatment of habitual drunkards, the expediency of political action, and the relative merits of moderation and abstinence. In Massachusetts, the 1832 license law helped to resolve at least one of these. The friends of temperance used various means to persuade selectmen and county commissioners that "the public good" was best served by granting liquor licenses only to a few of the most respectable, or to none at all. And in the middle 1830's, this limited form of political action succeeded in prohibiting legal sales in eight of the fourteen counties, and in many towns in the others.[11]

Even the Boston board of aldermen felt the fervor. In 1833, despite the new law, the board voted not to grant licenses to aliens, and to insist that licensees have lodging and a stable at least nearby. More and more applicants were turned down, more and more "referred to the city marshal" for investigation. The total number was reduced, by 1835, to three hundred, half the average in the previous decade.[12]

A climax was reached in 1838. At the February convention of the State Temperance Union, the delegates formally declared that total abstinence was their goal. Increasing militancy was recognized a few weeks later by the General Court, which passed the "Fifteen-Gallon Law." In addition to forbidding retail sales, this required licenses for all sales of any amount, and restricted the number of sellers to one for every two thousand inhabitants. The most radical law passed to that date in the United States, it was intended to eliminate not only public drinking but all drinking among certain classes. Only the threat of conflict with federal jurisdiction prevented some from pushing further to prohibit importation and sales over the fifteen-gallon limit.[13]

The unsettled political situation in the commonwealth, in a decade which witnessed the threat of a radical realignment of parties in almost every election, had given the most militant friends of temperance their opportunity. But just as the proponents of a looser law had over-reached themselves in 1832, so had the legal prohibitionists in 1838. The new act was widely condemned as an unconstitutional inter-ference with private habits, and as a threat to vested property rights in liquor. Moderates joined the opposition, and in 1839, a massive peti-tion of protest, headed by the name of Harrison Grey Otis and backed by many prominent citizens of Boston, was sent to the legislature. In the state campaign of 1840, the perennial Democratic candidate, Marcus Morton, made criticism of the law his leading issue. Judge Morton was a reformer himself, at one time President of the American Temperance Society, but belonged to the group which believed in voluntary methods. His election, although only by one vote, was interpreted in strongly Whiggish Massachusetts as an unmistakable repudiation of prohibition. The General Court in its next session repealed the Fifteen-Gallon Law, and the state reverted to license.[14]

But the issues were not dead. Throughout the preceding six years, the question of regulation had been argued in committee rooms, in pamphlets, in saloons, streets, and parlors. The morality of drinking was debated, and the constitutionality of limitation. But in the vigorous atmosphere of the 1830's, few respectable men, and fewer politicians, were willing to be counted openly against temperance. The opponents of prohibition insisted that they were the "true friends" of the movement, as public debate centered around the best means of reducing the evil. Relaxation was no longer in question; the three positions urged were prohibition, a stringent license law, and moral suasion, without either license or prohibition. All agreed on the need for "a vigilant police" and on the central importance of enforcement.[15]

Formal debate in the legislature was largely limited to those who favored the Fifteen-Gallon Law and those who would substitute strict license. During the committee hearings on the problem, in 1839, the latter argued that the law was undemocratic, possibly unconstitutional. Backed by the testimony of Boston's mayor and city marshal, who alleged an increase in small grogshops, they argued that it was un-workable as well. While 1,972,667 gallons of spirits had been manufactured in Massachusetts during 1828, ten years later, under the new law, the figure had risen to 3,190,681. Imports had risen also, those of 1838 exceeding the 1837 figures by 165,588 gallons.[16]

Supporters of the law had their own statistics: a decrease in distilleries from 118 in 1834 to 46 in 1838, and a 100,000-gallon decline in imports figured by using 1836 rather than 1837 as the base year. And, while admitting the difficulties of enforcement, they urged that an honest effort at least would drive out the respectable dealers, leaving the traffic in the hands of men whose character would illuminate its real nature. Even in balky Suffolk County there had been 181 prosecutions for liquor violations since 1836, with 119 resulting in conviction. And Mayor Eliot, cross-examined, could not deny that his own new police were vigilant enough to uphold the law.[17]

Both plans, in fact, depended upon a new kind of police action, which in Boston fell very largely on the new men. Mayor Chapman pointed out in 1842 that in "the very nature of the case, the offense of selling without license takes place, not in the open street, but in a house or shop, behind a closed door." The evidence to prove the offense could not be obtained "by eyesight only; but—to say nothing of tasting, which as a means of procuring evidence, no one would reject more indignantly than myself—the witness must remain long enough to hear the article named, before he can testify effectually." For the first time the police were called upon to act as detectives on their own initiative, to enter places without warrant, to return, search the premises, and seize the evidence. In charging them with such duty, the mayor had raised a political storm: "The passions of men are aroused, and the community is kept in a state of ferment."[18]

During the 1830's and 1840's the mayor and all of Boston's politicians were in a difficult position. Previously, the law had allowed them to grant licenses to the great majority of applicants. The city had rarely the means or the desire to disturb others who ignored it. But when respectable opinion demanded some kind of enforcement, and an end to a policy which granted the right to sell liquors to about one inhabitant in every ninety, the licensing power became an embarrassment. More applicants were disappointed than satisfied; and temperance men held the aldermen responsible for the behavior of the grantees, usually strangers, who had often misrepresented their qualifications. Doubtful cases were "referred to the city marshal," and lists of applicants were posted so that citizens might complain. But neither device relieved the aldermen of a responsibility of which they "would gladly be rid." And no moderate course would satisfy those who, desiring either total prohibition or "free rum," wanted no license at all.[19]

Its flexibility made this last alternative irresistibly attractive. There was a precedent for such a policy; in the latter part of 1832, following the change in the law, the aldermen, professing confusion, had issued no liquor permits and allowed anyone to operate without them. A series of cases which tested the constitutionality of the state's liquor legislation offered the same possibility between 1842 and 1846. And a new development within the temperance ranks added a moral to the legal sanction. The Washingtonian movement, which reached Boston in 1841 and expanded quickly, differed from previous efforts in the insistence that legislation was inexpedient and interfered with the true remedy, moral suasion directed at the individual.[20]

The no-license policy had several advantages. The prohibitionists were satisfied that the practice of drinking received no official sanction. The antimonopolists noted that the smallest grocers and confectioners were put upon the same footing as the hotels. The hotel-keepers had no bonds to forfeit. There were no rejected applicants and no licensees of ill repute.

But this plan simply shifted the problem to the marshal. Put forward as a reform, and on trial, it could not be allowed to result in disorder. Private and decorous drinking would not be interfered with: "As to the use of spirituous liquors within—leave that to individuals, and above all to the Washingtonians." But troublesome places would be prosecuted as "disorderly houses," or "common nuisances," and citizens were enjoined to "demand of your police to keep the outside in order—to see to it that the public peace is preserved, and the public proprieties in no way violated." The entire policy was in fact convenient only for the politicians. In design it encompassed a wide spectrum of opinion, but enforcement, in whatever degree, would immediately reveal the differences. Citizens were on watch for evidence either of negligence or of overzealousness. And inevitably the mayor had to note that "odious titles are affixed to your police."[21]

Other pressures in the same period also thrust the police into controversy. Much of the reform impulse was widely shared, even by Boston's conservative mayors. Theodore Lyman was a notable benefactor of the schools; Samuel Armstrong, in his youth, had been printer for the Massachusetts Temperance Union; Martin Brimmer and Samuel Eliot were officers of the Prison Discipline Society. But the caution of dominant opinion was reinforced by a fragmented political system. And the reform demand for a more positive use of police did not always fit the requirements of the majority, or of the police themselves.[22]

Increasing political pressure, resulting especially from the liquor issue, was clearly reflected in the status of the city marshal. The first appointee, Benjamin Pollard, had died in 1836, after thirteen years of service. His successor, former Deputy Sheriff Daniel Parkman, although less distinguished, was like Pollard a Harvard graduate and lawyer. Parkman resigned, however, after a few months, the week after a decision of the board of aldermen to issue no more liquor permits. Ezra Weston, Jr., appointed in September 1837, had not attended college but did have a degree from Harvard Law School. He resigned in January of 1840, and was succeeded by James Blake, the first nonlawyer to hold the post. Blake was followed in 1845 by Ira Gibbs, who had served a two-year apprenticeship as deputy marshal, after having been admitted to the bar without a college or other degree. Gibbs resigned after a single year, resuming his position as deputy to make way for Francis Tukey, the sixth marshal in a decade.[23]

This instability in the marshal's office was a symptom of a deeper uncertainty in the city government. Boston's local officers, by the 1840's, were no longer so firmly united by the ties of class and party as their predecessors of a generation before. The mayoralty was still largely reserved for representatives of the natural leadership of the community; Phillips, Quincy, Otis, Lyman, and Eliot were succeeded by others with similar qualifications, Martin Brimmer and Jonathan Chapman. But the monopoly could be broken, by men like Mayor Wells and shopkeeper Thomas A. Davis, the Native American candidate elected in 1844.[24]

The shift in class was more notable in the city council. The first group elected, in 1822, had contained a clear majority of merchants and professional men. But by 1845 the members were much more diverse. The aldermen included only one merchant, along with a doctor, a mason, a carpenter, a baker, one dealer in fish, one in lumber, and one with no listed profession. Ten of the forty-eight common councillors were merchants, three were lawyers, and others enjoyed such distinguished occupations as "Treasurer of the Worcester Railroad" and "none." But ten others were artisans and the rest were indeterminate "traders" and "provision dealers." There was no unity even within a single class. Reflective, educated citizens, the sons and grandsons of men who had been engaged in building a fortune or a commonwealth, could not safely be regarded as representatives of any family or group. Wendell Phillips and Charles Sumner descended, respectively, from the first mayor of the city and its sheriff; Edmund Quincy was a maverick in a manner quite different from his father.[25]

Boston remained a one-party city in the sense that candidates labeled Democratic or Locofoco had no chance of local success. There was a pool of willing candidates for mayor and council, only some of whom were included on the regular Whig ticket. Other factions held their own caucuses and posted their own lists. The "Firemen's," "Ex-Firemen's," "Grocers'," "Citizens'," and "Faneuil Hall" tickets usually duplicated each other in part but seldom entirely. In the kaleidoscope of local personalities and local issues those elected were twisted in several directions, and as a group lacked any clear position. A system of *de facto* proportional representation gave Whig conservatives a dominant but not exclusive voice in the city's affairs. Some spoke strongly, but more were tempted by a policy of avoidance and caution.[26]

The growing humanitarian reform movements of the 1830's and especially the 1840's created difficulties for these cautious municipal authorities. Even those causes whose focus was national or international presented practical problems. Should antislavery men, or, by 1850, Webster Whigs, be allowed the use of Faneuil Hall? Should they be protected in private meetings? Should the growing interest in the dignity of woman express itself in an attempt to end prostitution? Were gambling and other vices objectionable only when committed in public? Was truancy a matter for the police? Was drunkenness a crime, sin, or disease?

Two decades earlier these questions had not been raised. It was easy then for Boston's governing classes to ignore the social cripples, Negroes, prostitutes, and alcoholics who occupied the police. A conservative press occupied with ship arrivals, prices, legislative events, and national politics contained little noncommercial local news. The daily scenes in the lower courts went unattended by either sentiment or laughter at the breakfast table.[27]

Now not only the class but the newspapers had changed. The first cheap daily paper was founded in 1831, giving Boston a claim as "the mother of the penny press." Both the numbers and circulation of these papers climbed steadily, with the Boston *Times,* reportedly selling twelve thousand copies a day, leading even the established journals by 1836. All of the "pennies" left state and national politics to their older rivals, in order to concentrate on the local news which these had ignored, especially on violent or exciting incidents. Such stories could be gathered most easily each morning in court, and the popularity of this police court reportage led the more conservative press to adopt it. By the middle 1830's, even the *Advertiser* was devoting a paragraph or more to the courtroom.[28]

The treatment of such news varied with the case. Many were inclined to satirical accounts of hairpulling battles among the "frail sisterhood" of Ann Street, and to humorous courtroom excuses in brogue. But both conservative and popular papers also showed concern for the victims of a "Melancholy Suicide," a "Distressing Accident," a "Foul Deed." Stories of deviant behavior were moral lessons or warnings, and the police court furnished abundant examples of the effects of vice, especially of the impact of intemperance on guiltless wives and children.[29]

A heightened interest in the unfortunate was both an effect of the new humanitarian ethic and a contribution to it. And the police, for both reporters and reformers, became guides to this newly discovered underworld. Police work itself was as yet rarely publicized, but a few men, like Constable Derastus Clapp, became favorites with the press, treated as pundits and heroes. Legislators went out on watch, to talk to the men and observe firsthand the condition of Ann Street at night. William Ellery Channing hoped that a "preventive" police would be a major aid in promoting reform, since by improving the social environment they might improve those human souls who were shaped by it.[30]

But it was not clear that this was in fact what either the police or the procedures of criminal law were accomplishing, or whether this was what the city as a whole intended them to accomplish.

Drunkenness was both the basic problem and the test. Before 1836 the only recognition of this offense in the statutes was a law which provided for the arrest and punishment of "Common Drunkards."

The original law provided no specific penalties, but common drunkards were among those moral offenders whom peace officers could arrest, without warrant, in a public place or highway. In 1823, a maximum penalty was fixed at twenty dollars and sixty days in the House of Correction.[31]

The Supreme Judicial Court did not define the term "common drunkard" until 1855, as one "habitually drunk to the disturbance of the public peace and good order." But the meaning was always clear. Those arrested under the statute were notorious to the arresting officers as social drones, or complained against as a burden to their families and a nuisance to their neighbors. Single acts of overindulgence without reference to total behavior were made punishable by an English statute of 1606. But this provision was apparently ignored in the practice of Boston and Massachusetts until the codification and revision of the statute law in 1835. At that time the "crime of drunkenness by the voluntary use of intoxicating liquor" was added to the list of punishable moral offenses. Five dollars was charged for the first conviction, ten dollars and up to three months for the second. The offense was easier to prove than common drunkenness. And the number of drunk arrests in Boston, slowly at first and then more quickly, jumped from the few hundred annually during the 1830's, under the old statute, to several thousand in the later 1840's and 1850's, under the new.[32]

Many regarded this increase in arrest totals as an opportunity. The reform of prisons and prisoners was one of the oldest concerns of Boston's humanitarians, and the Boston Prison Discipline Society, under Louis Dwight, was one of the most active in the nation. The Revised Statutes of 1835 for the first time provided for an early version of parole, meeting part of Josiah Quincy's recommendation by allowing the courts to release moral offenders, on sureties, before they had served their full sentences. If the penal apparatus was not yet doing all it was supposed to, reformers were confident that with continued progress it would. The new generation, too, decisively reversed Quincy's distrust of the agents of police, and welcomed them as part of the reformatory process. Theodore Parker thought the day approaching when policemen would serve as "moral missionaries." Even in the 1840's he believed that the "rude tuition" of courts and constables was improving the drinking habits of Irish immigrants.

And the Society for the Suppression of Intoxication petitioned, in 1841, for a doubling of the police force, in order to help them gather subjects for rehabilitation.[33]

But not all of the rising arrest statistics resulted from such socially ambitious motives. Many temperance men, more vindictive than humane, were interested in punishing sin. Most citizens were satisfied that the arrests cleared the streets of disorder and potential violence. And some peace officers, under the fee system, still had a direct pecuniary stake in the process.

Some of these problems were illustrated by the work of John Augustus, "The Howard of Boston." Augustus, a bootmaker, belonged to no organized society, but had been impressed with the Washingtonians, and was troubled by the suffering exposed each day in the lower courts. Clearly the prevailing method of treating drunkenness was a failure; a legislative committee had already shown that the typical inmate of the House of Correction had been convicted five times of the same offense. With the cooperation of the judges of the police court, Augustus proposed an alternative. He would furnish bail and be given custody of the prisoner for a month; if at the end of that time there had been some improvement in character and prospects, the judge would set sentence at one cent and costs. Forty common drunkards received this treatment, in 1841, with apparent success. Augustus somehow fed and lodged his charges, and in two years extended his private probation system to the municipal courts and to cases of prostitution, petty thievery, and other offenses of the desperate. By the middle of the decade he was dealing with over a hundred cases each year.[34]

The cooperation of police, watch, and constables was useful, and Augustus was sensitive to their attitudes. They had, he found, no clear opinions as a group; lacking directions from superiors, they were free to act as individuals. Captain James Whitwell, of the west watch, was especially helpful, a "kindhearted as well as an efficient officer." His men and others brought in cases directly, bypassing the courts. "Respectable women and girls," in particular, who had applied for shelter in the watchhouses, as was customary on cold nights, were often taken to Augustus.[35]

But for many officers sympathy was countered by the pull of interest. The fee system, more inherited than designed, did not encourage philanthropy. And the beneficiaries of Augustus' work were of the helpless and tractable class who could most easily furnish quick arrests and seventy-five cents in witness fees. The police and watch ordinarily had enough to do, and perhaps a sense of shame was encouraged by the frequent chorus of jeering bystanders. But the constables at court, who got sixty-two cents for transporting prisoners to jail, were often openly hostile. Augustus was still widely regarded as an eccentric, and in the later 1840's these officers were able to make things uncomfortable for him.[36]

Meanwhile another incident, in 1842, demonstrated an even more threatening conflict of interest between police and reformers. That October, George Latimer, a fugitive from slavery, was captured on the streets by a group of constables acting without warrant in behalf of the owner. The case created an uproar. While the seizure was technically invalid, and not an arrest, it proved legally impossible to free the fugitive, and the abolitionists of the state were forced to buy him. This individual solution did not settle the deeper issue for the fearful population of "Nigger Hill" and their sympathizers. The use of constables as mercenaries had not before been questioned, and there were frightening possibilities in this new application of a traditional custom. Placards denouncing "HUMAN KIDNAPPERS" were circulated shortly after Latimer's capture, and followed by petitions calling for remedial legislation. Sixty-two thousand signatures helped convince the General Court, which in March 1843 passed the first of the northern personal liberty laws, forbidding peace officers and other public officials to cooperate in reclaiming slaves. No case arose, for a while, to test the act, passed largely by rural legislators. And it remained to be seen how it would be regarded by the federal courts and by the authorities in conservative Boston.[37]

The slavery problem was one of a series of political issues which threatened, during the 1830's and early 1840's, to involve the police in serious controversy, partly as a reflection of deep divisions within the whole city. To these were added other demands created simply by physical growth. While not so charged with emotion as those created by the reform movements, they had the same potential for future trouble.

Boston had had a population of approximately forty-nine thousand in 1822; this had grown to one hundred twenty thousand by 1846, and the rate of increase was not slackening. Transportation, formerly a casual matter of coaches, carts, and wagons, by the later date involved a system, with omnibus lines for intracity passengers and several railroads leading inland. The business of the port was still rising, with a regular passenger service established with England. The prosperity of New England manufacturing was reflected in Boston's importance as a financial center, and the city itself continued to develop a diversified economy of small industries and trade. "The Hub of the Universe" to its older inhabitants, it seemed equally attractive to the thousands of rural New Englanders who migrated to it. And if the foreign immigrants had less choice in the matter, their numbers too kept increasing, and the city was on the verge of a truly massive influx from the Old World.[38]

All administrative machinery had to be enlarged to keep up with this growth. The municipal budget had nearly quadrupled, from $264,721.24 in 1822 to $974,102.14 in 1845. With the greatest capital expenditures still in the future, almost the whole of this amount was spent on current services. With the exception of the fire department, which had begun with few expenses, the various branches of police accounted for the biggest rise, from $8,899.52 in the year of incorporation to $73,351.90 by 1845, not including the money spent by the department of internal health.[39]

The marshal's office, in 1837, had lost one important function, when administration of the sewer system was taken over by a separate department, headed by former Deputy Marshal Charles A. Wells. This encroachment on the marshal's extended responsibilities was desirable as technical progress encouraged specialization, and the loss was made up in other ways. The marshal had always helped to administer the grants of various licenses. He and his agents, too, had often, at least extra-officially, done service as criminal detectives. During the 1840's, these two duties were expanded beyond previous experience.[40]

The confusion and especially the anonymity of city living was an impetus common to the development of both functions. Men who had spent their lives in Boston could not keep up with its current growth, and to the immigrants from Vermont or Kerry it was entirely bewildering. The mayor, in 1848, noted the social effects of the transport revolution: "Railroads have changed the character and destiny of Boston—our narrow streets are thronged with a population that was never anticipated, and our marts with men of all nations and languages." In practice, he figured, if regular visitors and the non-residents who worked in the city were included, the population would be nearer two or three hundred thousand than the one hundred and twenty thousand officially counted.[41]

Not all of this transient population consisted of sober commuters. Sailors ashore and other rootless individuals were familiar in any port, but now adventurers, criminals, and homeless men could move in and out more easily than ever before, finding hiding places in the city unknown to the official society and uncontrolled by it. The presence of these groups made all of the population more difficult to identify and classify.[42]

One means by which the authorities dealt with this problem was through the licensing of various occupations. This practice, inherited from the English, had served many uses through the history of the commonwealth. Sometimes it was a means of ensuring standards of service, with a semimonopoly as the reward. The monopoly was itself the primary purpose in encouraging hazardous economic undertakings. Lawyers and doctors sought licenses in order to protect the professional reputation of their groups. Still another purpose, as in liquor licensing, was not only to protect standards but to keep track, to give authority the right to count, inspect, and control.[43]

At the time of the incorporation of 1822, the word "license" was often synonymous with "police," as "police" was with "government." The aldermen were responsible for a wide number of these permits. They were required of auctioneers, with vestiges of official authority; for theatrical exhibitions, to ensure decency; of users of gunpowder, to guarantee safety; and of chimney sweeps, porters, drivers of trucks and hacks, and others. The list grew, in succeeding decades, to include common criers, dogs, owners of glass furnaces, and newsboys, with the responsibility often shifted to the city marshal. This expansion did not involve the currently unpopular monopoly argument, and with the exception of those for exhibitions, the licenses brought in little revenue. Almost any individual could obtain one after paying a dollar and promising to fulfill the conditions.[44]

The use of all these permits was in various ways helpful to the police. The grantees were required to show them on request, thus identifying themselves. The licensing of newsboys and sweeps controlled juveniles without parents; shopkeepers had to admit inspection of their premises. In practice many of the licensing ordinances went unenforced, but sporadic efforts were made to exercise control. And between 1839 and 1850, several types were enforced with especial care, all of them designed to help in identification.

One of the most important was the licensing of pawnshops and dealers in secondhand articles or junk, required by a statute and ordinance of 1839. A special police officer, under the marshal, was assigned to superintend these establishments. Stringent conditions were imposed, which forbade irregular hours and purchases from minors or apprentices. Shop owners were required to keep elaborate records, with the date and hour of transactions, together with the names and addresses of sellers.[45]

These regulations were especially useful in identifying criminals, a function which was nearly becoming a public responsibility. The police agents were called upon increasingly as the injured citizen, traditionally his own detective, was hampered even more than the authorities by the transport facilities, size, and anonymity of the city.

By the 1840's, the growing sophistication of the criminal profession added still another obstacle to private effort. In 1822, professional crime in Boston and in America generally was a primitive occupation. There were schemers eager to defraud the countryman come briefly to town, as there were pimps and prostitutes and various vicious or desperate men. But none possessed the skills dangerous to citizens who walked in daylight and retired at night behind bolted doors. James Faxon, author of the *Record of Crimes in the United States,* a compendium published in 1833, was forced to apologize for his thin material, and to explain that the prosperous institutions of America made crime a shameful rarity. His book, largely a catalogue of domestic crimes and acts of madness, recorded only two kinds of professionals, the traditional, pre-urban highwayman and the pirate.[46]

Criminality was no more sophisticated than the economic and social system within which it operated. The elaborate confidence schemes, the organized bank robberies, forgeries, and burglaries which flourished later in the century were largely absent in the earlier period. Movable wealth, especially negotiable paper, had not as yet multiplied. Neither had the urban population, nor the intercity railroad systems which provided the anonymity essential to successful professional crime.[47]

The long hiatus in immigration during the late eighteenth and early nineteenth centuries also contributed to American ineptitude even in those criminal skills which were practicable. The art of picking pockets was exercised but not to the extent common in England or on the Continent. Even the clumsy iron locks of the period provided too great a challenge for its lawbreakers; the turbulent common jail of Philadelphia, typically, was the scene of many escapes, but it was noted that throughout the early nineteenth century, while bars and walls proved vulnerable, the locks were never solved. The development of criminal craftsmanship required a degree of patience and training for which, as Mayor Eliot and Editor Faxon were convinced, there were better rewards in the United States.[48]

Americans had a particular advantage in only one criminal enterprise. The rapid growth of banking institutions, and the confusing variety of notes, made counterfeiting relatively easy. The rewards were large, and during the 1820's the practice flourished, the only crime other than piracy which could seriously affect the propertied classes. Individual protection was useless, while state and local authorities were helpless because the problem was regional and even international.[49]

The first major reaction was mounted not by the state but by a private agency, the New England Association Against Counterfeiting. The directors of Boston's banks, accustomed to other forms of mutual help, met in November 1832 to join in combating the common problem. The local banks subscribed a hundred dollars each, and the association also sought out other members; while 92 institutions, mostly in New York State, refused to help, 126 others joined in the first twelve months. With the funds provided by their subscriptions, the association was able to achieve important results within a year.[50]

The officers considered the British Provinces the most important source of counterfeit, and a special effort was made to enlist the three banks of Canada. Horatio Gates, an influential banker in Montreal, was made the chief correspondent there. With the aid of information supplied by the New Englanders, and of pressure from Gates, the Canadian government, "zealously supported by the inhabitants, who assisted in making the arrest," captured twenty-five offenders in a single raid.[51]

In the United States, agents discovered twenty-three forged plates, and five packages of counterfeit Boston notes totaling over twenty thousand dollars. No one was captured in the city itself, but several were arrested in Massachusetts, with others scattered over the Northeast.[52]

The official agencies of law enforcement proved cooperative once the initiative had been supplied. In order to secure the help of a high constable of Philadelphia, the association had to bring him to Boston, give him two hundred dollars on account, and promise three hundred more upon the capture of an especially wanted criminal. There was no difficulty in obtaining warrants in Massachusetts. The attorney general, in some cases, agreed not to enter charges against repentant informers, although counterfeiting was punishable by up to life imprisonment, and two men were so sentenced. Whatever the demands of the commonwealth, the bankers were satisfied with discontinuance, and considered the forfeit of bond both sufficient reward for the state and sufficient punishment. The successes of the New England Association Against Counterfeiting were achieved on a scale impossible for others to match. But its approach was not fundamentally different from that of the individual victim of fraud or theft, who had still to rely on himself or to persuade a constable or other peace officer to undertake his case.[53]

However, as the conditions which had held back the development of crime were rapidly overcome, there was a felt need for more official responsibility. In 1829, Mayor Joseph Gates of Washington had written to the government of Boston, and probably elsewhere, asking for a regular exchange of letters between an official in his city and "any one who may be designated in this, in order to give and receive information in relation to convicts and stolen goods." While no formal detective service resulted, the aldermen were interested enough to grant the mayor authority to establish a correspondence. It was often repeated that lawlessness was growing faster than the city, and the incidence of burglary, especially, seemed to be rising during the 1830's and 1840's. This concern had contributed to the strengthening of police, and in order to encourage detection the city began to offer rewards more frequently. Arson, a general threat to the community, had often prompted the government to post a reward, as had an especially brutal murder or the destruction of its own property. The more nearly private threat of burglary was added to the list for the first time in 1834. The total rose steadily: following three in the decade of the 1820's and four in the 1830's, nine rewards were offered between 1841 and 1845.[54]

The effect of these offers was to increase the amount of detective work done by the various city police, but this remained extra-official. In adding to the private funds already available, the city implied that the kind of effort required was not normally expected. When the crime involved stolen goods, restitution by whatever means was the principal object. The city or state, not officially involved in the process, asserted no different claim. Neither law nor current opinion in fact made any clear distinction between the public and private interest in this area. There was legislation in England, often ignored and even officially flouted, which forbade the compounding of a felony through arrangements between police officers and thieves. The most nearly equivalent statute in Massachusetts did not mention police officers, and the only case in which it was tested in the Supreme Judicial Court involved private blackmail.[55]

Detective methods were not yet fully shrouded in romance, and the bargaining involved was reported quite openly. In the spring of 1841 the city was plagued with burglaries, culminating in the ten-thousand-dollar robbery of Davis & Palmer, jewelers. The newspapers were excited, and when the aldermen voted a two-thousand-dollar reward, Constable Clapp set out to earn it. The thieves were skilled professionals, one at least from England and others from New York. Clapp knew they were in Boston, and when one was arrested on an unrelated charge, he managed to obtain the return of the money in exchange for release. When directed to a room in a boardinghouse, the constable found in addition to the stolen articles a collection of what one paper described as two hundred burglar's tools and keys, which the thief "begged lustily for Mr. Clapp not to take. Mr. C. replied that the law required it."[56]

None of the parties was prosecuted, but Clapp nonetheless applied for the public reward and got a part of it. Sheriff Eveleth had approved the release, but otherwise, except for the reward, the state was not involved. Clapp was acting essentially as an agent for the jewelers, and there was no outcry about either the legality or the morality of the transaction.[57]

But the city could not remain apart indefinitely. There was a movement by 1845 to create a detective branch of the police, on salary, whose members would be available to the whole community and work in its interest. The action would fill a need; by accepting responsibility the city might provide detective service with a system and sanctions that had been lacking. At the same time, it would have to accept responsibility for the methods used, and for resolving the potential conflict between the public and private interest.

In the terms originally set by Mayor Eliot, the police at the beginning of 1846 were continuing to do their jobs well. They had been established mainly to deal with riots, and while it was difficult to hold an antislavery meeting in Boston, especially one involving imported speakers, this was widely supposed to be public policy, and no disorder since 1837 had gotten out of hand. In 1845 an aldermanic investigating committee declared that enforcement of the ordinances, the main task of police, was proceeding smoothly. The council had entertained complaints about the watch, in 1843, and the aldermen agreed in 1845 that a few of the forty-five constables were "intemperate" and should not be reappointed. Neither problem was regarded as serious, and it was stated, at the same time, that the new police, twelve of them, were "uniformly of a high order."[58]

But the aldermen were aware already that there were police issues which went beyond the state of the sidewalks and the preservation of the peace. Even the well-established routines of watch and constables were creating frictions. And since the reform of 1837, a series of important questions about the use of the police had been raised but not yet fought out or resolved.

CHAPTER FIVE

A Vigorous Police: Marshal Tukey, 1845-1853

The inaugural address of Mayor John Prescott Bigelow in 1849 gave the ultimate expression to the mercantile optimism of contemporary Boston: "The long winter of New England Isolation is broken,—she warms and flourishes in friendly and thrifty intercourse with the luxuriant West; and it is not too much to anticipate that the day will come, when there will be no greater or more prosperous city upon the American continent than the City of the Pilgrims."[1]

Bigelow was speaking especially of the possibilities opened by the new railroads. Business was excellent. The city was still growing at the high rate, between 40 and 50 per cent a decade, which had been maintained since incorporation. And its citizens were still supremely confident in the future, in the vitality of progress and reform.

Governmental expansion between 1845 and 1853 kept pace with commercial growth. Between 1845 and 1847 the budget tripled, leaping from $974,102.14 to $3,293,579.92. In 1846 ground was broken for the public water system, the largest and most dramatic of capital projects. Handsome school buildings were completed in the next few years, as the educational system expanded. Several parks were established, and the Public Library opened in 1852. As ordinary departmental expenses continued to mount, in the years after 1845 "the expenditures of Boston were on a municipal basis."[2]

But confidence in size was in the same period beginning to be clouded by social and political doubts. During 1845-46, as the waterworks was brought to Boston, the potato famine came to Ireland. Irish immigration reached a peak during the late 1840's and early 1850's. The newcomers brought problems more obvious than their gifts; increase in drink and poverty strained the institutions of charity and police. Their coming also helped to exacerbate a tense political atmosphere. As the Free-Soil and Know-Nothing movements grew and the older parties splintered and regrouped, men's hopes for the material future were balanced by fear for the political. Humanitarian reform in the city, no longer new, was in some ways accepted. In others the movement was discouraged, brought to a peak and then frustrated.[3]

In an atmosphere of expansion, many of these developments created demands for more vigorous police activity. The local authorities, still unused to the possession of force, were called upon or tempted to use it in a variety of new ways, some of which provoked popular excitement. In the process of experiment, both the government and the citizens began, often painfully, to discover the limits necessary to a politic use of the police force.

In December of 1845, the doubts had not yet begun to temper the optimism. The results of the municipal election that month were interpreted with especial enthusiasm in the press. The regular Whig candidate, overwhelmingly elected, was Josiah Quincy, Jr., in many ways the ideal choice. Quincy was a reformer, and by heredity and in his own right exemplified the tradition of aristocratic involvement in local affairs. As treasurer of the popularly subscribed Worcester Railroad, he was a forceful spokesman of public improvement. His belief in progress was measured by his willingness to multiply dramatically the city's spending and debt. And his program for dealing with the attendant problems was equally uncompromising. Crime and disorder, disease, drink, and poverty would all be met by a vigorous police, expanded for the purpose.[4]

To assure this vigor the mayor chose Francis Tukey, a personal friend, to head the department. Only thirty-two years old in 1846, the new marshal had originally come to Boston from Maine, as a mechanic. But he had shown his ambition by working his way through law school in two years, and his enormous gusto made him well suited to take on responsibility for the most rapidly growing department in the city. The regular force was more than doubled at the time of his appointment, as eighteen new men were chosen with him, raising the total to thirty. Eight were detailed as a special night force. And three more, within months, were added to serve as detectives, the first on the public payroll.[5]

During and after Quincy's administration the regular police expenses continued to climb. The $12,232.14 spent in 1845-46 mounted
to $49,251.27 in 1851-52, exclusive of the money spent on internal
health. By 1851 there were twenty-two night men, usually detailed
to patrol the business district as a supplement to the watch and often
used as a flying squad of raiders. Most of the forty-four day men did
ordinary patrol service, covering beats of three to four miles each.
The detectives were assigned to the central office, together with
several headquarters officials, the marshal himself, and the two
deputies.[6]

This great growth in the marshal's office overshadowed the more
modest gains of the watch, which, moving from 150 men in 1840 to
190 in 1851, roughly kept pace with the population. The effect was
felt more severely by the constables, whose numbers were cut back,
in 1848, from forty-four to thirty men. The reduction in number
reflected a change in duty. The constables like Derastus Clapp and
William Eaton who had shown a talent for thief-catching were transferred to the police, as detectives. The rest, in practice, virtually ceased
to operate independently of the courts. While occasionally serving
criminal warrants, they were increasingly confined to civil business.
The new model police could handle the rest.[7]

Respect for the reorganized police department, and the number
of men available, enabled the city to expand their activities. Some
of the new duties were merely odd jobs, as when members of the
force were used as messengers to deliver official reports. Others were
extensions of existing practice. The men had always helped to provide
emergency aid to the unfortunate, for example, and during the later
1840's this service was made official. Budgets for the police and
watch included fifty or a hundred dollars a year to cover medical
treatment for the victims of accident or sudden illness, and a similar
amount made up "cash disbursement for the immediate relief of suf-
ferers in various ways."[8]

Still other responsibilities were entirely new, reflections of growth
in both the department and the city. One resulted from the need to
regulate the city's thriving "intelligence offices." These were employment bureaus, open to "domestics, servants, or . . . other laborers
except seamen." Pregnant with possibilities for the cruelest kind of
fraud, they were subjected to license and control in 1848, under the
charge of a special officer who joined the superintendent of second-

hand shops at headquarters. His inspection of the books of these companies provided information about that growing pool of transients and immigrants which was in many ways a subject of concern.[9]

More important still was the city's first systematic attempt at traffic regulation. Since 1797 the commonwealth had had a statute regarding hacks and trucks, which required both rate regulation and the prominent display of a license number. But despite an occasional petition this had not been enforced between the incorporation and 1846. In that year the marshal was ordered to keep the licenses on record, collect the fees, and check on the conditions. A third special officer was employed to do this work full time, and to answer complaints about lost articles, high rates, or conduct in violation of a series of strengthened traffic ordinances.[10]

A fourth special officer joined the force in 1850, in response to a long-continued agitation. Nothing was more obviously essential to progress than the instruction of youth, one of the major concerns of the younger Quincy. The increasing emphasis on universal education demanded that as many as possible be reached. A special committee of the city council reported in 1846 that "the mischief caused by habits of truancy, which prevail in many of our schools can hardly be overrated. No valuable or permanent reform will ever be carried into full effect until this obstacle is removed." Existing law required only that "the resident ministers of the gospel, the selectmen, and the school committees, in the several towns . . . exert their best endeavors that . . . youth shall regularly attend the schools provided." But like so much of the legislation of the commonwealth, this did not fit conditions in the mid-century city. In 1850 educational reformers accordingly secured an act which set penalties for truant children, and especially for those parents who profited from "their wretched gains or . . . dishonest pursuits." The law also enabled Boston to detail a policeman to enforce it. The whole force made arrests for truancy, and the special officer, Theodore Parker's "moral missionary," offered counsel to several hundred delinquents and their families. His work, in company with that of the other new officers, demonstrated again the flexibility of the police department and its usefulness in dealing with the emergent problems of the municipality.[11]

But for Mayor Quincy and many who supported him in three successful campaigns, the most important function of the police was dramatized in the city's first major campaign against vice. The growth of reform sentiment had been reflected earlier in city politics, but the more uncompromising reformers had never won a majority in the city council, and between the two Quincys the mayors had generally been moderates. Before 1846, the government had neither the force nor the purpose required for a concerted attack on immorality.

Because police estimates and statistics were not published before 1850, it is difficult to measure the city's efforts to deal with vice. But the temperance campaign did have some effect. It is clear that between the early 1830's and the middle of the 1840's the number of places selling liquor in Boston declined, possibly in absolute terms and certainly in proportion to population. It is more difficult to estimate the extent of gambling and prostitution. The latter problem probably increased, at least absolutely, with the number of unskilled and homeless girls seeking work in the city. The existence of numerous houses of prostitution was acknowledged openly and lightly in the popular press. Disorderly houses were sometimes prosecuted, and individual nightwalkers arrested when complained against. Arrests on the initiative of police officers themselves were probably made only when aggravated by circumstances. The elder Quincy had seen the problem as insoluble, capable at best of being hidden away. And despite increasing intolerance toward this and other moral offenses, nothing more ambitious had been done.[12]

But the younger Quincy abandoned this fatalistic attitude. Although more moderate than some of his supporters, the new mayor was definitely a reformer. He supported Horace Mann's program for the schools; his brother was an abolitionist; and he was the only firm prohibitionist ever elected to head the city. He was willing to use the law and the police to enforce his ideals, and his election tipped the balance in the city government.

Since 1842 the aldermen had cited legal uncertainty as the official reason for failure to grant liquor licenses. But in 1847, the decisions of the United States Supreme Court in the License Cases made it impossible any longer to avoid the issue, and the policy was reviewed. When the board split, four to four, over the wisdom of granting liquor permits, the mayor cast his deciding vote against them. His reasons were not based on caution, or like those of Mayor Chapman, earlier, on a professed abhorrence of monopoly. Instead he firmly stated his belief in both the benefits and the possibility of prohibition. Marshal Tukey's views, if nonideological, were equally stark. When the aldermen later asked him how best to check the increase in crime, "he contented himself with the simple statement—'execute the law.' "[13]

This process was begun in the easiest manner, in the fall of 1846, through the Sunday laws, where proof was required only of the fact of doing business and not of its nature. But after the official decision in 1847, the license law itself was used to justify arrests and raids by the night police. The business of executing the law, urged on by organized groups, developed a momentum of its own under Tukey, which survived Quincy's three years in office. The continual harass-ment of sellers increased even during the administration of the con-servative Mayor Bigelow, elected in 1848. Bigelow's opposition to prohibition was overridden by a unanimous vote of the aldermen. In 1850 the police made 417 arrests for violations of the license laws, and over 41 for keeping noisy and disorderly houses. In 1851, the figure for license violations reached 718, the largest single cause of arrest other than simple drunkenness itself.[14]

At the same time, the police under both the Quincy and Bigelow administrations intensified their efforts against other kinds of vice. Gaming arrests increased. The numbers of those taken in for drunken-ness continued to climb. And for the first time action was taken to curb prostitution.[15]

Quincy ordered the first move against prostitutes as a class, to end the ancient connection between vice and the stage. Many of Boston's theaters hired special policemen to eject trouble-makers, but they made no effort to limit their use as places of assignation. It was notorious that the drama often only raised the curtain on the evening, and in some places a special section, the "third row," was set aside for prostitutes. The aldermen in 1847 voted to clean up this situation through the use of the licensing power. All theater owners were re-quired to hire regular officers from the city, who were ordered to keep liquor and prostitutes out of the premises. The wages, while charged to the police appropriation, comprised the license fee.[16]

More dramatic was the "descent," or raid. Begun under Quincy, the practice was extended by Marshal Tukey and reached its height during the late winter and spring of 1851. By that time it covered not one place but several and attacked gambling and other offenses as well as illegal liquor selling. On Saturday night, March 8, eighty-six people were arrested for "shaking props" in a gaming resort, to the especial delight of the penny press. Afterwards the marshal invited the public to the police office, to inspect the captured gambling instruments. Twenty-seven more arrests were made the next Friday, and were followed by a similar exhibition. A month later, on April 23, Tukey staged "the Celebrated Ann Street Descent," aimed partly at gamblers but largely at prostitution.[17]

Nothing before had been organized on the scale of the Ann Street venture, which originated either with private reformers or the police themselves. The whole street was raided, and the one night's work netted sixty men and ninety women. Thirty-five were sentenced as "keepers of brothels, noisy and disorderly houses, violaters of the license and Sunday laws, etc." The remaining men were prosecuted as "tipplers, vagabonds, pipe players, etc.," and the women as prostitutes. Most significant was the advantage taken of the pioneering of John Augustus: many of the women, by arrangement with the courts, were given suspended sentences and hired out as domestics to private families.[18]

All of this was fascinating for the press, but the exploits of the marshal's detective bureau were the subject of an even greater and more continuous interest. The detectives, when first organized, were formally distinguished from the other day police only by their function. But they were beginning, in the later 1840's, to acquire a special glamour. In part this was a reflection of interest in their antagonists. The police court news introduced in the 1830's had concentrated sometimes on misery, sometimes on humor, but almost always on the violence and petty offenses of a class that was more perishing than dangerous. But in the 1840's and 1850's, this was supplemented by news of professional roguery of a different kind. The detectives were now engaged with "noted" or "notable" thieves, often from out of town. And the papers assumed a readership which needed no help in identifying men like "Bristol Bill" and similar characters.[19]

The three full-time detectives were selected in this period largely for "their knowledge of rogues and their schemes." Two were former constables, who continued to work as they had before being brought under public direction—with one important exception. Late in 1845, after a watchman claimed $2,000 offered for the arrest of an incendiary, the government had objected. In the case of *Poole* v. *Boston,* the city solicitor argued that persons performing paid duty should not be eligible for rewards from the treasury. Although none of his precedents involved peace officers or criminal rewards, the Supreme

Judicial Court upheld his view. And in 1846, when the detectives were organized, the aldermen ruled that public rewards would be granted policemen only by special vote. More important, it voted to forbid both witness fees and later private rewards under the same condition.[20]

In practice, these rules could be evaded; one way was to make semi-official the arrangements which had before been private. Those requesting detective work were often asked to contribute to a "discretionary fund" kept by the marshal for use in procuring evidence and witnesses, and sometimes the city was billed in small amounts under the same heads.[21]

Many of the applicants were sailors and others victimized by "panel thieves," who specialized in robbing loose clothing in bawdy houses, and the detectives were often occupied in policing these places and restricting them to their primary functions. At other times they simply circulated in crowds in order to spot pickpockets. But there was higher work to do as well. Marshal Tukey was once authorized to pursue offenders all the way to Canada, on behalf of the New England Association Against Counterfeiting. As detective service became less a private and more a public responsibility, the city on at least one occasion furnished half the salary of a Boston-based agent of the bankers' organization. At other times, since it employed the only regular detectives in New England, the city lent them out to pursue safe robbers in such places as Provincetown and Lynn.[22]

Tukey basked in his reputation as "Our Vidocq," after the famous French inspector, and his talent for publicity magnified the intrinsic interest that these operations held for the press and public. In January 1848, the police drew a crowd by mysteriously digging into Boston Common to uncover a cache of allegedly stolen money. And in 1851 the marshal introduced, as a regular institution, a weekly "show-up of rogues," designed to identify suspicious persons for the benefit of both police and public. At the first of these spectacles, "Seventy-six pickpockets, burglars, panel thieves, etc."—among them twelve women —were "shown up to the whole of the police force." None were legally under arrest, and all, upon leaving the office, were forced to run a gauntlet of crowing citizens who tore their clothing and marked their backs with crosses in chalk.[23]

The "show-up" was an almost totalitarian display of power, fully appropriate for a man who had become the most important local officer in Boston. The marshal was still superintendent of the department of internal health, although most of the work was delegated to Deputy Hezekiah Earle. The department's two large yards employed a number of full-time artisans, blacksmiths, and painters, in addition to the casual labor required in sweeping the streets. The marshal was responsible for the vaccination program. And he possessed all the old power of the board of health to institute proceedings of eviction, condemnation, and transportation to the South Boston institutions for the contagious. By 1851-52, the various expenses of the internal health department, including the cost of buying horses and grain, fuel, paint, and lime, reached $79,573.87. Tukey's other job as head of the police was strengthened by the fact that he was able successfully to demand the right of approving appointments. His salary had been raised in 1847, at Mayor Quincy's suggestion, to $1,800, a figure exceeded only by the mayor, the treasurer, and the city solicitor. This put him on a level above the municipal judges; and his deputies, at $1,100 each, earned more than many department heads.[24]

But his official position did not fully explain Tukey's remarkable hold on the public. He had arrived in Boston just as the always latent excitement in police work was beginning to emerge, and he was well equipped to exploit it. Unlike earlier men who had dominated the local scene, he had no aristocratic pretensions and no family connections. Once, when he was fined for his persistently reckless driving, the *Daily Mail* observed that "the spirit of the b'hoy" had triumphed over "the dignity of the officer." But for most readers of the penny press, the marshal's frankly coarse behavior had an appeal of its own. And few papers treated him so lightly; he was hard, and rude, rather than familiar. A big man, with curly hair and an impressive, heavy face—one editor called him "beautiful"—he kept his own men at some distance, and most of them were afraid to speak to him unasked. The fact that he was a popular hero, admired by temperance men and bankers as well as reporters, made his elective superiors equally hesitant to interfere with him. He was obviously ambitious, and it was said that Mayor Seaver, elected in 1851, owed Tukey his election.[25]

But despite the marshal's commanding position, his power rested on an uncertain base. The same activity that made him newsworthy to all and praiseworthy to some made him offensive to others. He was always in controversy, "a terror to evildoers and to some who were not evildoers." And as remarked in the *Bunker Hill Aurora,* the maxim that "it is easier to get than to retain popularity" was especially applicable to officers of police.[26]

The same methods which excited admiration when applied to gamblers were not so acceptable when used against other citizens. The drive to enforce the traffic ordinances goaded the owners of omnibus lines into carrying the issue all the way to the Supreme Judicial Court. And the technique of mass arrests was used as frequently in connection with the bylaws as with moral offenses. On February 2, 1848, 91 people were arrested for failure to clean up icy sidewalks. On two occasions in the same year, 50 more were brought in for keeping unlicensed dogs. On April 21, 1851, 101 were arrested for dog law violations, and on December 23, 112 for neglecting icy sidewalks. Some 83 more sidewalk offenders were brought in on February 5, 1852, 65 dog law violators on March 9. The gentle tactics of Marshal Pollard were exploded for "a policy to have as many cases of this kind before the court, at the same time, as possible, giving the defendants but little opportunity to complain of partiality, and plenty of time to wait in court." There was no provision until late in the century for issuing summonses in minor criminal cases, and no means of transportation for those brought in. An arrest in the 1850's meant a long walk through the streets with a policeman, accompanied by howls in disreputable areas and stares in the respectable.[27]

The activities of the marshal's detective bureau also opened up an area of vulnerability, this one of more long-term importance. Official detective work was still a novelty, and its publicity brought it close attention. The men had no scientific aids, no files or photographs, only a few handbills. But since the proposal of Washington's Mayor Gates, in 1829, the invention of the telegraph was beginning to make it possible for detectives in various cities to communicate. Some states, New York and Pennsylvania the most important, made public announcement of the release of convicts from prison. Descriptions were relayed to the marshal's office, and if it appeared that an ex-convict or suspected thief might head for Boston, his agents stood watch at the railroad terminals. The keepers of pawnshops were useful in local cases. And the detectives had skills of their own; the term "shadow" was already used, and many men developed extraordinary memories for the faces and habits of criminals. But with all of these aids, criminals themselves were the most essential to detective work. It was necessary to overlook some offenses to concentrate on others, as in panel thievery, or to overlook the crime to concentrate on recovery.[28]

One ex-detective who had worked in New York during the middle of the century explained, "There are but two great classes in civilization—the oppressed and the oppressors, the trampled upon and the detective. He is dishonest, crafty, unscrupulous, when necessary to be so. He tells black lies when he cannot avoid it, and white lying, at least, is his chief stock in trade. He is the outgrowth of a diseased and corrupted state of things, and is, consequently, morally diseased himself." The same authority concluded that there was no alternative; the detective was useful, even necessary. So long as there was a demand, the business of bribery and extortion, the harassing of ex-convicts, and the compounding of felony were inevitable.[29]

But since this inevitability was not widely recognized or accepted, so far at least as it concerned public officers, the detective system was a weak spot in the reputation of any police force. The first attack on detective procedures came soon after the agents were officially connected with the force; critics remarked that while Tukey was proud of the amount of stolen goods his men recovered, a total worth $16,121 in 1850, he never talked about the means of recovery. For those who knew, the information was potential ammunition, all the more valuable since the marshal's popularity with several groups was beginning to wane.[30]

One new complaint centered on Tukey's published attitude toward juvenile delinquency. The marshal, together with many other citizens, was disturbed by the number of neglected children in the city, estimating that some fifteen hundred, between the ages of six and sixteen, were beyond the reach of parental or other discipline. But he saw the problem not as an educational reformer but as a policeman, concerned only with keeping children off the streets, where, drifting into petty crime and vicious habits, they made trouble for his men. The courts, Tukey believed, were too easy on young offenders under the new truant law. His recommendation was that guilty juveniles be bound out as apprentices or domestics until their majority, a proposal denounced as reactionary by the friends of Horace Mann.[31]

This attack, while minor in itself, reminded reformers that while the marshal was sometimes with them he was not of them, and it came at a time when many of them were disillusioned with his performance for other reasons. The more ardent spirits in the temperance movement had from the beginning called for vigorous enforcement of the no-license policy. Drink was regarded as the primary agent of all of the evils of contemporary society, the most widely recognized cause of poverty, crime, and disease, of seduction, broken families, prostitution, irreligion, and corruption. The temperance ideal was part of a wider vision of the progress of civilization, and specifically of Boston. And while in some respects this vision reached a height during the late 1840's, in others it was beginning to fade.

The decline was in part a natural reaction to exaggerated hopes. In part it was related to increasing concern for the Union and absorption in the national problem of slavery. But for many it was precipitated by the evidence that there had been no social progress in Boston, a problem aggravated by the irony that the decade of reform overlapped the decade of the Irish coming.

The tensions that the Irish presence created had occasionally erupted before 1845. But the immigration following the Great Famine was unprecedented. The number of arrivals shot up until by 1850 thirty-five thousand of the one hundred thirty-six thousand residents of the city were Irish by birth. More revealing of their impact are the statistics of misery. The wretched economic and physical condition of the newcomers was partly reflected in the amount annually spent on institutional poor relief, which rose from $43,700 in 1845 to $136,217 in 1852. Smallpox became a problem again after 1845. Cholera struck in 1849. And the death rate, boosted by dirt and overcrowding in the Irish districts, averaged 29.4 per thousand in the five-year period before 1850, a record for the century.[32]

The coming of the Irish was an enormous shock to the police of the city. As superintendent of internal health, the marshal was the official most concerned with rapidly deteriorating sanitary conditions. The increase in minor criminality was equally troublesome. Irish mores and misery made the prohibitory liquor policy, especially, impossible to enforce. The friends of temperance later recalled the early 1840's as the period when the movement in Boston had reached its peak. Whether or not the voluntarism of the Washingtonians and their imitators was more effective than the harassing tactics of Marshal Tukey, it was clear by the later 1840's that the policy inaugurated by Mayor Quincy was not achieving its ends.[33]

The mayor, and more especially the marshal, blamed the failure of their crusade upon the courts. In fact, the vice laws themselves were the result of compromise. They recorded official condemnation of immoral behavior, to the satisfaction of puritans and reformers. But in a large city, where thousands of inhabitants were habitual violators, prosecution was necessarily partial. And when the police brought in large numbers whose conduct was not considered extreme, and who had not prompted private complaints, the courts were often lenient. Judges had considerable latitude in fixing penalties, and were dependent both upon political favor and the willingness of juries to convict. Tukey complained that liquor dealers were fined an average of only twenty-four dollars each; the victims of the great gambling raids in 1851 were assessed at three dollars apiece, as first offenders.[34]

But these complaints, reflecting an increasingly intransigent majority opinion, only emphasized that police action in itself was insufficient. Mayor Bigelow's plea, in 1849, for a careful return to the license system, did not move the aldermen, who had a variety of reasons for supporting the existing policy. But it did express a widespread disillusion. Quincy's "experiment," he noted, had had a fair trial, "aided by an efficient police, and backed by . . . a large and influential body of his fellow citizens. What has been the result?" The answer was more than disappointing. An appalling increase in intemperance and attendant crimes made it seem "as if the saturnalia of Bacchus, or some more malignant of the heathen deities, took date from the vote which was to overthrow his altars, and confound his votaries."[35]

The marshal's own figures bore out this complaint. In 1851, Tukey estimated, there were 227 houses of ill fame operating in the city, and 26 gambling places. An even 1,500 shops sold liquors, 900 run by Irishmen. These were not taverns, or even groceries; 1,031 of them sold nothing else.[36]

Almost in proportion as critics were discouraged with these returns on their hopes for a better city, they turned to the most distant problem of slavery. In this battle there were fewer daily reminders of failure, and less frustration. Here was no apparent victory lost but a movement still gathering force. Under the administration of Mayor Quincy there were no local incidents involving mob violence. But active antislavery sentiment was still minority opinion, and conflict again developed during the tenure of Mayor Bigelow. While reformers had urged a more vigilant professional police force for other reasons, they discovered in this context that the marshal was not merely a disappointing ally but actually an opponent.

The problem had become more acute since the Latimer case in 1843. The Mexican War and its aftermath, including Webster's Seventh of March Speech, the Compromise of 1850, and the evident Southern determination to enforce the new fugitive slave law, had all contributed to political fragmentation in Massachusetts. To Mayor Bigelow, for many years an intimate associate of Governor Everett, the disintegration of the long dominant Whig party was especially painful. But despite its usual caution, the city government was unable to avoid involvement in controversy beyond its limits. Marshal Tukey, stationed at Faneuil Hall in November of 1850, failed to take action when a great abolitionist meeting to denounce the apostate Webster was broken up by a disorderly invasion. Edmund Quincy, brother of the former mayor, demanded that the city council rebuke the marshal for neglect of duty. While Tukey was absolved, the point was made. In future, both abolitionists and Webster Whigs were denied the use of Faneuil Hall, a move which satisfied neither group.[37]

The city government also took a vacillating attitude toward the fugitive slave act in actual operation. Since the Latimer affair, the city had successfully avoided involvement in any of the infrequent incidents involving fugitives in Boston. But in the first case which tested the new personal liberty law, the antislavery men abandoned their usual peaceful tactics. The change was precipitated on February 15, 1851. Fully nine Deputy United States Marshals arrested the escaped slave Shadrach in a Cornhill coffee shop, in full view of the patrons. Deputy Patrick Riley, fearing trouble, notified both Bigelow and Tukey, neither of whom took official notice. With Boston's jail facilities legally unavailable, Shadrach was confined in the federal courtroom, a place without bars or means of defense. When a writ of *de homine replegniando* and a petition of *habeas corpus* were both denied, a crowd of free Negroes stormed the courtroom and carried Shadrach to safety. For those who believed in the recent national compromise, the rescue was a clear breach of faith, an outrage against law and property. The conservative press was furious. In New York, the affair was branded "a deep stain upon the city of Boston," and it was remarked that no member of the marshal's office, down the hall from the courtroom, had taken any note of the mob and its action.[38]

Both Bigelow and Tukey were sensitive to these criticisms, one as a Whig politician, the other as a professional policeman. Both got a chance at redemption a month later, when a search was begun for seventeen-year-old Thomas Sims, from Savannah, who had stowed away on a brig and slipped off into Boston Harbor. While the law forbade any overt aid either in catching or holding a fugitive, the mayor and the marshal could still take such steps judged necessary to prevent a public disturbance.[39]

When United States Marshal Devens received a warrant for Sims, he asked for help from Tukey, who commanded an experienced group of officers fully familiar with the city. Tukey in turn passed the warrant on to two of the police, who were then deputized by Devens. The city marshal later explained that he would not ordinarily help the arrest of a fugitive, but that riot and bloodshed had to be avoided. It had been shown that the federal officers, in contrast to his own, had "neither courage, shrewdness, or strength to do it." And it was the two deputized policemen who finally did overtake Sims, on the night of April 3. As in the Latimer case, the fugitive was first told that he was being arrested for theft. When he became suspicious and resisted, he managed to stab Officer Butman seriously with his knife. But despite this scuffle, the affair was consummated swiftly, and Sims locked up on the third floor of the courthouse.[40]

The circumstances of the arrest were of doubtful legality, and the conduct of the individual policemen was further obnoxious. Asa O. Butman, especially, became notorious for his "generous" refusal to press assault charges, an action which might have rescued the fugitive from federal jurisdiction and would certainly have helped the argument that the police were only doing their duty. Once again the Boston Vigilance Committee distributed placards denouncing police officers as "Slave Catchers" and "Kidnappers."[41]

More maddening than the arrest itself was the scene at the courthouse. By the time Sims's friends got in to see him the building was surrounded by a guard consisting of every patrolman on the force, day and night men both. The sight left no doubt about the position of official Boston. When United States Commissioner Curtis asked for help, Bigelow had given Tukey a generalized order to preserve the peace about the courthouse, leaving the details to him. In the nine days of Sims's incarceration the marshal's men not only held guard but were otherwise obtrusive. Tukey himself often slipped into the surrounding crowd, warning off countrymen with pitchforks and feeling for weapons in pockets; at one point he was arrested by a deputy sheriff when a Negro, roughly searched, pressed a suit for false detention. In preparation for the final march to return Sims to the harbor, the police were drilled with borrowed United States sabers, their first official experience with weapons other than the customary short club. Borrowing an idea he had developed during the famous Parkman-Webster murder trial, Tukey had the courthouse surrounded by a heavy chain, waist high, to hold back the crowd. Only those on legitimate business, and with passes signed by the federal marshal, were allowed to go through. The symbolism was not lost on the abolitionists and others. There were no openings in the chain, and no gate; some insisted that they be let in by unfastening the corners, and Sims's attorney generally vaulted over. Chief Justice Lemuel Shaw, however, the man who had turned down the writ and petition in the Shadrach case, was observed habitually to duck or stoop under. "This was the hour of the deepest humiliation in Massachusetts."[42]

After a rescue plot was aborted and all legal counters failed, Sims was marched off on April 12 with a police and militia escort, the first fugitive ever successfully returned from the city. While the whole affair helped the Boston force to win a reputation in some quarters as the most efficient in the country, it also made bitter enemies for the officers in general and the marshal in particular. When questioned by abolitionist T. W. Higginson, Tukey averred that he was only doing a painful duty: "I know I am violating the state law . . . but I am acting under orders, and it is the mayor and the aldermen who are responsible." But while this was ultimately true, it was clear that Tukey had acted with excessive zeal. An investigation was carried out by the state Senate, then in control of a reform coalition of Free-Soil men and Democrats. The mayor was obviously a weakling, and no testimony implicated him either in the original arrest, in Butman's refusal to press charges, or in the offer of fifteen hundred volunteers, "Marshal Tukey's gentlemen," to help keep the peace. Tukey's remark to Higginson, publicly relayed to the investigators, did not save his reputation with reformers and simply inflamed his relations with the mayor and other members of Boston's conservative Whig machine.[43]

The marshal was a confident and outspoken man, and a bold actor, at a time when caution was the rule in local politics. Some kind of conflict was inevitable, and whether or not the Sims case began it, it had fully arrived later in the year with the fight over the appointment of Barney McGinniskin to the police force.

The Whig ascendancy in Massachusetts had been broken in the state election of 1850, which resulted in a controlling coalition between Democrats and Free-Soilers in the legislature. The Sims affair had contributed further to that Whig division exacerbated by Webster's Seventh of March position. In Boston, the center and strength of regular Whiggery, there was no real hope of winning back the reformers in number. But there was a chance that the conservative Irish Democrats, themselves unhappy with the reform coalition, might be persuaded to join an opposing alliance. Evidently as part of this intended *rapprochement*, it was proposed, in June of 1851, to add an Irishman to the police.[44]

Custom dictated that this or any political use of the department had to be carried out within narrow limits. None of the seven city marshals had been a political chieftain, and in fact none had held elective office before or after appointment. The fragmentation of local politics made it impossible that watchmen or police be subjected to any rigid political test. The blatant political use of appointments was inhibited also by the fact that police and watchmen did not serve annual terms, like constables, but during good behavior. In order to remove one man to make way for another, it was necessary not merely that he fail of reappointment at a given date, along with a number of his fellows, but that he be fired individually. This was a drastic course, which often stirred up petitions for a hearing. Usually the annual turnover was low. But occasionally a list with a few additions and subtractions was drawn up and voted "in place of all those now serving." And with applications running between two and three times the number of jobs available, prospective members did seek to exercise influence. Many presented the aldermen with petitions signed by merchants and other citizens. Others, in place of these extended references, undoubtedly had individual sponsors on the board.[45]

The movement to appoint McGinniskin was calculated not to violate any of the customary procedures. A number of businessmen signed a petition in his behalf, and Marshal Tukey reported on June 9 the results of the usual investigation; the candidate was temperate, a taxpayer, forty-two years old, twenty-two years a resident of the

United States. With his eligibility assured, the board of aldermen on September 19 confirmed his nomination, although he did not immediately report for duty.[46]

The subsequent controversy built up all during the state campaign season. Only one alderman at first opposed McGinniskin, and he received a ringing rebuff from the mayor. In a speech delivered on October 8, and later reported as far away as London, Bigelow noted that the principal objection offered was "that it is a dangerous precedent to appoint a foreigner to stations of such trust." But he had himself served with two respectable Irish members of the legislature. The city crier, David Hill, a veteran of the Mexican War, had been appointed without reference to his Irish birth, and so had the late constable Michael Riley. Nativist intolerance was not ground for objection, and McGinniskin's personal qualifications could not be challenged when "he stands the scrutiny of our lynx-eyed city marshal."[47]

But in the months following, the marshal himself became the leader in the fight against McGinniskin, in defiance of the mayor and apparently as spokesman for the force. Although it was true that Irishmen had served the city earlier, the men were convinced that their own department was something different. The police were no more prejudiced than other groups; given the fact that the Irish, during the 1850's, comprised the vast majority of those arrested for all crimes, it is notable that the force did not develop a more fearsome reputation as an engine of nativism. Marshal Tukey's first annual report, written in 1851, directed its bitterness not at the immigrants but at their poverty and plight. His men customarily aided the residents of the Irish districts with gifts of firewood and other necessities in emergencies, and organized a regular charity for the benefit of the poor, principally Irish. But there were instances of discrimination and violence. And the gap between a rough compassion and acceptance onto the force was not easily bridged.[48]

Unlike the constables, the police acted not solely as individuals but as members of a group, with a developing professional pride. Their two dollars a day was about twice the pay of common labor. And the attractiveness of the job was measured above all by its year-round security and the prospects of permanence. The men were drawn from the class of apprentices, artisans, and mechanics, and the number of working days in the year raised their annual income well above that of the typical master mason.[49]

In an open letter to the press, published on the day of the state elections, Marshal Tukey objected above all to McGinniskin's imperfect credentials, a threat to the status of every other member of the force. Not a respectable worker, he was a "common cabman," from Ann Street, the most notorious in the city. Ten years earlier he had been convicted of a criminal offense, as a participant in a riot at St. Mary's Church. And although the marshal disclaimed any prejudice, the candidate's behavior as well as his name was outrageously Irish: he had arrived at work, for the first time, on the afternoon of November 3, announcing himself to the night force as "Barney McGinniskin, fresh from the bogs of Ireland!"[50]

The marshal refused to assign him duty, and the mayor took no action. Bigelow and the incumbent aldermen had won considerable unpopularity, partly because of the Sims affair. With a major turnover in the city government expected, the impasse was left to the next administration. Since things looked "a little squally" to the marshal and his men, they decided to "dabble a little in politics." The first December election resulted in no choice, and John H. Wilkins, the regular Whig nominee, was forced to follow tradition and withdraw. The police were then instructed to vote for Chairman Benjamin Seaver of the common council, who replaced him, and Seaver was able with their help to win the needed majority.[51]

But united political action by the police was a novelty in Boston, and not appreciated. Mayor Seaver, once inaugurated with a sympathetic Whig council, felt no obligation. He ordered McGinniskin kept. And he followed this by firing the whole night police force, which had most conspicuously marched to the polls in a body; its duties were abolished, and the night left entirely to the watch.[52]

The abolition of the night force was another blow at Tukey. His only previous defeat had come in 1850, when the total number of night men was cut from twenty-two to seven, and much of his 1851 report was devoted to an argument for their restoration. They had been, he argued, a fine lot of men, all young, all married, full-time workers serving a probationary period before appointment to the day force. And through the several years of their existence they had captured more criminals than the entire rival body of over two hundred watchmen.[53]

Their activities as night raiders accounted for their favor with the marshal, but also for their unpopularity with regular politicians and much of the public. And their services as the especial guardians of mercantile property were outweighed by their roughness, and by hints of venality confirmed when at least one ex-member was indicted for burglary. Neither the cutback in 1850 nor the total abolition of 1852 was seriously protested in the press, which was showing other signs of impatience with Tukey's methods. The weekly "show-up" was becoming notorious, as its novelty declined and its abuses were more apparent. Many were indignant at the showing up of a young woman transvestite from New York, obviously displayed as entertainment. By 1852, even the *Mail,* ordinarily inclined to the marshal's support, was calling for the abolition of the practice, unique to Boston.[54]

In April of 1852, the mayor and aldermen cut further into the marshal's authority by voting to limit the tenure of policemen to one year. It was argued that this procedure would help in firing incompetents, by subjecting them to a close annual review. Tukey had in fact suggested a similar change earlier, in order to get rid of some whom he considered "unfit to be policemen." But he had since been satisfied by a promise, obtained from earlier administrations, that all new applicants must be cleared through him. With the exception of McGinniskin, the force by 1852 was largely composed of his men. The timing of the new rule made it clear that Seaver was determined to choose policemen more sympathetic to his own views.[55]

At the same time, the administration was showing its intention to abandon prohibition, the policy which had originally inspired the marshal's appointment and activities. As the reform legislature prepared a new liquor law, more drastic than the original Fifteen-Gallon Act of 1838, the board of aldermen reversed its ten-year-old no-license policy. During the winter and spring, the city granted a total of 612 liquor licenses. The move was not made in open defiance of the friends of temperance; as Mayor Seaver suggested, the licenses were no more than existing law allowed, and less than a majority of applications. Their issuance would allow discrimination, making enforcement easier by enabling a drive against those remaining unlicensed. In fact the board voted to stop issuing permits on May 17, the day that the new prohibitory bill was vetoed by Governor Boutwell. But when five days later the bill was repassed, it became clear that whatever the city's intention with respect to the license law, it was not going to cooperate in the enforcement of prohibition.[56]

This showdown had been approaching for several years. Even before the 1850 election of the Free-Soil–Democratic coalition, the state had tightened its liquor legislation. Chapter 232 of the Acts of 1850, which in a few words substituted the term "intoxicating" for "spirituous" in the basic license law, brought wines, beer, and even the countryman's cider under regulation for the first time. But the new statute, Chapter 322 of the Acts of 1852, was still more drastic than anything passed before. The private sale of liquor was forbidden entirely; state agents alone could sell for medicinal and scientific purposes. Far-reaching search and seizure provisions were designed to help enforcement. And violation, for the first time in the history of the commonwealth's liquor legislation, was made a jailable offense, upon the third conviction.[57]

Most important for local politics was section seven, which decreed that "It shall be the duty of mayors and aldermen to prosecute" violations upon complaint. Outright defiance of the whole law, by an open policy of granting yet more liquor licenses, was defeated in the board of aldermen by a five to two vote. But with the aid of the city solicitor, the Seaver administration did find legal means of evading the spirit of section seven. Among these was a reform of the police department, the agency through which any prosecutions would have to be instituted.[58]

In June, the council passed a new police ordinance. In most respects this simply summed up existing rules and legislation. Following the order of April, police appointments were to be made annually. The title of the "City Marshal" was changed to "Chief of Police," although the chief was specifically given the same duties that the marshal had had. He was to post a $2,000 bond with the city treasurer, to appoint his own deputies, and to have "precedence and control over constables and police officers when engaged in the same service." To this end he was entitled to make departmental rules and regulations. His office was to be open at stated hours for the reception of complaints, and he was to attend to the prosecution and trial of those acted upon. He was to be a full-time officer, in charge of the "peace, order and cleanliness of the city," charged especially with the removal of nuisances and obstructions in the streets. The only thing omitted was mention of the law, as distinct from the ordinances, and the stipulation, as had been the case with the marshal, that the chief be sworn as a constable. Constables and sheriffs, as officers of the state, were charged with carrying out the search and seizure provisions of the new liquor act; "chiefs of police" were not mentioned. As Mayor Seaver explained, the services of the chief were highly important, and "these services could not be had if that officer is employed in searching for and removing property."[59]

When the new ordinance was followed by no announcement appointing a chief, it was clear that Marshal Tukey was in trouble. The newspapers chose up sides with spirit; the Whig *Mail* commented, "There is a great deal of feeling existing in this community in regard to the selection of a chief of police." The *Congregationalist* was outraged; linking Tukey's firing with a proliquor policy, it estimated that three-quarters of the city's businessmen and voters were for him. The *Mercantile Journal* made this "four-fifths of business men and legal voters," and the *Mail* put it at 90 per cent. When the job was finally given to Gilbert Nurse, a former councilman then serving as assistant clerk of the Faneuil Hall Market, even the *Bunker Hill Aurora* was disturbed. That paper had complained in June that "the city marshal was in a fair way to become the entire government," but it wondered in July whether any new man could match Tukey's achievements in office. And while most other journals were noncommittal, and some hostile, few could defend the administration's refusal to explain. The aldermen, on July 15, unanimously tabled Tukey's request for a public hearing.[60]

With local candidates still bent on ignoring more distant issues, it was natural that the Tukey affair should dominate the fall campaign. The regular or "partisan" Whigs renominated Seaver in December. The Democrats, with no more hope than usual, put up one of their own. And the combined opposition, organizing as the Citizens Union Party, chose Dr. J. C. V. Smith, three years earlier fired as physician of the Port of Boston and ever since an opponent of the dominant Whig faction. Smith had earlier found common cause with the Native Americans, but it was possible to claim him on several sides of the wider reform issues which troubled many of his supporters. The regular Whig newspapers regarded him as a puppet, and reserved their fire for ex-Marshal Tukey, "the Warwick of the Citizens' Movement."[61]

A committee of aldermen, officially appointed to consider further reforms in the police department, was active throughout the campaign season. Although it did not formally report until the day after election, pro-administration papers did not wait to print their own versions of its findings. "The Great Caesar fell for his ambition," wrote the editor of the *Atlas*, "The Great Tukey, because, like the Sons of Levi, he took too much upon himself." The accompanying story condemned the marshal's questionable accounting methods and his secret auctions of unclaimed stolen property; it reminded readers of his frequent lawsuits and of the doubtful character of his night police. The editorial was especially outraged at his lust for power, his defiance in the McGinniskin case, his political use of the force, his evident intention to "run the city."[62]

Direct accusations of this kind went far beyond the decorum which the papers ordinarily maintained in covering local elections. Together with an even more heated campaign of rumor, and the natural excitement surrounding the liquor issue, they made the canvass in 1852 the largest in the history of the city. The outcome was a triumph for the Whig strategy. Mayor Seaver, with the help of many Democrats, won a total of 6,018 votes, Dr. Smith 5,021, the regular Democrat 899.[63]

The formal report of the aldermanic investigating committee, when released the next day, proved less personal and more significant than the newspaper accounts. It was couched as an argument against the then current proposal for a union of the watch and police. In warning against an undue concentration of power in the hands of a single man, it did mention that "the previous head of the department" had once interfered in local politics and had been heard to use profanity. But the bulk of the report was an impersonal defense of changes already made, of decreased expenses, annual appointments, and the abolition of the night force. Its central criticism of the earlier regime concerned not Tukey's integrity but his purpose and methods.[64]

An undue and overpublicized emphasis on criminal law enforcement tended, in the opinion of the committee, to create a morbidly excitable public opinion. The amount of crime in the city could easily be exaggerated, damaging its reputation. Large numbers of those arrested were visitors seeking excitement. The police had earlier been overzealous, pursuing offenders beyond the city and even out of the country, while the watch had in recent months without theatrics quietly reduced the incidence of burglary. The main business of the chief and his men, the report concluded, was the enforcement of the city's own rules and ordinances, and they should concentrate less on roguery and more on the removal of obstructions from the streets. "The police, while it should be argus-eyed, seeing all things, should be itself unseen and unobserved."[65]

On the day this report was delivered, the former marshal also appeared before the board with a formal claim of election fraud. While this was rejected, he was given a final chance to redeem his reputation. An alderman's death created a vacancy on the board, and it was necessary to call a special election on February 1. The Whigs nominated Sampson Reed, a member of the outgoing board and principal author of the report on the police. The Citizens, in January, countered with Tukey himself. With both men running at large, the anti-Tukey campaign lost none of its fervor. And this time it was aimed at the most sensitive aspect of the police business. The marshal had been accused before of dictatorial ends and methods; now he was accused of personal and professional immorality, of compounding felonies, possible bribery, and "abetting with rogues."[66]

To answer his critics, the Citizens' candidate on the Friday night before the election held a mass meeting in the historic forum at Faneuil Hall. Ushered in to a "perfect storm of applause, mingled with hisses, catcalls, unearthly yells and sounds infernal," he maintained a cool command of the packed house despite constant interruptions, "great merriment," "laughter," cries of "pickpockets!" and "Barney!" And he proceeded, with occasional difficulties, to make his case.[67]

Tukey disposed of the older charges in the familiar way. He had never denied his role in the 1851 elections or his hostility to Barney McGinniskin. He only regretted in both cases that he had been betrayed. In one he had been battling political partisanship, in the other the appointment of a convicted rioter. His audience had heard it all before. What they had come for, knowing the marshal's gift for invective, was his arraignment of the clique of aldermen who ran the ruling Whig machine.

The talk lived up to expectations. He had been accused, Tukey noted, of living rent free in the house of a gambler. In fact he owned his own home—but certain members of the city council lived in a West End bawdy house, and there were others "whose family relations have been to this city, and tried to bargain with burglars to break open the bank in the towns where they live." There had been talk of the "misuse of obscene books and prints—when they or some of their supporters were always the first callers for any such . . . as were taken by the police." "They" had accused him of profanity, whereas "they can go into a house of ill-fame in the city of New York, and set in it with a prostitute on one knee, with one arm around her waist, and the other holding a glass of champagne at the expense of the City of Boston. (Laughter and shouts)." "These things are facts and I know it, for I was in New York City with them. (Great merriment)." His opponent was "an honest old fogy," the marshal concluded, but it was time for a change: "Some members of the city government had been in city hall so long that their seats stank. (Laughter and shouts)."

It was a grand performance, but largely irrelevant to the main charge, that of malfeasance in office, first by misappropriating money and second by "abetting with rogues." Tukey's defense here was more reasoned and careful than his flamboyant countercharges. As to the first, the mayor had authorized the auction of stolen goods unclaimed after a year. He had kept books, and the money had gone to a charity administered by the police. The second charge the marshal freely admitted. He was proud in some cases to have saved reputations by failure to prosecute for panel thieving. In others he was ordered not to. And in more important cases, this was simply the system; he mentioned several in which the district attorney, the sheriff, or some other official had interfered on behalf of a victim seeking to recover his property. "Such bargaining is right and cannot be helped."

The voters next Monday had a unique chance to pass judgment upon this defense and the whole system of police administration under Tukey. And the judgment was unmistakable. The December election had been close; the special election resulted in 4,936 votes for Reed, 2,354 for Tukey, and 620 for the Democrat. The defeated candidate, in humiliation, quit the city to try his energies in the bold new State of California.[68]

Between 1846 and 1853 the city had had its first experience with a tough cop. And after the initial period of hope and excitement it had clearly rejected that experience. The February vote signaled more than a personal repudiation of Marshal Tukey. The duties of police in general and of the marshal in particular had been growing steadily. While the emphasis had shifted from the original concern for internal health, only the superintendence of sewers had been subtracted from the marshal's responsibilities, and a host had been added. Neither the legislature nor the courts had intervened in the process. The citizens and their local representatives had voluntarily used the police to the utmost, raising their expenditures in every year between 1838 and

Seaver's election in 1852. But by mid-century there was an apparent desire for a check.[69]

A number of administrative reforms were needed. Equally important, the police had to be confined within limits which would not antagonize any substantial sections of the community. There had been little trouble in an earlier period, under a system of popular administration. In the 1820's and early 1830's the peace officers of the city had dealt only with those who had injured a specific complainant, or with a voiceless class of unfortunates. But the growth of the city had made the system of private complaints by itself obsolescent, so that it was necessary for the police to take the initiative. At the same time new duties brought them into contact with a larger proportion of citizens. A continuing revolution in politics and social attitudes, added to the older one in publishing, was beginning to give voice to the class which filled the watchhouses and jails.

The new organization of police made it possible for the first time in generations to attempt a wide enforcement of the criminal code, especially the vice laws. But while the earlier lack of execution was largely the result of weakness, it had served a useful function also, as part of the system of compromise which made the law tolerable. Even the ordinances were often resented where applied. And especially in a time of severe political tension, there was need for caution in enforcement.

By 1853 the city had had fifteen years of experience with the new police. The government during that time had been controlled by both reformers and conservatives. And both groups had found that a vigorous police was in itself no solution to their problems. The force employed in raiding a barroom might be used again in guarding fugitives. The department needed strength in order to maintain the peace, protect property, and alleviate misery in a city still swelling with immigration. But it also needed discretion, in order to serve as a buffer between the literal demands of the law and the desires of the citizens.

CHAPTER SIX

Adjustment and Definition, 1853-1860

Just before the Civil War it was evident that Boston had passed an important turning point. The experience of the 1850's justified neither the reformist hopes of Mayor Quincy nor the commercial visions of Mayor Bigelow. Loss of political dominance in the state accompanied a noticeable decline in the social caliber of local political leadership, while national problems heightened all tensions. Increase in the proportion of immigrants and the children of immigrants continued to create social problems and friction. At the same time, the loss of vitality was measured by a declining rate of growth in both general population and real estate values.[1]

None of these indices was a wholly accurate measurement of the health of the city. Many problems had their compensations. The presence of the Irish nurtured a factory industry which revivified Boston's economy in a new form. A lessened interest in local affairs, among the leaders of both reform and conservatism, allowed the city to reach a kind of political truce, during which it was able to meet its municipal needs successfully. The police especially were transformed rapidly and with success. For the department this was a period of definition, in terms of law, organization, and function; it managed at the same time to increase its usefulness and to avoid damaging involvement in controversy.[2]

In a decade wracked by tension, Boston's fundamental political achievement was simply the maintenance of enough stability to prevent the breakdown of civic order and administration. Partisan politics posed one potential threat to this stability; others emanated from divisions over three substantive issues: abolition, prohibition, and immigration. Boston was unable to solve these problems. But the tradition of a cautious, balanced politics, reflected in a judicious use

85

of force through the police, prevented any of them from disrupting the normal activities of the city.

Boston's political machinery had always been geared to the avoidance of party issues. The city always chose its officers at least a month after the state and national elections. The local Democratic organization, after taking a stand in the earlier contests, rarely made a serious effort in the city election, and sometimes commended the Whigs on their well-made nominations. The only excitement came when the dominant party split into rival tickets; whatever their real differences, these always framed their appeals in terms of such local issues as the waterworks or the tax rate. The neglect of party labels, dictated partly by circumstance, was reinforced by the policy of many newspapers, which made nonpartisanship an ideal.[3]

The events of the 1850's strengthened the ideal. The decline of Whiggery left Boston without a majority party, and no "regular" nomination held any sure value. At the same time a new municipal charter accepted in 1852 made an important change in election procedure. Thirteen times in thirty years the December mayoralty contest had resulted in no choice, and it was necessary to hold new elections, sometimes repeatedly. Now a plurality rather than a majority of votes sufficed; the effect was to discourage extremist splinter parties and to encourage moderate nonpartisan coalitions. Benjamin Seaver was the last mayor to serve as a Whig. He and ex-Mayor Bigelow were defeated by Dr. J. C. V. Smith and the Citizens coalition in two trials held in 1853-54, before the new charter went into effect. The indecisive Dr. Smith won re-election as an "American" in 1854. But Alexander Hamilton Rice followed with two terms and Frederick Walker Lincoln with three more as nonpartisan candidates.[4]

The city's political truce was institutionalized in 1857 by the creation of regular nonpartisan machinery. In that year the Democrats, Whigs, and Know-Nothings held a joint nominating convention. Bolters from this group set up a parallel system, so that the two tickets presented, the "Faneuil Hall" and the "Citizens," were both nonpartisan. This arrangement continued for the next three years, producing a series of local candidates intent upon hiding their political identities, and bridging their differences over state and national issues.[5]

Caution in referring to affairs outside of the city was matched in the same period by moderation in dealing with affairs within. None of the mayors of the 1850's approached their predecessors in social influence and prestige. Seaver was an auctioneer, Smith a doctor, Rice a small manufacturer, and Lincoln, who went on to serve more terms than any man in Boston's history, a skilled mechanic. The new charter prevented any of them from essaying the hard-driving, autocratic techniques of a Quincy or Eliot. The charter, drawn up by the city council, granted the mayor a limited veto, but in other respects diminished his effective authority by excluding him from the deliberation and votes of the aldermen. The real executive power was lodged in aldermanic committees, which met in secret, without the presence of an outstanding mayor to compel action or publicity. While this diffusion of responsibility was the bane of later students of political science, it met the political problems of the period.[6]

The most immediate of these problems was created by the state prohibitory law of 1852 and its successors. It was soon obvious that this law would not be enforced in Boston, but open defiance might have serious repercussions either in the legislature or at the polls. Through skillful maneuver, the city's politicians were able to hold the prohibitionist vote in Boston to 20 per cent at its peak, and to avoid censure by the legislature.[7]

The law in itself was distasteful to many genuine friends of temperance, who doubted the expedience of prohibition. Other moderates were alienated by the use to which the law was put. The miserable effects of drink among the poor, making them unfit for labor and reducing their families to pauperage, was almost universally admitted. But the prohibitionist organizations attacked from another direction. In accord with the strategy set forth during the earlier battle over the Fifteen-Gallon Law, they determined to win public opinion by driving out the respectable liquor dealers and leaving the evil in evil hands.[8]

Many lawyers were troubled in any case about the implications of the new statute. Its confiscatory features, allowing for the uncompensated destruction of illegally held liquor, upset a tradition which made the sanctity of private property the highest end of law. The prohibitionist assault upon established hotel and restaurant proprietors strengthened these doubts by making the law in practice seem more an attack upon property than a legitimate exercise of the police power. And their efforts courted ridicule as well as hostility; once when reluctantly forced to prosecute Peter Brigham, a leading restauranteur, the embarrassed district attorney delivered a rapturous description of the defendant's chicken salad by way of a charge to the jury.[9]

The policy of city officials, first set a dozen years earlier by Mayor Chapman, was refined under the Seaver administration and followed by its successors. Its essence was the shift of responsibility for enforcement back to the citizens, a reversion to the older system of indirect administration. The theory was stated explicitly by the city solicitor, who advised the mayor to refuse to act unless given written complaints, with the names of witnesses, together with evidence which in his judgment would hold up in court. "Until such information is given, and such proof furnished, . . . the terms of this section impose no duty upon the Mayor and aldermen to commence a prosecution."[10]

Mayors Smith and Lincoln also felt obliged to explain their performance under the act, blaming conditions upon the insufficiency of complaints, crowded court calendars, grand and petit juries. No candidate for mayor, however, felt the need to repudiate the support of temperance groups, and several bid actively for it. Even Mayor Seaver was able to claim that he was "an enforcer": "The board have at all times been ready to receive and hear complaints." In fact, all administrations did enforce the law to a point, the point where they would have enforced a license law. There was a purpose to the hurried grant of 612 permits in the first part of 1852. In July, after the prohibitory law went into effect, the board of aldermen sent the list to the local judges, who indicated that only those not previously licensed would be punished. The police were instructed to prosecute accordingly, pursuing those whose practices were the most widely condemned. Under this understanding the police did institute proceedings in several dozen cases.[11]

But during the first eighteen months after the passage of the act there were no convictions in Suffolk County. The liquor dealers of the city and the state responded to prohibition with a blizzard of bills of exception and constitutional challenges; the first unappealed sentence in the municipal court was not received until December 1853. The Supreme Judicial Court of Massachusetts had never before declared any part of any liquor law unconstitutional, and turned down the great majority of exceptions. But the delay helped grand juries and prosecutors to refuse indictments. And the dealers did finally score a success in the case of *Fisher* v. *McGirr,* heard early in 1854. After having upheld several sections of the law, the court in this instance invalidated section fourteen on two grounds: first, that it allowed the destruction of property without fully due process, and second, that the loosened means of procuring search warrants encouraged "unreasonable search and seizure."[12]

The effect of this decision was to reinforce public suspicion of prohibition. It became impossible to enforce the law in Suffolk County. Shortly after the McGirr case the strongly proliquor aldermen voted to replace Chief of Police Gilbert Nurse with one of his subordinates, Captain Robert Taylor. In 1855 not one case was prosecuted under the prohibitory act. The policy was continued under Chief Daniel J. Coburn, a former deputy sheriff chosen by the city council from among its own members to head the force in 1856. And the General Court, in attempting to break this resistance, only succeeded in making prohibition a dead letter entirely.[13]

In 1854 the voters of the commonwealth, continuing a political reaction begun several years earlier, elected a new legislature containing a great majority from the new Know-Nothing party. The result was due partly to a suspicion of immigration but even more to resentment toward the conservatism and factionalism of the older parties. Among the several reform measures it passed was a new prohibitory law, which while eliminating the unconstitutional provisions of the 1852 act was in other respects more severe. "Chiefs of Police" were specifically charged with enforcement. Several ingenious provisions were designed to discourage the trade; in case of damages committed by drunken persons, for example, the sellers were held equally liable. Receiving deliveries of liquor was made prima-facie evidence of intent to sell. Arrests for either the sale or the transport of liquor might be made without warrant. Any individual arrested for drunkenness might have his case excused by disclosing the name of the seller. In addition to a fine, common sellers faced mandatory jail terms of thirty days even upon the first conviction.[14]

The product of a notably inexperienced and often inept group of legislators, the whole act was widely regarded as outrageous. The last two provisions mentioned were especially calculated to arouse the new suspicion of legislative tyranny and the traditional hatred of the informer. And in compounding its mistakes the same session of the General Court provided a legal safety valve. In a move ostensibly aimed at crippling the federal fugitive slave act, Massachusetts juries were given the right to determine questions of law as well as fact; in practice this enabled jurors to nullify prohibition. At the same time the legislature codified and ameliorated the common-law provisions against nuisance, providing an alternative means for proceeding against the notorious. Chapter 405 of the Acts of 1855 declared that "All buildings, places, or tenements, used as houses of ill-fame . . . or for illegal gaming, or used for the illegal sale or keeping of intoxicating liquors, are hereby declared to be common nuisances." Landlords as well as tenants might be prosecuted, and the maximum punishment, $1,000 and one year, was greater than that for common selling. But as imprisonment was not mandatory, juries were less reluctant to convict. And from 1855 on, all sellers prosecuted by the police were indicted under this nuisance act.[15]

This course provided a politic solution to a difficult situation. Local politicians were able to suggest the impracticality of prohibition without defying it. The Boston police, never involved in odious search and seizure activities, could pursue the most flagrant offenders without endorsing it. The courts were given all the cases they could or would handle. And as public attention passed to other matters the Act of 1855 ceased to be a threatening issue.

The Know-Nothing legislature also helped inadvertently to remove the slavery issue from the local arena. The city had itself been moving to settle the two problems, harassment of abolitionists and reclamation of fugitives, which had involved its police and elected officials in national controversy. The General Court, in passing a series of unbreakable personal liberty laws, sealed a decision already in the making.

The growth of antislavery sentiment had been shown in the storm after the Sims rendition, when the mayor and aldermen responsible were defeated. The next board fired Officer Asa Butman, who had arrested Sims. After the Thompson meeting of November 1850, there were no further abolitionist complaints about police laxity and disorder at their gatherings. In fact from April of 1851 until the 1860 elections there was only one serious clash between the local authorities and the opponents of slavery. The circumstances of that case, the famous rendition of Anthony Burns, made it in several respects less damaging than the Sims incident to the reputations of the local police and officials.[16]

A fugitive stowaway like Sims, Burns was arrested on May 24, 1854, a few weeks after escaping from Virginia. As in earlier cases, his captors used a pretended charge of larceny. But the chief arresting officer this time was not a local policeman, but the notorious Asa O. Butman, now permanently employed, under a Democratic administration, as a United States deputy marshal. The friends of Mayor Smith in the previous campaign had praised his opposition to "putting chains around the courthouse," and the city at first took no more official notice of Burns than it had taken earlier of Shadrach.[17]

On the night of the 26th, however, the abolitionist attempt to free the fugitive changed the nature of the case. The Reverend T. W. Higginson, remembering the success in Shadrach's case, led an assault on the courthouse which resulted in bloodshed, killing a guard. And on the following day, when requested by the federal authorities, Mayor Smith called out two companies of militia to prevent further riot.[18]

As United States marines and regulars were summoned, one of these companies was dismissed, despite objections from the federal officers. The police were called in only on June 2, the day when legal efforts failed and United States Commissioner Loring made his decision to send Burns back to slavery. The case by that time had become a test between the Democratic administration in Washington and all the opponents of the fugitive slave law who could be gathered in Boston. That afternoon there were roughly two thousand uniformed men in Boston, militia and regulars. It was the job of the police, about two hundred in all, to clear the streets ahead of the soldiers so that Burns could be marched to the harbor and Richmond.[19]

In all other respects the city government tried to maintain neutrality. In the board of aldermen the only notice of the affair was taken in a pair of back-to-back votes, one authorizing a $200 reward for the person guilty of an assault on R. H. Dana, Jr., the attorney for Burns, and the other offering the same amount for the murderer of James Batchelder, the courthouse guard. While the mayor and police could not so easily escape criticism, neither felt the full weight of antislavery anger. Many of the officers acted with obvious reluctance. During the long walk to the harbor, the spectators were less conscious of the unarmed local force in plain clothes than of the military, with their sabers and bayonets, some of whom had orders, in case of trouble, "to fire upon the people without notice." These were not the orders of Dr. Smith, "that poor shoat," as Dana called him, "raised by accident to a mayoralty." The case was for the Free-Soilers actually a victory. Their mood this time was exultant, rather than frustrated, and they had more important targets in mind than the mayor and his police.[20]

Commissioner Loring, principal object of Free-Soil contempt, was eventually removed from his state job as judge of probate. Burns was bought and freed. Mayor Smith was re-elected, in the fall of 1854, without significant reference to Burns. And the legislature in 1855 took several steps to ensure that there would be no similar incidents in the future. Juries were made responsible for judging law. And peace officers cooperating in the return of fugitive slaves were subject to a heavy fine and a mandatory prison sentence; those found guilty were to be fired and "forever disqualified from holding any office under the laws or constitution of this state." No further cases arose, and the police of Boston were not again called to act as "Slave Catchers."[21]

There remained only one more serious threat to the peace of the city, as hostility to immigrants reached a peak during the 1850's. No American city had a larger proportion of Irish Catholics. Even during the 1830's, when their numbers were far smaller, attacks on them had erupted into menacing riots. Yet, although Boston elected a Know-Nothing mayor and voted for a Know-Nothing governor, the city was able to avoid the kind of violence which broke out in New York, Baltimore, and Philadelphia.

The Know-Nothing movement in Boston and Massachusetts never became so outrageous as it threatened to. The party was never so strong as it seemed; aside from Senator Henry Wilson, few respected political leaders joined it with any enthusiasm. The sweep of state and city in 1854 was only partly a result of nativist sentiment; it was a revolt of laymen against professionals, countrymen against the city. On many issues the Know-Nothings were split along the same lines as their older rivals. While usually promoting reform measures, they also had a "pro-rum," anti-abolitionist, "Hunker" wing, composed largely of old Boston "Americans" who resented the diversions of their party into new channels.[22]

Once in power the party showed another basic weakness. Neither in Boston nor in the state was there any real target for a separate and political attack upon Roman Catholicism. The Know-Nothings were agitating for a twenty-one-year naturalization law at the national level. But they had no local issues. In New York and Philadelphia the Irish had established themselves politically and had real power with which

to excite resentment. But in Boston they had no such organization. At
the time of the Know-Nothing agitation, no Irishman had ever been
elected to any office in the city. Even the Irish nationalists were led
locally by John W. James, a native Protestant lawyer.[23]

The Jacksonian leader David Henshaw had been accused in the
1830's of trading rum for Irish votes. But his following subsisted
entirely on federal patronage; Democratic influence in the city could
be safely ignored. Only taxpayers were eligible to vote, and without
organized machinery to see that poll taxes were met, few of the poorer
members of any group apparently qualified.[24]

What influence the Irish had during the 1850's was thrown to the
conservatives. Suspicion of a series of reform legislatures, and of a
proposed new constitution, was fanned by Father John Roddan,
editor of the Catholic Boston *Pilot*. Nothing infuriated reformers more
than the apparent alliance between Ann and State Streets. But the
Irish vote against the reform constitution, which would have robbed
the city of representation, was only a part of the huge Suffolk County
majority which defeated it. And on most of the other issues which
separated them from reformers, the Irish also stood with majority
opinion in Boston.[25]

As a result of Irish political docility the Know-Nothing city administration in 1855 had little to do. Barney McGinniskin had already
been fired, and except for common laborers there was no one left to
harass. The General Court accomplished little more, dismissing a few
Irishmen from state jobs and disbanding their militia companies, a
move already suggested by the *Pilot*.[26]

In fact the Know-Nothing legislature of 1855 resulted in a para-
doxical blend of achievement and failure. It helped decisively to end
the fugitive slave question in the state and mistakenly to settle the
liquor issue in Boston. Its third service to the city was ironically to
discredit itself and the movement which had led to its election. A series
of blunders, culminating in the goatish misbehavior of a committee
chosen to investigate a Roxbury nunnery, turned even sympathizers
against it. Together with the national split over the slavery issue, this
effectively killed nativism as a political movement in the state. In
Boston, Mayor Smith had been elected narrowly, in 1854, against the
combined opposition of all other parties. The vote in 1855 was 5,390
for the Know-Nothing candidate and 7,398 for the Citizens'.[27]

With the political party dead, there was no other permissible outlet for nativist resentment, and the city was well prepared to deal with the antisocial manifestations of No-Popery. Several conditions made Boston difficult territory for mob violence. The police force, originally organized in response to anti-Catholic rioting, was able to prevent its recurrence.

Smaller places, like Ellsworth, Maine, where a priest was tarred and feathered in 1854, had no force at all to oppose to popular violence. Cities like Philadelphia had considerable areas which were not covered by police protection. And in most larger centers, even New York, which had policemen in adequate number, gangs of toughs, "Stingers" and "Killers" and "Blood Tubs," served as the nuclei for mobs.[28]

Boston's small area made it possible to bring the whole city under patrol. Not since the elder Quincy's raids in the West End had there been any district beyond police control. And the city had relatively little trouble with organized gangs. The fire department, troublesome in the days of Quincy and Eliot, had been transformed; the companies had been progressively cut in numbers and the members raised in pay. With the installment of a fire telegraph system and steam engines, the firemen in the 1850's were too few and too thoroughly professional to engage in serious rioting.[29]

City officials had always taken precautions during holidays and other periods when excitement combined with freedom from work. Temporary special police were still appointed on the Fourth of July, but as the regulars proved adequate they were rarely called in the 1840's and 1850's "in anticipation of a riot." And a new law in 1850 helped demonstrate the meaning of "preventive force." The police were given the right that year to order any assembly of three or more persons to "move on" or be subject to arrest, a useful method of breaking up incipient fights.[30]

There were plenty of smaller affrays, and the police were often called to stop them. But until the assault on the jailers of Anthony Burns, there had been apparently no lives lost in mob violence since the incorporation of the city. Until the Sims affair, the militia had been called only once, to Broad Street in 1837. Boston's police had been cited for their peerless record in maintaining order, and they were proud of it. Riot duty brought out professional esprit as no other could; the police as a group were bigger and stronger men than any like number of opponents, and their appearance when running toward a disturbance or surrounding a courthouse produced a satisfying respect. By the 1850's, at least, this professionalism was proving stronger than private prejudices or politics. Many members of the force, when interviewed, expressed distaste for the proceedings against Burns. But only one man, Captain Joseph Hayes, quit rather than help to clear the streets. And his action was regarded as squeamishness rather than moral courage, as backing off before difficult and unpleasant duty.[31]

All the conditions which helped in general to keep the peace in Boston proved especially useful during the Know-Nothing era. Serious violence came close to the city but never entered it. A church was blown up in Dorchester, then a separate town, and a cross was torn off another in Chelsea. In Charlestown, during the spring of 1853, nativist excitement led to a threat to the church there. Trouble was headed off with the aid of marines, militia, and one hundred men borrowed from the Boston watch and police. The incident proved the last of its kind.[32]

A number of changes in its police strengthened the city's ability to keep the peace during the 1850's. Boston's needs, together with the experience of other cities, suggested reforms in organization and equipment; and political peace enabled the department to stay clear of controversy.

At incorporation three sets of peace officers, watch, sheriffs, and constables, shared with the selectmen and ordinary citizens the responsibility for enforcement of the criminal code. In the next thirty years the growth of police headed by the city marshal had shifted these responsibilities. Private citizens were no longer expected to contribute, and the sheriffs and constables were mostly confined to the service of civil warrants. But the city had still no uniform or specialized system of police. The regular police and the watch cooperated only in emergencies. The marshal still did double duty as head of the internal health department, and the captain of the watch as superintendent of lamps. The arrangement was increasingly criticized as inefficient.

Boston was always willing to borrow technical and administrative ideas from other places; the fire department in Quincy's day had drawn on the methods of New York and Philadelphia, and the police had been loosely inspired by "the system of London." By the 1850's imitation was institutionalized. Members of the government visited and corresponded with officials of other cities, which also engaged in the search for better methods. A joint special committee of the city council thus learned from London in 1851 that information on that city's police had recently been sent to New York.[33]

All information indicated that the watch was outdated. Two committees so reported, in 1850 and 1851. But no action came for a number of months. Some politicians perhaps dreaded the necessary business of firing the watchmen. Others argued that it was uneconomical to pay policemen two dollars a day when watchmen might be had for a dollar a night. And the report issued late in 1852 warned that consolidation would put enormous power in the hands of a single man, perhaps a Marshal Tukey.[34]

But during 1852-53 a number of events combined to ease a union of watch and police. The Boston *Herald,* with the largest circulation in the city, conducted a campaign that winter against James Barry, the captain of the watch, who, it charged, was too busy with his butcher shop to pursue his job properly. From the argument that the captain was an old man fifty years behind the times, it was easy to extend the same criticism to his men and the system.[35]

In many respects the watch was managed as it had been under the town. The hours had been extended, but the "Charlies" were still governed by the same simple rules published in 1821—they were to walk the rounds singly rather than in pairs, forbidden to sleep on the job, and fired for three consecutive and unexplained failures to show up for work. Although by the 1850's there were two hundred and fifty watchmen, there were still only two supervisory offices, the part-time captain and the constables in charge of the watchhouses. Discipline was slack, and there was no real means of checking to see that the men were actually making their rounds; and the installation of a fire telegraph and alarm boxes in 1851 made fire patrol duty less necessary.[36]

Further, the watch was not capable of filling certain needs. It could not furnish protection against well-planned thievery; and the fact that it stopped in the early morning hours, before the day police arrived, indicated that it was not expected to. Marshal Tukey had pointed out that the watch was never of much use in catching criminals. In the busy second quarter of 1853, of a total of 3,516 persons arrested, only 64 were held for stealing or attempting to steal in any degree, ranging from simple larceny to highway robbery. In that

quarter 1,048 persons received lodging for the night; 1,399 were arrested for drunkenness, and another 506 were listed as "drunken persons taken home." An addition to the basic watch act, in 1850, gave
the men the right to enter "any building" rather than "any disorderly
house," in order to quell tumults. And there were 539 occasions when
the men were "called to stop disturbances," many and perhaps most
of them family quarrels in private homes. A number of miscellaneous
cases were reported: 32 stray horses put up, 120 stores found open
and locked, 29 physicians called, 7 children found. But it is evident
that the primary function was simply to clear the streets and maintain
quiet. Beyond those mentioned above, the largest number of arrests
reported were for "fighting," 79 persons; "peacebreakers," 64; "assault and battery," 46; "abusing family," 34; "nightwalkers," 30.[37]

It was a reflection of the relatively trivial nature of the offenses
which occupied the watchmen that only about one-quarter of those
arrested were actually held for trial. The others were released by
mutual consent. Justice Russell of the Police Court attempted to settle
doubts about the legality of this procedure in 1853 with a ruling that
no arrest by a watchman was fully legal until ratified by a constable
of the watch. But the more persistent problem involved not those released but those detained.[38]

Charges of favoritism were inevitable in a situation in which some
guilty of the same offense were kept and others let go. The watch was
more vulnerable to this criticism than the regular police. Nearly all
their arrests involved matters of discretion, in which many individuals
taken not only felt innocent but questioned the law itself, which condemned as illegal what they held either necessary or harmless. While
the police could plead the impartial performance of professional duty,
all the actions of the watchmen were open to suspicion on account of
the witness fees, which they alone continued to receive. Indeed, the
Herald's crusade was based largely on the charge that minor offenses
were manufactured for profit.[39]

Marshal Tukey's downfall in February 1853 removed the most
serious barrier to a union of watch and police, and the *Herald's* popular criticisms helped overcome several other obstacles. First the council
abolished the office of the superintendent of lamps, and turned the
business over to the Boston Gas Light Company. On February 21 the
aldermen unanimously ordered the witness fees of watchmen diverted
into the city treasury. In April the council created the office of super-

intendent of health, relieving the marshal from his original function and allowing him to concentrate on his police duties. And in the same month, upon application, the General Court authorized the city to combine its watch and police under one chief and to create new officers, captains and lieutenants, to serve in place of the constables of the watch. The act was accepted by the city on June 2. All that remained necessary was an ordinance to unite the two departments.[40]

At this point an endemic jurisdictional dispute between the aldermen and the common council interrupted the smooth course of reform. The city charter clearly placed the executive power in general and "the administration of police" in particular in the hands of the mayor and aldermen. But the common councillors, having tried vainly during the 1820's to obtain a voice in the appointment of the marshal, attempted now to secure some kind of influence over the police. They insisted on a clause subjecting the department to "the orders of the city council" as well as to those of the mayor and aldermen.[41]

But the aldermen found a way to break the deadlock in the spring of 1854. The board, as the executive power, was able within statutory limits to define the duties of both departments, and it took the initiative in unilaterally uniting the two by order. Watchmen were appointed and then given additional warrants as policemen, entitling them to two dollars a night as members of the "Watch and Police Department."[42]

The most important immediate effect of the change was the creation of police divisions like those of the watch. The men were based in eight stations, each under a captain, assisted ordinarily by two lieutenants. The thirty-one men available for daytime patrol and many of the line officers were largely drawn from the police proper. The former watchmen, 166 of them, did the less desirable night duty and hoped for promotion to the day force. Their officers, the constables of the watch, filled the remaining jobs as captains and lieutenants.[43]

Although the number of men was less than the former total of watch and police, the new arrangement made the patrol more effective. The local neighborhood stations made it easier for citizens to seek help and for the day men to reach their beats. There were no longer any gaps in time: the day men worked from 8:00 A.M. to 6:00 P.M., and the night men in each station were divided into two companies, one serving from 6:00 P.M. to 1:00 A.M. and the other from 1:00 A.M. to 8:00 A.M. In addition, the companies were split into three sections, which served in rotation as day reserve forces, waiting at the station for emergency calls and special duty. The lieutenants, when not relieving the captains of duty, were "roundsmen," walking the divisions to make sure that the patrolmen were actually covering their beats, the first such check introduced.[44]

The five divisions established on the main peninsula varied considerably in area, wealth, and population. There was no explicit statement of the reasons for deciding how many patrolmen were assigned to each. But clearly the most important criteria were the extent of business activity and of vice.

The largest number, seven day and thirty-four night men each, were assigned to divisions two and four. Station two, located at Williams Court, was the center of a territory between Union Street, Hanover Street, and the markets on the north; Howard, Somerset, and Beacon Streets on the west; Park, Winter, and Summer Streets on the south; and the Fort Point Channel on the east. In area it was the second smallest of the districts, but it covered the Irish neighborhood around Fort Hill, and the business and financial center of the city. Station four, situated next to the Boylston Market, served a much larger and less crowded area, bounded on the north by division two, on the west by Beacon Street and Western Avenue, and on the south by the Western Railroad tracks. Its territory included a portion of the business district, together with Irish slums to the east and the Common, Public Garden, and Back Bay to the west.[45]

The next largest number of men, at station one on Hanover Street, covered the smallest division in the city, marked off on the south by division two, on the west by Portland Street, and on the north and east by the waterfront. This crowded North End of the city, the location of its largest vice area, was patrolled by six men in the daytime and twenty-six at night.

Division three was located to the west of divisions one, two, and four. Covering residential Beacon Hill and the "Black Sea," a small Negro vice district behind it, the territory also extended in a long narrow strip along the Charles. Four day men and twenty at night worked out of Leverett Street headquarters.

Station five, on Canton Street Place, was headquarters for only three day and eighteen night men. Its territory was the largest in the city, bounded on the northwest by division four, on the south by the Roxbury line, and on the east by the channel and South Bay. The inordinate length of the beats in this South End was justified by the fact that neither the wealth of shops nor the character of settlement created many problems.

East and South Boston, off the main peninsula, were also provided with a minimum of police. Station six, in South Boston, had two day men and eighteen at night, and station seven, East Boston, had two day men and sixteen at night.

The last division, number eight, covered the harbor and the islands. Marshal Tukey had suggested the need for a water patrol to protect anchored ships and wharves from depredation. A series of such attacks during 1852-53, involving the use of chloroform on ships' crews, helped to convince the city council. In July ten men and a captain were commissioned as harbor police, the first in the United States. The officers showed their worth during their first week on the job by capturing a ring of river pirates. They went on to prove their usefulness, rescuing persons from drowning, retrieving lost boats and bodies, and explaining the harbor regulations to incoming vessels. Special favorites of the merchant community, the harbor police were easily accepted into the regular organization.[46]

But for a full year this entire divisional scheme of organization remained unrecognized by the common council. Jealousy and a substantive dispute over the departmental rules delayed passage of a confirming ordinance. Through 1854 the councillors insisted on a flat prohibition of all extra money for policemen, either in the form of witness fees or rewards. Several times they rejected more permissive proposals, until a compromise provided that "the chief of police and other officers shall receive such compensation as the city council may from time to time determine to be meet and proper." The rule was incorporated into an ordinance adopted May 19, 1855, which finally recognized reorganization and turned the "Watch and Police" into the "Boston Police Department."[47]

The aldermen had in fact won the battle. Even the Boston *Herald* recognized that at least those called to testify in off-duty hours needed some compensation, and in practice they often received fees. The councillors were mollified by the grant of warrants confirming them all as "special policemen," entitled to leather badges which enabled them to pass through fire lines and assume an air of authority in other situations. In later years this mass issuance of badges furnished critics of municipal extravagance with an issue almost as juicy as the annual aldermanic dinners. More important in 1855 was the fact that it focused some attention on the one outstanding anomaly in the new police department.[48]

One group of police still remained outside the reorganized force. The need for a more constant and specific protection of certain business establishments than the regular peace officers provided was met in the 1820's by private watchmen, and after 1838 by "special police," privately paid. These officers were usually issued warrants giving them full powers within designated areas. Some served as night watchmen. Others kept order and prevented loitering during business hours, especially at theaters and terminals. Warrants were given to regular employees, conductors and ticket takers, simply in order to add to their authority. The city itself took advantage of the practice for the same reasons; Chief Nurse, before his regular appointment, had been made a special policeman to facilitate his job as assistant clerk of the Faneuil Hall Market.[49]

The rule requiring the old special watchmen to report weekly to the captain had never been applied to special police, and there was no means of checking their activities. Their badges resembled those worn by the ordinary members of the force. Yet since they had no standards of behavior, pay, or qualification, the regulars despised them and feared that the public might confuse them.[50]

Mayor Rice, in the summer of 1856, voiced doubts about the special officers; and an investigating committee reported that no law or ordinance governed their appointments. The Supreme Judicial Court in 1838 had in effect condoned the practice in *Commonwealth* v. *Hastings,* validating the right of a special officer employed by the National Theatre to make arrests without warrant, in the vicinity of the premises. But the decision had raised as well as settled an issue; it was still unclear whether it was possible to abridge a policeman's authority by area, and, if not, the city might face unexpected liabilities. The mayor added another objection. The whole practice of giving warrants to men free to hire out to private firms was "liable to bring the officers into trials of integrity between interest and duty. No police officer should ever be placed in such a position."[51]

Neither the mayor nor the committee insisted that the specials be abolished outright. Dozens of men, many businesses, and the entire common council had a stake in the practice. The total number of special warrants did not shrink noticeably. But the men were more carefully supervised, required to conform to regular rules and to make weekly written reports to the divisional captains. With the adoption of these regulations the special officers ceased to be an issue.[52]

One more class of officers introduced in 1857 completed the reorganization of the police department. The lieutenants had proved too busy acting as deputy captains and as divisional detectives in minor cases to operate effectively as roundsmen. At the suggestion of the chief, a number of sergeants, three for each division, were appointed to relieve them of the duty.[53]

This move was a part of the continuing effort to introduce paramilitary discipline into what had become quite a large body of men. An important advantage was the attractiveness of the job and the large number of applicants; there had been no trouble inducing the watchmen, who theoretically held two jobs, to abandon both for two dollars a day as patrolmen. But there were no official standards of appointment. The chiefs and mayors complained constantly of the quality of the men for whom citizens signed petitions; and those appointed to the force often resented controls, remembering earlier experience with the carelessly supervised watch. No officer below the chief could take action against patrolmen, who had the right of appeal to the aldermen's police committee in anything involving more than minor changes in duty, small fines, and suspensions. By contrast, most other city employees could be fired outright by their department heads. These restrictions made it difficult for the chiefs to get the new rules obeyed in practice.[54]

Nevertheless their efforts were successful. Chief Taylor had noted in 1855 that within months of the union Boston's police system was already regarded as a model. He took pride in the impression made on visitors, and his office was a center from which flowed a host of suggestions for further improvement. Reporters and councilmen often dropped in to exchange ideas and news. The police, through the telegraph, had long since established contact with their counterparts elsewhere and put to use the information gained through this network. Of the changes made during the 1850's, Boston pioneered only in the establishment of the harbor police. All the others were borrowed; and all, except for the annual appointments, were first officially suggested by the marshal or chief.[55]

One matter which concerned the whole department was the physical change-over from watchhouses to police stations. The city was prodded into adopting a program of building and alterations as soon as the divisional system was organized. The stations, unlike the watch-houses, had to be equipped to receive citizens with complaints, as well as to house sleeping policemen on reserve duty. And they would ideally hold prisoners not simply until taken to a central jail but for the full time between arrest and appearance in court. In 1855 the city did embark on a building program with handsome results. The fifth district station, for example, completed in 1857, was a solid edifice measuring thirty-six by fifty-five feet. It contained in the basement twelve separate cells with no means of communication between them, four for female prisoners and eight for males. Upstairs were nine rooms, not counting the washroom and bathroom. There was a public office, a private office for the captain, a muster room, a property room, a sleeping room for the lieutenants and four for the men. In the opinion of the chief, it was the best-designed station in the United States.[56]

Telegraphic communication among stations was modeled on the fire telegraph set up in 1851. The idea, suggested by the chief in 1855, won quick approval; when the system went into service it became possible instantly to summon the entire reserve force to the scene of a disaster or riot.[57]

In his first annual report after the union, Chief Taylor also noted that the traditional equipment of the watch was unsuitable for the police. The rattles were cumbersome, and the billhooks were easily seized in a scuffle and turned against the men who carried them. The regular police had never used either, but many customarily carried short clubs tied to the wrist. The General Court, in the spring of 1855, authorized peace officers to carry clubs no more than eighteen inches long, which became standard equipment.[58]

No more authoritative weapons had ever been issued, except for the borrowed sabers used in guarding Sims. No one had ever raised the question of whether peace officers should be supplied with guns. It was perhaps considered inappropriate to arm the sheriffs and constables, who had civil as well as criminal duty to perform; and the watch was not fully trusted. But the business of the criminal police was physically dangerous. The men walked their beats alone and dealt in violence every night. They had no handcuffs, no signal boxes for summoning help on the beat, no wagons to escort prisoners back to the station. Three watch or police officers were murdered in the years before the Civil War, all shot to death by men they pursued.[59]

Not many criminals in fact carried arms, even after the invention of the revolver made it possible to do so inconspicuously. But the few who did met no direct opposition from the law. The legislature, in 1850, made possession of a "sling shot" under some circumstances a criminal offense; and in 1859 extended the measure to cover "metallic knuckles," "billies," or "other weapons of a like dangerous character." Firearms were never listed. In practice, the police could be hard on those "going unduly armed," but the General Court was wary of any head-on conflict with the federal Bill of Rights.[60]

The murders of peace officers, which on all three occasions produced a deeply excited reaction, also inspired demands that they be allowed to take stronger measures of self-protection. The *Mail*, commenting on the death of Watchman Daniel Estes, in April 1848, noted that:

Had Mr. Estes, instead of attempting to seize the burglar, knocked him down with his club, he would have taken away his power mischief [*sic*], but a watchman is not privileged to strike except in self-defense . . . the law is too rigorous . . . it may be presumed that a man running away from a watchman's cry of "stop thief" is provided with the means of adding murder to his crimes, and he should be treated accordingly.

Nine years later the murder of Officer Hodgson in East Boston created a great stir; hundreds gathered at the station house, as "most of the prominent men of the ward left their beds . . . to join in the search for the desperadoes, or proffer their advice to the police." Reverend Daniel E. Chapin, at the funeral, commented that he had served many years as a Methodist pastor in the city, but that "he never knew before that the billet of wood which they carry was their only defense against midnight assassins who are allowed to go armed."[61]

In fact, when Officer Hodgson was shot, some members of the force were equipped with pistols, without formal permission or notice. The harbor police during their first week on duty had used guns in "an armed battle" with harbor thieves. The affair was not reported in the press, and the guns were not authorized by the city government or General Court. But the men continued quietly to carry them, almost certainly with official knowledge.[62]

The issue of uniforming the force was the last and most controversial of the 1850's. The police had worn numbered leather badges since their appointment, but in 1857 the chief urged that distinctive uniforms would make them more useful to citizens seeking help or to strangers wanting directions. Equally persuasive was the potential aid to internal discipline; uniformed men were more easily spotted by the roundsmen, and less likely to sneak a drink or a nap. This logic impressed the committee on police and the mayor. But many councillors and a few aldermen sensed that opposition might be more popular; a petition, some debate, and a number of delaying actions held up the motion for several months.[63]

In the end the protesting common councillors could do no more than pass a resolution of "astonishment and regret." The papers did not get excited, and the issue did not loose the storm generated in other cities. Letters sneered at the "popinjays" whose livery would expose them to criminals. But the matter was essentially interesting only to the men themselves, not to the general public. New York had taken years to uniform its police; and the Philadelphia city administration had shared the fear that officers thus identified would more frequently be assaulted. But the Boston department was not so concerned because the men were not embarrassed by their membership on the force; many had voluntarily adopted uniforms already— Kossuth hats, white silk toppers, jackets in varying shades of blue. The elaborate blue outfits designed by the chief were expensive, but the aldermen granted each man an allowance of twenty-five dollars. The department was fully outfitted by 1859; two years later the Civil War erased any lingering stigma attached to a uniform.[64]

The reorganization of the police also occupied other cities in the commonwealth. An act of 1851 enabled any municipality to create a force on the Boston model and many did so. As a result the number of officers rose steadily and provoked some hostility, which ultimately led to a review and definition of the police power by the courts.[65]

The Supreme Judicial Court had started the process in the case of *Fisher* v. *McGirr*. The invalidation of section fourteen of the prohibitory act of 1852, on the grounds that it permitted illegal destruction of property, was in full accord with the legal traditions of the commonwealth. But the second reason, that the section allowed "unreasonable searches and seizures," came rather as a surprise, unanticipated even by the opponents of the law.

Until then it had seemed reasonable that since licensed places had always been open to inspection, that illegal ones should be at least equally liable. For thirty years the General Court had extended the common-law right of search without legal or popular objection. For forty years after the revolution, the common law in Massachusetts had recognized only stolen goods as legitimate objects of search warrants, use of which had been restricted to the daylight hours. But the legislature in 1823 made counterfeit money an object of legal search; and it added gunpowder in 1828, gaming houses and gambling instruments in 1834, and in 1835 property embezzled or obtained by false pretenses, lottery tickets, and obscene books and prints. In 1835 also searches were permitted at night, if two magistrates signed the warrant.[66]

The only one of these provisions challenged in the Supreme Judicial Court, the right to search for lottery tickets, was upheld. The court further allowed considerable latitude to peace officers searching without warrant. Thus *Banks* v. *Farwell* held it legal for a constable to break into and search a shop under the common-law doctrine that the stolen goods sought were "in possession" of the arrested shop owner. Before 1854, newspapers and local officials were no more sensitive to the issue of search than the court and legislature. The objection in *Fisher* v. *McGirr* was that it was too easy to get search warrants without specifically naming either the owner of the premises or the objects sought. But in 1852 Mayor Seaver, while defending his administration against the charge of laxity, paradoxically complained that the legal requirements made warrants inordinately difficult to obtain.[67]

The McGirr decision gave focus to public suspicions. Complaints about search and seizure and about the tyrannous invasion of privacy by the police re-entered the vocabulary of popular rights, strengthened opposition to the liquor laws, and contributed to a growing tendency to question other police activities. Tightened liquor legislation inspired defendants and their lawyers to probe the limits of a policeman's competence. Before 1845 the Supreme Judicial Court of Massachusetts had ruled on the powers of peace officers in only two cases, which had confirmed their rights to act under warrants. But between 1845 and 1861, it heard fully twelve such cases. Some of the decisions confirmed the authority of the officers. Others tended to curb it. All indicated a widespread disposition to challenge and define it.[68]

Rohan v. *Sawin* affirmed the power of arrest without warrant and for the first time in Massachusetts confirmed the difference between police and private citizens in this respect. A Boston officer, having tried and failed to get a warrant against a suspected receiver of stolen goods, went ahead on his own authority to make the arrest. The court upheld his action:

> The public safety . . . imperiously requires that such arrests should be made without warrant by officers of the law. As to rights of private individuals . . . it is a much more restricted authority and is confined to cases of the actual guilt of the parties arrested.[69]

On the other hand, *Commonwealth* v. *Carey* clearly limited an officer's common-law right to arrest without warrant. The shooting of a constable in Lincoln was held to be manslaughter rather than murder, because the officer had been pursuing the killer, without warrant, in order to arrest him for a misdemeanor committed some time earlier. Such pursuit was held illegal, for there was no right to arrest for lesser offenses not committed in the presence of the officer. The court in *Commonwealth* v. *McLaughlin* avoided the more difficult question of whether an officer could arrest when unsure not merely of the identity of the felon but of the existence of a felony. But in the same case, it did rule that there was no right to arrest on suspicion of a misdemeanor, and that a boatload of men, stopped by the call of "Boat Ahoy," were within their rights in resisting arrest when so charged. This last rule, however, was in many cases impractical, and in *Commonwealth* v. *Presby* the court recognized this by affirming the legitimacy of arrests for drunkenness. The decision by implication covered other minor moral offenses in which officers could never be positive of guilt.[70]

Two cases, both significantly involving the liquor laws, contributed to a substantive definition of "reasonable grounds" in arrests without warrant. The decision in *Mason* v. *Lothrop* declared that "reasonable grounds" must rest on something positive; suspicion confirmed by proof discovered afterwards did not of itself justify the original arrest. *Kennedy* v. *Favor* expanded this doctrine. Arresting officers, the court explained, needed more than good faith and a "reasonable cause to suspect" in order to establish "reasonable grounds":

> The authority to seize liquors without warrant, though sometimes necessary, is a high power, and being in derogation of common law right, it is to be exercised only where it is clearly authorized by the statute or rule of law which warrants it.[71]

The officers' rights of entry and search, like those of arrest and seizure, went through the same cycle of affirmation and definition in the 1850's. The earlier case of *Commonwealth* v. *Dana,* like *Fisher* v. *McGirr* and others, dealt not directly with the powers of peace officers but with the powers conferred by warrants, matters for which the responsibility lay with the courts and legislature. But others concerned the manner of executing various writs, and the use of authority without them. *Barnard* v. *Bartlett* affirmed the right of an officer armed only with a warrant of arrest and not search to break into a private dwelling after having been refused entry. That the offender sought was not in fact there was immaterial; a man's home was his castle only in civil cases. Somewhat later in *Commonwealth* v. *Irwin* the court ruled that there was no need even to show the warrant—a policeman's uniform itself was "reasonable notice" of his authority. The ability of peace officers to "enter any building in the night time" to suppress disturbances was never tested. But forcible entry was by implication legitimate. In the one contrary case, the offending constable was held in error not because he was pursuing a misdemeanant without warrant, but only because he had failed first to ask for admittance peaceably.[72]

There was confusion in some of these rulings, and more in the understanding of them; it was only clear that any citizen with a lawyer was prepared to assert his rights against the police. The city council was aware of the threats of political repercussion and legal liability for any acts of roughness, and departmental rules during the 1850's stressed politeness and caution. The officers were ordered to give their badge numbers on request in order to facilitate individual complaints. They were forbidden to use abusive language or unnecessary violence in making arrests in order not to inspire "hostile feeling among the bystanders." And they were instructed fully in the limits of their authority, as outlined by statute, tradition, and the courts.[73]

The experience of the 1850's helped to confirm the ancient belief that there was danger in controversy and virtue in cautious attention to the city's own affairs. The ordinance of 1855, which defined the duties of the chief, conformed to the spirit of that which had thirty years earlier established the office of city marshal. Section two, on the role of the chief, made no mention of the general laws, requiring only that:

He shall devote his whole time to the municipal affairs of the City of Boston, to preserve the peace, order, and cleanliness thereof, and to this end he shall execute and enforce the special laws relating to the city, the orders of the city council, and the orders of the mayor and the Board of Aldermen. He shall take notice of all nuisances, impediments and obstructions . . . and . . . take proper measure in relation thereunto, according to law, under the direction of the mayor and aldermen.

The ideal had been set in 1852: "The police, while it should be argus-eyed, seeing all things, should be itself unseen and unobserved."[74]

It was not always possible to apply this rule, especially among the detectives, who continued to work in the light of newspaper publicity. The headquarters staff expanded to five, supplemented by the local work of the station officers as well as the superintendents of hacks and secondhand shops. Marshal Tukey's men had recovered $16,121 worth of stolen property in 1850; during the next decade this total climbed to a peak of $62,415 in 1860. Detective work was by this time an essential part of police business, and the increase in activity was not hidden. But the chiefs did refuse to dramatize it in their annual reports. The rising figures were given one line each year, without boast or particulars.[75]

The political ideal in police work was routine municipal housekeeping. Both the watch and members of the marshal's office had always been instructed, when on patrol, to remove minor obstructions from the streets and sidewalks, to put out fires, test doors, and turn off running water. While some departments had been split off from the police—streets, lamps, health—the patrolmen continued to serve as "the eyes and ears" of all of them. They rarely did physical labor, but it was still their job to note potholes, smells, and broken lamps, and to report these for reference to the appropriate agencies.[76]

The enforcement of various ordinances necessarily involved some friction. The department shared responsibility for removing major obstructions on streets and sidewalks with the superintendent of streets. In practice, this work devolved largely on the police, who were better organized to serve notice or prosecute, and who had the job of keeping traffic moving. New building construction was supervised jointly but unevenly by the police and firemen. While the aldermen granted permits, the police kept the records and watched construction in progress. The aldermen occasionally demanded "strict enforcement" of the various rules applying to such construction and to blockage in the streets. But in practice these rules had always to be applied against taxpayers, builders piling lumber on the sidewalks, merchants with overflowing warehouses, storekeepers receiving heavy deliveries. Chief Coburn believed in flexibility, and urged that citizens think of the effect upon businessmen before complaining to the police.[77]

The most difficult set of ordinances to enforce were those which regulated traffic in Boston's narrow and twisting streets. Rules governing the rates of hackney carriages, and restricting vehicles to "a moderate trot," or seven miles an hour, had been established before the city was incorporated. But regulation, by licensing and by a traffic code, dated only from the middle 1840's. During the 1850's the ordinances were revised in accord with changing need and the situation created by three new horse railroads to the suburbs.[78]

Rules limited the size, weight, and number of horses allowed various classes of vehicles, and the length of time during which they could stand in the street, especially in front of places of amusement or in the business district. Unoccupied hacks could park only at places assigned by the aldermen, and the city's twenty-nine omnibus lines were restricted to set routes. These provisions made some streets one-way at all times to some vehicles and some streets one-way at some times for all vehicles. There was no general rule about keeping to the right, although state law anciently required that drivers in a narrow passage must do so, and in some sections omnibuses were required to pick up passengers on the right only.[79]

The general superintendence of these regulations belonged to the two full-time men at headquarters. But the patrolmen every day faced the drivers, traditionally a fierce and competitive lot, not tamely amenable to any set of rules. The job entailed unscrambling sweated teams and teamsters and mediating fights. However well it was done, it generated constant if minor resentment.

But police work sought to reduce friction. As in Marshal Pollard's day, strict attention to the ordinances was the primary task of the department, but success was best measured as the inverse of the number of prosecutions. Marshal Tukey in his last year had set a record with 685 arrests for such violations. His successor immediately cut that total in half, and Chief Coburn reduced the annual figure to less than two hundred through the patient use of notices and warnings. There were some complaints of laxity and favoritism, but very few of tyranny.[80]

The official stress on a gentle enforcement of the ordinances was one means of avoiding the execution of unpopular law. But there were other issues too pressing to ignore; the most notable expansion of police responsibility in the 1850's involved the old problem of poverty, vice, and misfortune.

Chief Coburn testified that there was no change in the accepted attitude toward these ills: "It is an admitted fact, that intemperance is the direct origin of more poverty, more crime, and more human suffering than all other causes combined." Only those who read the statistics of health, or who had reason to visit the city's Irish slums, were fully aware of the misery in Boston. But all who walked the streets could see its public face, and it was easy to use drunkenness as the index to it.[81]

The widespread impression was that drunkenness was on the increase. Before the temperance reform had gotten under way, the number of places that sold liquor legally or illegally was estimated at about one to every sixty-five inhabitants. The relative figure decreased during the 1830's and 1840's. Then Irish immigration precipitated a steep rise, and by 1860, with an estimated 2,220 liquor shops serving a population of 177,902, the earlier proportion was approached again.[82]

There is no way of gauging what these estimates meant in terms of alcohol consumed. Between the 1820's and the 1850's, intensive education in temperance and an increase in the use of milder beverages had probably improved the drinking habits of the nation as a whole. But prohibition in Massachusetts had eliminated lager beer saloons "like dew before the sun." Beer was relatively bulky, expensive to transport and to store, and not easily manufactured locally "for use in medicine and the arts." The opponents of prohibition, at least, insisted that the liquor drunk in Boston during the 1850's was strong and poisonous in quality.[83]

The effects of intemperance were more crippling during the 1850's than they had been a generation before. The self-employed teamster or artisan of the 1820's could afford some loss of time and money. Thirty years later a real proletariat lived barely over the level of existence, and the more complex economic organization of the city was less tolerant of inefficiency and delay. After three decades of agitation, both law and respectable opinion were hostile to drunkenness. But while the enormity of the problem was recognized, there was no agreed treatment for this or any of the vices of the mid-century city.

Josiah Quincy and the generation of municipal leaders after him believed in significant human as well as material progress, and hoped to reform the vicious through the courts and the penal system. They had built and supported the houses of Industry, Reformation, and Correction, in which the poor and evil would be confined and changed through useful employment in the arts and agriculture. They had attempted to coordinate public and private charity to make both more effective; and the temperance ideal, basic to the hopes of all, had gained steadily through the 1840's.[84]

But not all those involved in the temperance crusade were humanitarians. Intimately related to the movement for prohibition was the old notion that the law and the penal system were simply agencies of punishment. Fines and imprisonment for those guilty of drunkenness and similar offenses were ends in themselves, rather than first steps in a program of individual and social regeneration. The Supreme Judicial Court of Massachusetts expressed this view in 1858, in the case of *Commonwealth* v. *Miller,* when it ruled that publicity was not required for conviction under the 1835 statute regarding simple drunkenness. Quiet intoxication in a private room was adjudged criminal, and the language used made it clear that the justices believed it sinful as well.[85]

Most opinion in Boston was not so severe. In practice the treatment of drunkenness followed no coherent plan. Many reformers, either discouraged or obsessed with the problem of slavery, paid little attention to this problem during the 1850's; and the local authorities were neither so philosophical nor so hopeful as their predecessors, partly because of the shift in class and partly because of the sheer weight of immigration. After more than a generation of experience, the penal institutions were still not rehabilitating their inmates; no marked improvement resulted in 1858 from putting them all under a single board of directors. All experts condemned the system of public out-door relief, which was continued but without enthusiasm. Private charity was not adequate to fill the gap. The government, moved by a genuine if unreflective popular humanitarianism, simply followed the easiest course, dealing as it could with the most pressing social needs and providing a limited, symptomatic response to vice and crime.[86]

The treatment of drunkenness reflected these limited aims, as well as a desire to avoid antagonisms. The rise in drunk arrests, during the last years of the watch, was regarded with some suspicion in the popular press, as being too harsh and possibly inspired by the desire for witness fees. But the agents of police faced an opposing pressure to rid the streets of disorder and distress. Police and watch statistics were even then remarkable not in the number taken in but in the few prosecuted. The police in 1849 did not make a single prosecution for drunkenness. In the last quarter of 1852, the watch arrested 2,053 persons for this offense; only 16 were held for trial. After 1853, when the police and watch were combined and there were no more complaints about witness fees, the number of annual drunk arrests continued to climb. There were 13,157 in 1860, nearly double the 6,983 for 1854. But there was no great increase in the proportion of prosecutions.[87]

This was a simple solution to a difficult problem. Neither the police nor the city authorities were eager to inflict five dollars and costs on the unfortunates rounded up at night. About four of every five arrested were foreigners, often desperately poor, and one in five was a woman. A night in the cells often saved them from exposure and self-injury, and most were let go in the morning. Several hundred more, each year, were "helped home drunk," a total which apparently included the most sympathetic cases, the most influential, and those known personally to the officers. One in four or five of those arrested for all causes came from outside of Boston; many of these were held for trial.[88]

The ultimate tendency was to eliminate prosecution and punishment altogether. But the court's decision in the Miller case clearly denied this. The next year Representative Ben Butler of Lowell, always sensitive to urban opinion, led his judiciary committee to sponsor a solution. His bill, passed in 1860, stated simply that "no person shall be fined or imprisoned for drunkenness, except as a Common Drunkard, anything in the laws of the Commonwealth to the contrary notwithstanding." Temporary arrest and detention was permitted, however, so that the law had little effect in Boston, where it had been anticipated in practice.[89]

This approach to the problem of drunkenness was matched by the city's treatment of poverty and misfortune. While charitable reformers still hoped to adopt some form of the strict British poor law system, the elective overseers of the poor continued to distribute a wasteful outdoor relief; and the municipality permitted a supplementary charity administered by the police.

The police, on patrol throughout the city, were in more intimate contact with its misery than any other representatives of the government. The practice of admitting the homeless to the watchhouses was an old one. During Tukey's administration his men occasionally distributed coal to the tenants of Ann Street, in addition to setting up a charity of their own. None of this was authorized by statute or order, but by the end of the 1840's the department was regularly reimbursed for out-of-pocket charitable expenses. In the 1850's the police began to act as agents for the overseers of the poor, investigating and recommending action on several hundred cases a year.[90]

New and larger station houses after 1854 allowed an enormous increase in this activity. In 1856 the stations began to do officially what they had previously done unofficially; they provided "lodgings" to dozens of strangers each night. In the first year the police put up 9,037 individuals, not including those arrested for drunkenness. By 1860 the total reached 17,352.[91]

In the absence of any alternative, the cells and floors also served as temporary hospital facilities. Although the chief by then had lost his function as superintendent of health, during the cholera epidemic of 1854 the dead and dying came or were carried to the stations. The police removed the victims, searched and closed their dwellings, and fitted them into sealed coffins for burial. A movement in the 1850's to build a municipal hospital proved abortive, and the city council rejected a motion to attach salaried doctors to each station house. But the city physician and some volunteers visited the stations daily; others were called in emergencies. In almost every annual report after 1855, the chiefs urged the aldermen to establish a free hospital for the poor.[92]

Exposure to misery must have hardened many policemen, but there was no hint of callousness in these annual reports. The chiefs were sensitive to social conditions, and especially to the problems of juvenile poverty, prostitution, and intemperance. Tukey and Coburn, in particular, wrote vivid descriptions when moved by the neglected death of a consumptive Irish girl or the disintegration of a drunkard's family. Sometimes among the statistics and suggestions there appeared little jeremiads, bitter comments on the cruelty and squalor of contemporary society.[93]

Sensitivity to social conditions, together with direct corruption and popular opinion, governed the efforts to deal with vice. In contrast to the prohibitionists, the city was not concerned with the immorality of the rich. While not tolerated openly, as even reformers admitted, "palaces of gilded vice," catering to "the upper ten," were allowed to operate. Power and influence accounted in part for the undisturbed existence of faro rooms and brothels. So did the fact that "officers who are chosen to enforce the laws protect the one, and patronize the other." But there were less venal motives also.[94]

Majority opinion, as reflected in jury actions, prevented any major reform. Some lawbreakers were jailed for running houses of ill fame, but the fine for keeping gambling rooms or liquor shops was too low, between twenty and a hundred dollars, to serve as a deterrent. Anything higher, or the threat of imprisonment, often resulted in refusal to convict. Juries were plainly skeptical of the possibility of institutional reformation.[95]

It was difficult in mid-century Boston for a policeman to escape a belief in the inevitability of vice, and discreet and well-regulated places were preferable to "common nuisances." If refining the grossness from vice did not eliminate half the sin, at least it mitigated the social consequences, disorder and misery, which brought in the police. There was undoubtedly hypocrisy but also some truth in the frequent claim of officials and police that they were concerned only with those who could not afford to misspend their money.

The handling of prostitution clearly illustrated the fact that the police as individuals were often prompted by humane as well as corrupt motives. Chief Coburn, in explaining their attitude toward vice, called the men a cross section of the public. In fact it was a narrow section. There were no rich men on the force, and except for the erratic tenure of Barney McGinniskin there were no Irish. The police were not quite typical even of the "mechanics." A survey of their nativity in 1855 revealed that only 32 of the city's 238 policemen had been born in Boston. Some 49 came from elsewhere in the state, 2 from Rhode Island, and 1 each from Connecticut, Delaware, Pennsylvania, and New York. The greater number were from upper New

England—17 from Vermont, 56 from Maine, 77 from New Hampshire. Coming down from the small towns and farms, they got their first employment as apprentices or self-employed teamsters and drivers. But with wages uncertain, they found it more secure to offer their youth and strength as policemen. In all but this last step, in fact, the typical biography paralleled the personal history of the prostitute.[96]

A man like Captain Edward H. Savage of station one—New Hampshire bred, handcart-jobber turned policeman—needed no Victorian literature to suggest that many of the girls about Ann Street might have been his sisters. The police naturally developed a hatred, not of prostitutes, but of prostitution. The annual reports were filled with anger at the panderer or seducer; many of the several dozen arrested each year as "idle and disorderly persons" belonged to this class. The newspapers, too, reported acts of gallantry. In one such affair, after a pimp had beaten a girl in especially vicious fashion, Savage pursued the offender all the way to Portland. And the captain returned to manage a trial which was covered like a drama, with the defendant's villainous lawyer, asking the complainant "And what do you do for a living?" brought up by her bitter reply: "You know very well what I do for a living, without asking!"[97]

Some reformers in the early 1860's accused the police of a growing tolerance toward prostitution. But the statistics indicate rather a determined effort to discourage it, at least among newcomers and those not connected with established places. During the 1850's and on into the early 1860's, arrests for nightwalking were absolutely higher than at any other period in the century. Over four hundred such arrests were made annually. When this course proved ineffective, the police organized another, as in the Ann Street Descent of 1851. During 1858 the men reported to Captain Savage that there were too many new faces, young girls, soliciting on Ann Street. On October 22, forty men went out in plain clothes, and in thirty minutes served fifty-one warrants issued by Judges Wells and Chase of the Police Court. The former tactic of providing local jobs, usually as domestics, had been discredited when the girls disrupted families, turned to petty thievery, and drifted back to old associations. This time forty-seven of them, all new arrivals, were given suspended sentences and sent back home, away from the corrupting atmosphere of the big city.[98]

An uneasy acceptance of vice was typical of a decade in which Boston was forced to come to terms with itself. Its citizens had to accept the fact that the Irish population was there to stay, that the city had lost its position as political hub of New England, that no miracle would make it the leading commercial center of the continent. But these setbacks did not produce despair. While ambitions were limited, there was still faith in the future. And while the city was threatened with cleavage, political moderation could still hold it together.

The police were an integral part of this process. By limiting their use in controversial areas, local officials kept tensions from erupting into violence. Governed by a conservative consensus, the police were no longer considered agents of reform, whose primary function was to "execute the law." But they were able to meet the increased demands of municipal administration and to deal with the most pressing social problems of the mid-century city.

By the end of the decade, the police had arrived at basic patterns of organization, duty, and even appearance which would remain stable for a long time. Important questions of function and control were still to be settled. But there was no serious challenge to the standards according to which the men were doing all that was wanted. The attorney general wrote in 1859 that "at no time in the history of Massachusetts have life, liberty, and property been more secure than at present." And observers with wide experience shared the opinion of the local press and government that the Boston police department was the best in the Union.[99]

CHAPTER SEVEN

The Violent Years, 1860-1869

The experience of Boston during the decade of the Civil War, like that of the nation, was marked both by severe disruption and by accelerated growth. The threat to the Union, at the outset, shattered the fragile political truce achieved in the previous period. War itself upset the operations of the government; and the strain was magnified by a rapid increase in activity, expenditures, and area.

No department of the city was more deeply or typically affected by these conditions than the police. The force had to deal with many wartime problems. Its size and the scope of its activities expanded. Most significant, it became the subject of the leading local controversy of the decade.

For many citizens the excitement of war stimulated the dormant urge to battle with sin at home. Outside reformers joined dissatisfied residents in condemning the character of the police of Boston. As the experience of other cities suggested new means of realizing an old ideal, critics pressed for important changes in the objectives and conduct of the force.

The controversy over the Boston police in the 1860's was the climax of a dispute inherent since the founding of the department. Most American police systems developed without fundamental reflection or debate, in response to specific problems of riot, theft, and disorderly behavior, which were generally condemned. They combined a variety of organizational patterns and functions, some inherited, some based on unique experience, others borrowed from each other or from abroad. The paramilitary European systems, and especially the London metropolitan police, were often used as models. But as the American forces gained strength there was a fundamental division over the extent to which these models should be followed in practice.[1]

118

The ideals of discipline and efficiency were universally attractive to municipal governments and taxpayers. The adoption of uniforms, and of officers with military titles, was part of a continuing effort to make the police a more useful tool of administration. During the 1860's, in Boston and elsewhere, this movement was spurred by the new prestige of the military, and by the need to meet problems aggravated by wartime disorder.

But for the city government, admiration for the London model was confined to limited matters of internal discipline and organization. American policemen were emphatically not soldiers but citizens, required to be voters and taxpayers, preferably married, familiar to their neighbors, and sensitive to their needs. The duties of the department, as of all other branches of municipal administration, were shaped by the demands of the populace and by representative local government.

This emphasis upon organic involvement in the community and in the normal political process was in direct contrast to the system of London. The English metropolitan police commissioners recruited their men from the pool of common labor outside of the capital or from the lower ranks of the army. Once on the force, the officers were denied the vote. Bachelors were assigned to barracks, married men restricted to designated neighborhoods. And in order to assure impartial execution of the laws, the force was responsible not to the population it served but to Parliament.[2]

It was impossible in the United States to adopt the London personnel policies, and there was no movement to restrict the individual liberties of policemen. But there was considerable admiration for the purpose behind these measures, and the provision for central control commanded wide attention. Some Americans sought to imitate the British pattern by transferring the direction of the police from city to state, especially in a period of rising political tensions.

New York State led the way in 1857 by creating a metropolitan commission, appointed by the governor, with full authority over the police of New York, Kings, Richmond, and Westchester counties. Maryland established a similar commission for Baltimore in 1860. As Civil War came to Missouri, in 1861, the police of St. Louis and Kansas City were also brought under state direction. Detroit followed in 1865, Cleveland in 1866, New Orleans in 1868.[3]

A number of considerations prompted these arrangements: the

existence of an emergency, a demand for economy, a frank desire for power and patronage. But there was another motive as well. In the case of *People* v. *Draper,* which upheld the constitutionality of the metropolitan commission in New York, Justice Shankland questioned the city's ability to govern itself, and particularly to enforce the statutory law: "How have the local authorities of that great city discharged its duty of local government to its citizens and to the state at large, in protecting them in their liberty, life, and property? Let the statistics of crime answer." The state had made the law, the justice concluded, and it was "bound to protect the citizen . . . irrespective of locality."[4]

Shankland's argument expressed a conviction which gathered strength in Massachusetts as well as in New York. In the 1850's the performance of the Boston police had not met the high expectations entertained by the citizens in the previous decade. By the 1860's, there seemed no hope of achieving the old hopes through local political action. The social problems which had long distressed reformers still beset the city. In the North End each night dozens of spectators, "pickpockets," "petty knucks," and "females with vermillion cheeks," gathered in fetid rooms to make bets on the contestants in rat pits and dogfights. In a tenement in another section there was "a room twelve feet square, where thirteen people live, and they are all drunkards, and keep rum in the place." The police chief acknowledged that scores of open brothels and dozens of gambling rooms catered to the passions of degraded residents and invited countrymen from all over New England to ruin. The police were incapable of eliminating this viciousness because, of the eleven or twelve thousand citizens who participated regularly in municipal elections, "at least five thousand are pledged by instinct and interest against the enforcement of the most wholesome laws of the Commonwealth." The board of aldermen, as a result, was merely "a standing committee appointed by the grog-shops of the peninsula."[5]

The argument of the city government was also expressed in *People* v. *Draper,* in the dissenting opinion of Justice Brown: "Under popular systems of government, laws depend for their enforcement upon the enlightened moral sense of those upon whom they are to operate, and it is as unwise as it is unwarranted, to pass acts which impair inherent rights, in the vain hope of useful or beneficial results." The police in a democracy could not and should not attempt to enforce such laws.

They were legitimately used only for local prudential purposes, or to preserve order according to standards not in controversy.[6]

The Civil War accentuated the opposing concepts of police responsibility, and magnified the substantive issues at stake. The result was an alternating round of conflict, renewed almost every year; as the city continued to exercise and improve the department according to its own standard, its critics, seizing on a variety of complaints, attempted more fully to realize the London ideal.

The city made the initial change itself in the summer of 1860, after the first proven scandal in the history of the force. Six night patrolmen of the second division for several years had been stealing cigars and similar items from the shops along their beats. The Boston *Herald* protested that the department was still "a model for the world," rarely guilty of sins more serious than levying small contributions from illicit liquor dealers. But the discovery precipitated two revisions in the departmental rules.[7]

In line with earlier efforts to increase efficiency, all new applicants were required to submit to an examination by the city physician who was to certify that they were in good health, between twenty-one and forty years of age, and at least five feet eight inches tall. Also, to prevent a recurrence of the trouble in division two, the council abolished the distinction between day and night patrolmen, which had made the latter second-class members of the department. All men were to rotate beats, so that none would feel slighted and none would become dangerously familiar with their colleagues or the places that they were supposed to protect. These corrective measures were considered enough, and the *Herald* announced that the department "needs no further purifying."[8]

But this show of satisfaction did not survive the fall campaign. Abraham Lincoln swept Massachusetts in the excited November elections of 1860, and so did the Republican state ticket. But in Boston, Lincoln took only 9,727 of 20,371 votes cast. By the time the municipal contest was begun the effect of his election was already apparent. A convention of all the other parties nominated a Democrat, Alderman Joseph Wightman, to run for mayor on a "Union and Citizens" ticket against the Republicans. The contest, for the first time in years, was largely and bitterly concerned with the national issues of slavery and union.[9]

In this heated atmosphere, the Union men revived the earlier police scandal as their leading local issue. Mayor Lincoln, elected three times as a nonpartisan, had emerged as a Republican. Since the embarrassment of his administration seemed bound up with the fate of the nation, the *Herald* changed its position and denounced blackmail, bribery, and officers in league with thieves. Wightman became the champion of police reform as well as of Union, and on December 10 defeated his opponent 8,834 to 5,674.[10]

Once inaugurated, Wightman proved to have no radical reform in mind. Chief Coburn was replaced by General L. C. Amee, an elderly militia officer and political ally of the mayor. The new rule requiring physical examinations was retained. So was that which ended the day and night distinction. But the last one had inspired complaints from businessmen, politicians, and the police themselves. Familiarity between patrolmen and the inhabitants along their beats was an essential part of the city's police system, an important bulwark against overzealous enforcement of the laws and ordinances. This innovation was rescinded as Amee took office, and the men went back to the three-division system and their regular routines.[11]

That winter the dominant concern of the city was not the state of the police but of the Union. The position of official Boston, as excitement mounted, was clearly established. The board of aldermen, on January 14, unanimously requested Wightman to petition the General Court for repeal of the personal liberty laws. On January 21, again unanimously, the members requested Congress to take "conciliatory measures" in the face of secession. But the emergency provided many citizens, who disagreed with both proposals, with the occasion for a new and radical attack on the management of the police force.[12]

Temperance men had long condemned Boston's record on the enforcement of prohibition. The recent city campaign had stressed illegalities and immoralities in the conduct of the police. Beginning in December there had been a revival of mob attacks on abolitionists, which the force on two occasions had encouraged rather than prevented. And in January, the Supreme Judicial Court of Massachusetts delivered a significant decision in the previously obscure case of *Buttrick* v. *Lowell,* a suit which came to involve the liability of municipal corporations for the actions of their police. No such liability existed, the court held, because police officers could "in no sense be regarded as agents or servants of the city." Their control simply devolved upon the local authorities, "as a convenient means of exercising a function of government." And in terms more forceful than those of *People* v. *Draper,* the justices concluded that "The preservation of the public peace, the enforcement of the laws, and other similar powers and duties with which police officers are entrusted, are derived from the law, and not from the city or town under which they hold their appointment."[13]

The timing of this decision fitted perfectly with other events to advance the plans of the reformers. On January 21 Senator Whiting of Plymouth moved to create a special legislative committee to consider a metropolitan police for Boston. Three days later the Anti-Slavery Society held its annual meeting at Tremont Temple, barely a block away from the State House. Thirty patrolmen stood by as the convention was mobbed; the mayor and Chief Coburn ordered it closed, and the society adjourned until evening. Wightman then announced that the police would be unable to protect it, and ordered Coburn to lock the doors. Governor Andrew and several members of the General Court witnessed the whole disturbance; few agreed that a vigorous force could not have controlled it. Whiting's committee was appointed, with only one dissenting vote, and began hearings on February 7.[14]

The bill brought in by the petitioners was closely modeled on the experience of New York. It created a board of three commissioners, with staggered three-year terms, chosen by the governor from among the citizens of Boston. All rules then governing the department were to remain in force, except that the men were to serve during good behavior, and could be fired only after hearings on written charges. The city government would have no voice in matters of policy or appointment, but the budget, drawn up by the commissioners, would be met by requisitions on the municipal treasury.[15]

The opponents of the city clearly felt that their proposal was well timed. But during this first set of metropolitan police hearings they failed to manage their case with skill. No one denied that Boston ignored the prohibitory law, and had failed to protect the abolitionists. But their chief other arguments, that the police were deeply involved in partisan politics and in corruption, were difficult to prove. The petitioners called four main witnesses: ex-Chief Coburn, ex-Deputy Chief Luther Ham, ex-head of detectives Galen Holmes, Jr., and ex-Captain William A. Eaton. Coburn and Ham had just been fired by the incoming administration; Holmes had been dismissed earlier by Coburn, and Eaton had resigned after a dispute with Ham. All four had complaints against the system and each other. But Coburn had been in charge of the force during the period under discussion, and none of the other three was barred from possible re-employment.[16]

Coburn's annual reports had urged that the police, like judges, serve during good behavior because the recurrent springtime sense of insecurity adversely affected their work. He also admitted rather reluctantly that his final report had suggested that the department be managed by a board of commissioners, and he had stricken out the passage at the insistence of Mayor Wightman. But on the whole he concluded that "Our Police Department compares favorably with that of New York—our men are better, there being no foreigners in our department." Some appointments were tinged with politics, his own included, but removals for political reasons were unknown. And excepting recent work in circulating petitions in behalf of the Crittenden Compromise, the men were forbidden to engage in political activity.[17]

None of the others contradicted this testimony, except when Holmes noted that some policemen had furthered Coburn's own attempt to win the nomination for sheriff in 1858. For the press, and the officers concerned, accusations of individual corruption were far more important than this line of questioning.[18]

Eaton testified solely to improper relations between Deputy Ham and Abijiah Jenkins, a secondhand dealer and convicted fence. Holmes first charged that although intemperance was ordinarily considered a high crime in the department, a few favored members were notorious for drunkenness. At this point he was taken into secret session. When he emerged, he was asked whether he knew of any case in which an officer had been bribed by an arrested thief; he did not, although he had heard of such a case. When asked to "state what you know of corruption," he listed four cases, all involving Ham and Coburn: the two had illegally shared a reward for solving an out-of-town burglary; Ham had once refused to arrest Jenkins, merely returning some goods; Coburn had padded an expense account; Coburn had extorted money from a liquor dealer.[19]

The opponents of the metropolitan bill chose to ignore the more general issues, and treated the hearings merely as a slanderous attack on individual policemen, who were simply called in their own defense.

Various members of the force testified to their sober habits. Ham said he had not at first had enough evidence against Jenkins and claimed credit for the eventual conviction. Coburn admitted that Ham had bought him a suit of clothes after solving the Frederickstown Bank robbery, but said that the "extortion" which Holmes alleged had been an act of gallantry; he gave the money to an unfortunate girl made pregnant by a saloon-keeper.[20]

The special committee, on April 8, reported five to two against the metropolitan police measure. The majority asserted simply that "nothing has been elicited by the investigation which should impair the high character of the Police of Boston . . . for intelligence, efficiency, and integrity"—the best in the United States. If the liquor law was not enforced, the trouble lay not with the police but with balky juries; and there was no remedy for the mobbing of abolitionist meetings which would not violate the spirit of the constitution and the age. The trend of a generation had been toward more democracy, not less, toward popular election, as of sheriffs, toward local autonomy and away from centralization.[21]

This report killed the bill. Even a Republican legislature had little sympathy with Wendell Phillips, who managed the case for the petitioners and set the tone of the hearings. The political course of the local authorities did not seem wholly outrageous. Governor Andrew had refused to call out the militia on the occasion of the Tremont Temple riot, claiming a lack of authority, and the legislature that spring did follow the city's recommendation in repealing the personal liberty laws. There was as yet no war, and Massachusetts was not in a militant mood.[22]

When fighting did break out, only days after the settlement of the police bill, city and state united in common purpose. Wightman and the city council followed the example of Stephen A. Douglas in vigorously supporting the Northern cause. And for a time reformist sentiment in the Commonwealth was engaged with something larger than an investigation of the Boston police force.[23]

The conflict presented the police with a number of problems apart from politics. The city during its course spent over three and a half millions on direct war expenditures, largely for bounties and soldiers' relief. This extraordinary expense, roughly equal to the total prewar budget, combined with inflation to force curtailment of many ordinary services. But despite the demand for economy, it proved impossible to cut the police force, which grew steadily from the 294 men in 1861 to 375 by 1865.[24]

Some of this increase came in response to unique wartime conditions. The most important new function was the arrest of deserters and bounty jumpers. The city had a large investment in many of these, and during the first two years of war more than one thousand were recaptured by the civilian police. Patriotic rallies and parades required extra men to clear the streets, restrain crowds, and watch for pickpockets. The harbor police were called upon to guard military shipments and to transport men and supplies to the island base at Fort Warren. And on one occasion Chief Amee and eighteen men were sent to Washington, after the Peninsula Battles, to use their station house nursing experience to help care for the wounded.[25]

But in most respects, the city and the police department tried to maintain normal operations. Neither the prestige of the soldierly virtues nor the special demands of wartime affected the government's pacifist ideals. General Amee shared the belief that "the public good requires the power of the police to be felt rather than seen." And the board of aldermen continued to stress a circumspect enforcement of the ordinances. The police committee in 1862 established a special detail of eleven men to watch over the newly planted Public Garden, to guard against "persons crossing the turf and flower beds, or boys bathing naked in the ponds, . . . or dogs suffered to range at large among the flowers, tracking their way to destruction." This job had earlier fallen to a group of gardeners. There was need now, the committee believed, for the authority of a uniform "to secure unquestioning obedience." But it had no intention of inaugurating "that harsh system, which in Europe exposes individuals, infringing unconsciously some petty regulation, to indignity and penalties. The large powers confirmed by law to an officer, unless tempered by courtesy, easily become oppressive." The same committee ordered eight men to patrol Washington Street, the city's busiest thoroughfare, to enforce the traffic regulations, suggesting that the chief "require of them an attention to dress and deportment, which will satisfy the just expectations of the public for a post so conspicuous. Their example in neatness, as also in quickness . . . and courtesy of manner, good sense and intelligence, may possibly have its effect in raising the standard throughout the department."[26]

The committee also noted that the city had not used its power under the law to regulate outdoor sales by minors. Chief Amee echoed the earlier complaint of Marshal Tukey about an army of unruly children in the streets, many habitually drunk or prostituted at the ages of twelve or thirteen. The police committee recommended the licensing of newsboys, bootblacks, and others, both to expedite traffic and to curb truancy: "These rules will enable the truant officers to see at a glance which boys are authorized to absent themselves from school, and whether it is with the full consent of their parents." The full board made two hours a day of school attendance a condition of license, and restricted the holders to designated stands.[27]

The final recommendation of the committee was that the city council revise all rules governing the police department, in order to encompass and add to the many changes made since 1855. But while its suggestions as to the garden police and traffic squad were adopted easily, this proposal involved an extended battle much like that of the early 1850's.[28]

Most of the proposed new rules conformed to customary procedures. They required the chief to keep a daily "meteorological diary," for instance, and prohibited political and religious discussions in the station houses. They reviewed in detail the police responsibility for laws and ordinances. Captains were enjoined to familiarize themselves with their divisions, patrolmen to know the inhabitants on their beats, and to note all new arrivals and departures. The men were also reminded to give polite assistance to strangers and citizens. The main change in emphasis was the insistence on discipline and regularity, and on the need for careful records and roll-keeping at all levels. The duties of every rank were spelled out in meticulous detail in thirty-seven pages of close print. Over these matters there was no dispute. Nor was there a controversy over the politically significant provision that policemen serve during good behavior.[29]

But the question of witness fees and rewards again aroused the common council, and the rules shuttled several times between the two branches without ratification. The election of 1862 complicated the business. Former mayor Frederick Lincoln, in retaliation for Wightman's 1860 campaign, made the conduct of the police an issue and won. He then replaced Amee with another militia officer, Colonel John Kurtz. But the new rules remained unapproved, and as in 1861, many citizens were still unsatisfied and concerned with issues deeper than who should head the force or the proper manner of calling the roll.[30]

One of the long-term results of the Civil War was the dissipation of the reform energies generated in the 1830's and the 1840's. But in Massachusetts, the more immediate effect was to create among reformers a spirit of fierce intolerance, a demand for unconditional victory over all opponents. The state legislature elected in 1862 contained many uncompromising men who hated the South and slavery and also hated the city which had frustrated their earlier efforts. They were not primarily motivated by partisan politics; the governor was not entirely with them, and they cared little that a Republican had been elected mayor of Boston. The city was corrupt beyond redemption, and they were eager to reduce it.

These reformers found allies among other group within the city. The tradition of aristocratic involvement in municipal affairs continued to decline throughout the Civil War. None of the mayors and few councillors belonged to the class which had earlier governed the community. As the number of naturalized voters increased they joined political organizations, and several Irishmen took places in the common council. Many inhabitants of the richer wards, meanwhile, fled to the country every spring, giving up their voting rights in order to avoid Boston's personal property levy. Such people came to view local government with distaste and turned for help to the General Court, not for ideological reasons but to preserve their tax money from improper use.[31]

This process of alienation among the upper classes was still far from complete. But it was widespread enough to enlist many substantial residents in any effort to reduce the power of the city's politicians. These citizens found common cause with reformers in the metropolitan police movement. In February 1863, several hundred of them joined critics from outside Boston in another successful petition for a legislative hearing.[32]

This set of metropolitan police hearings was conducted very differently from those in 1861. This time, both proponents and opponents of the measure relied not on detailed testimony but upon abstract argument. Beginning on March 7, the committee listened principally to speeches by prominent men on both sides of the question, who engaged, in effect, in the commonwealth's first real debate on the proper nature and function of a police force.[33]

On March 16 Alderman Thomas Coffin Amory, one of the last aristocrats in the city government, "a gentleman of culture and refinement . . . chosen unanimously on the concurrent action of all parties," summed up the case for Boston. A Democrat, he had served four years on the police committee, two as chairman; and he was proud to announce his own qualifications as a student of government and comparative police systems. Citing the Greeks, the Italian and Dutch republics, and the Swiss Confederation, Amory noted that "History teaches us that free institutions are only practicable in small communities, or where there exists a subordination of part to the whole." The example of New York City, cited by the petitioners, was hardly inspiring: "In a country all aglow with the life and light of liberty, amidst a constellation of free states and cities, she sits alone in humiliating bondage." Less excusable, even shocking, were models drawn from abroad: "In monarchies, absolute or limited, the police force is less the watchdog of the cottage . . . than the blood hound of authority, every ready to strike its fangs into the feeble and needy." The alderman admitted that "from training and superior discipline in some of them it is made of greater convenience than with us—and their example in this respect is worthy of imitation." But the price was usually too high: "Long may it be before we have forced upon us a constabulary like that of Ireland, or a system of police and espionage such as exists in Cuba and the Southern States, or on the continent of Europe, where the traveller moves in fetters through the glories of nature and art."[34]

Amory identified three major groups with substantive complaints about the police of Boston: the abolitionists, the temperance men, and those who objected to the political use of the force. He dealt with each in turn.[35]

The alderman rehearsed in familiar terms the history and failure of prohibition, its dubious constitutionality, its repugnance to the sense of the community. Despite all of this the city had at first attempted in good faith to execute the Act of 1855. Indignant juries had frustrated the effort. Since that time, "it has never seemed worth while to subject either state or county to heavy criminal costs, merely to prove that the law might be violated with impunity." Responsibility for enforcement in any case belonged with the courts and individual complainants. "It is the duty of the police officer to serve . . . warrants, when directed to him. It is nowhere made his duty to initiate prosecutions." A system of spies and informers would not conform to the institutions of a free country. "The statutes impose no such ungrateful task. . . . Nor could we procure any but the most depraved of men for the protection of our lives and property if any such duty were exacted of them."[36]

Reformers had suggested that belief in the prohibitory law be made a test of competence for jury service or that liquor cases be tried outside Suffolk County. Amory rejected both plans as violations of the spirit and letter of the constitution. In any case the evil had been exaggerated. A mere one thousand people, taken in a dozen times each year, probably accounted for the size of the arrest statistics. And many of the three thousand groggeries were little places run by widows and cripples with no other means of support. The city was quite capable of enforcing a license law which met the test of public opinion and gave the licensed dealers an incentive to help prosecute others.[37]

The alderman dismissed the problems of the abolitionists with less argument. There had been a few unfortunate incidents in 1860-61, he admitted. But no one was seriously hurt; and large numbers had agreed, in that critical period, that "any freedom of discussion of the subject of slavery could answer no useful purpose."[38]

As to the business of politics and the character of the police force: "The changes on political grounds have been very inconsiderable." He belonged himself to the party of General Amee, but saw nothing wrong with his replacement by Colonel Kurtz. "The relation of chief to the mayor, necessarily from its nature, requiring the most implicit confidence, should not be disturbed by any doubt of his friendliness of feeling." Below that rank the annual turnover was slight. Great improvements had been made recently, and the force was composed of respectable, vigorous men, artisans and mechanics attracted by a liberal salary "higher than is thought advisable by some at the outset, at it deprives the public of skills it can ill afford to lose." All of the officers were expressly forbidden to engage in politics, and the tenure "has always substantially been, one of good behavior."[39]

The plan to appoint three commissioners from both parties, finally, would recognize rather than eliminate politics in the control of the police. The proposal was undemocratic and unfair, applying to Boston alone. And since it required the city to pay for the police without managing them, Amory concluded, it would constitute "taxation without representation," an insult to the traditions of the common-wealth.[40]

The last word in the hearings, however, belonged to the friends of a metropolitan police, skillfully represented by Charles M. Ellis, a veteran reformer and author of the state's first personal liberty law. He spoke on behalf of various "large property holders," in and outside of Boston, who headed the petitioners for change. His argument, less familiar and more closely reasoned than Alderman Amory's, closed the hearing on March 18.[41]

It was the purpose of the bill, Ellis declared, "to save the police from too intimate relations with the populace." His opponent "seemed to have in his mind for a policeman the common definition—one set to keep good order in the city, 'a man in uniform with a salary of $700 a year, to regulate the city, according to the opinion of the city.'" But it was absurd to speak of the men "as having for their chief function to sweep the streets, shut shop doors, and remove obstructions from the highways." They were in fact charged with a long list of statutory responsibilities, and clothed with vast powers by the common law, in order to administer "the most primitive, lasting, necessary, and inti-mate relations between the state and the citizen." No other power was so strong, or so ubiquitous. "With it, the state is safe; without it, the state is nothing but an oppression."[42]

The business of police was clearly too important to be entrusted to policemen. The force was a powerful engine. There was in Boston one policeman for every fifty or sixty houses; more significant, there was one to every fifty votes cast. And the men were, or became, of a special type: "They do not move equally among all classes of citizens." Indeed, "if they perform their duty, their ways are in the paths and dens of crime." "The dangerous classes," "the perishing classes," those who "are amongst us, but not of us"—these were the associates of the police.[43]

They in fact held the balance of power in the city: "Does property, does virtue, do the good citizens of Boston, control Boston?" Ellis compared the police statistics on the number of illegal establishments in the city with the number of arrests for each offense. There were about 3,000 liquor shops, but only 43 prosecutions under the nuisance act. Amee had reduced the number of gaming places to 16; there were but 2 arrests for keeping gambling rooms. There were 209 brothels in the city; only 75 had been disturbed. It would be time enough to say that vice could not be controlled when the city had had "for a while a power disposed to do it."[44]

Local politics tended to weaken and demoralize the force; General Amee had noted a ward politician's warning to "remember the ides of March." While Amory had spoken of the tyranny of state management, Ellis was not disposed to dismiss so lightly the use of police against fugitive slaves and abolitionists. He stressed that the police themselves understood the source of their troubles; one of them had appealed to a bystander, during the Sims affair, "For God's sake, don't scold us; we feel worse than you do." Ellis described the attack on Sims, the chains around the courthouse, the guard for Burns— "here is your Austrian and Roman despotism!"[45]

Counsel for the petitioners cited *People* v. *Draper* and *Buttrick* v. *Lowell* to prove that the police were properly agents not of the city but of the state. Their first task was not the ordinances but the law. Local control was against public policy, which should be "to create no direct relation between the police, the city, its government, and its populace; and especially certain classes of its populace—its criminal, its dangerous and perishing classes." Local control, finally, rested on a false theory:

They say in South Carolina, "local self-government." What is the reply? "National Sovereignty!" Mr. Chairman, is not the spirit of secession and treason—the *spirit* of it—sometimes whispered in our ears here?[46]

The prohibitionists, during the hearings, held a series of mass meetings to support the proposed law. Boston's city council hastened finally to approve its long-debated departmental rules and regulations. And without reference to party lines, the aldermen resolved by a vote of ten to nothing to denounce the metropolitan police scheme.[47]

The legislative committee, however, voted eight to two in favor of the bill. The majority felt it "the constitutional duty, as well as the right, of the people of the Commonwealth to provide for the faithful execution of the established laws." "The police officers are the primary, and where population is dense, the most essential of the executive officers of the Commonwealth." But in large cities, "the common sewers of the state," they were guided not by the laws but by "the lawlessness of the mob and the will of the populace." For a while in April it looked as if the police bill might pass the senate. But after being taken up, discussed, and laid over, it eventually was referred to the next session of the General Court.[48]

This narrow escape was a clear warning, and official Boston made some concessions. The hearings in March had precipitated a decision on the departmental rules, and Colonel Kurtz publicly announced a crackdown on liquor sales on Sunday. A more general drive against illegal establishments followed; at the end of the year the number of brothels had been cut to 146, and the number of gambling places to nine.[49]

But the city would make no further concessions, especially since attention was diverted by a new round of wartime problems. In the critical spring and summer of 1863, financial pressures mounted with the need for new recruits. Towns and cities throughout the state engaged in a spiraling competition to offer the most favorable bounties in an effort to fill their quotas and avoid a draft. The situation was especially acute in Boston. If there was danger at one social level in alienation from local politics, there was danger at another in a sullen attitude toward the policies of state and nation. When Governor Andrew ended the bounty competition and announced a draft, the city and its police faced a problem more immediate than any threat from the legislature.[50]

The great Boston Draft Riot began in a working-class neighborhood of the North End late on the afternoon of July 14. A crowd of angered women attacked two assistant provost marshals, come to serve official papers; a number of idle men joined and nearly beat to death the local patrolmen who attempted a rescue. As dinnertime approached and more men quit work, the protesting crowd became a mob too large for the police of the first division, who were forced to retreat until barricaded and surrounded in the north station house.[51]

Mayor Lincoln, called by police telegraph, assembled the three available militia companies in the Cooper Street Armory, where they were reinforced by regulars from outside the city. The armory, too, was surrounded; and an attack on the troops inside was repulsed by rifle and cannon fire. The mob then moved on toward Dock Square, where gunshops might provide them with weapons. But an advance guard of police held the ground until the mayor and the militia arrived. Their stand was the turning point, as the reinforcements effectively ended the riot.

There were two permanent effects on the history of the department in Boston. The police had entered the riot without arms, but they acquired and kept some pistols during its course. As in the earlier case of the harbor police, this action went officially unnoticed. But the next session of the legislature authorized peace officers to carry "such arms as the aldermen or selectmen may direct." From that time on about one-third of the patrolmen carried revolvers on their beats, some of them privately owned but others quietly issued by the city.[52]

The second effect of the riot was more widely publicized. Boston had handled its draft rioters more efficiently than had New York a few days earlier. The mayor had shown courage, the force had served well, and the actions of certain patrolmen were heroic. For the city, at least, this supplied the needed emotional reply to its critics. Ever since the Emancipation Proclamation, many months before, the old complaints of abolitionists had been losing force. Local officials and police had decisively shown their ability to move against the "danger-ous and perishing classes" in their midst. Now their opponents followed the lead of Wendell Phillips in avoiding charges about the caliber of the men, and even made a ritual of praising them. The city was more than ever set to resist insults to its management of the force.[53]

The events of 1863 changed the emphasis of attacks on the city and its police. But there was no loss of intensity. As other complaints became irrelevant, the ancient problem of the regulation of drink rose up once more; and the practices of Boston were, as usual, the central points at issue.

The authorities in Suffolk County and the prohibitionists took firm positions. But the liquor question was more complex than either would admit. Drunkenness and the sale of alcohol were not one problem but two, interrelated but separable; and quarrels among liquor dealers, prohibitionists, and voluntary reformers, between Re-publicans and Democrats, state and city, did not follow clear-cut lines of battle. Boston was not committed to either major party, and while the prohibitionists frightened the Republican state majority, they never convinced it. The problem had been quieted earlier by letting one side have the law and the other the liquor. But there was trouble when either pressed for a change, and the General Court wavered between them.

On the whole, the city won the continuing controversy over the treatment of drunkenness. The legislature had no clear views on how to handle the problem, and after one year's trial repealed Ben Butler's law eliminating the punishment of simple drunkenness as a crime. But the trend was still away from the harshness of earlier legislation. In 1862 the Butler law was revived, slightly amended; anyone accused of simple drunkenness could be freed on a written order and a promise to reform. Beginning in 1860 and continuing throughout the decade, the General Court voted annual sums, of from three thousand to six thousand dollars, for the support of the Washingtonian Home in Boston. In 1864, the legislature ordered that all convicted drunkards be sent to the House of Industry—the institution for paupers rather than criminals. It also authorized the city to set up a "Boston Asylum for Inebriates."[54]

No money was, however, appropriated for the Inebriates' Asylum, and the city and the police continued to treat drunkenness as scarcely distinguishable from poverty and other misfortune. Since the rising criminal statistics had been used to prove a special urban viciousness, the police were ordered in 1864 to make a minimum of "arrests" for drunkenness. They simply classified those taken in as "lodgers." Co-operation with such local temperance societies as the Washingtonians, which specialized in reformation, was institutionalized in the same year. The mayor appointed a temperance lecturer to serve as probation officer attached to the police force. Officer John C. Cluer attended the police courts daily, escorted children home at night, visited the homes of hundreds of drunkards, and recommended probation when indicated. Chief Kurtz, in commending Cluer's work, indicated his own belief in the theory that "dipsomania" was a disease, requiring kind treatment rather than punishment.[55]

During the war years, under the leadership of Mayor Lincoln, the city adopted a series of reforms which helped to relieve some of the police responsibility for dealing with drunkards and others needing help. After years of recommendation, the City Hospital finally began to function in 1863. In 1864 the board of overseers of the poor was reformed and assigned a temporary home on Charles Street, to which patrolmen were to direct applicants for shelter and relief. At the same time the city began work on a more ambitious building on Chardon Street, which would house a number of private charitable groups as well as the overseers and facilitate the kind of rationality and coordination which reformers had been demanding for decades.[56]

Despite these improvements, the police were still the main agents for handling intemperance; and it was obvious to John Cluer that there was no solution in existing law and social arrangements. Significantly reversing the earlier and simpler notions of causation, he observed that "I know of two blocks in this city where there are sixty-four families, and where . . . I conceive it to be utterly impossible for any human being to breathe the pestiferous air and be a sober decent man."[57]

Cluer's argument was a rebuke to the prohibitionists, who still conceived of drunkenness as both sin and crime, and who pressed more than ever to make a reality of the prohibitory law. He was backed by a strong delegation of local ministers, priests, and temperance reformers, who agreed on the complexity of the problem and the futility of any simple legal solution. These men, the voluntarists, voiced fundamental objections to the substitution of "Be it enacted" for "Thus Saith the Lord." Convinced that the situation had worsened under prohibition, they were ready to testify on behalf of a license law which might better regulate the traffic in liquors.[58]

But the prohibitionists were well organized, and had the support of a number of societies and of the overwhelming body of the clergy outside of Boston. In 1866 the Reverend Edward Otheman polled all of the approximately 1,400 clergymen of the commonwealth. Of those replying, 962 were in favor of the existing law, 56 for license, and 7 undecided. The 56 were doubly suspect; 25 of them were Roman Catholic, 8 Episcopal, the rest scattered. Only 2 "Orthodox Congregationalists" were in favor of license, and no Baptists or Methodists.[59]

The clergy was not hesitant to use its massed influence in politics, much of it in the continuing movement for a metropolitan police, considered an integral part of the wider cause. The prohibitionists worked hard in the Republican primary caucuses, pressing candidates for pledges of support. Many legislators were privately reluctant. And Governor Andrew was especially so; as an opponent of prohibition, he wanted no responsibility for enforcement. Nevertheless, the police bill passed the Senate in 1864, and a year later it clearly had the votes to pass both branches of the General Court. In the House, Boston members fought for support through an extreme amendment to bring the police departments of all cities under gubernatorial control. Despite bitter opposition the prohibitionists accepted the amendment and the bill passed the House, 112 to 107. At that point, with the minority close to open rebellion, Representative Sawin of Natick proposed a compromise measure.[60]

Sawin's bill left the ordinary operations of police in the hands of the cities, except that the governor might direct them in emergencies. But it created a new body of supralocal "Constables of the Commonwealth," appointed by the governor. These officers, like police, would have all but the civil powers of constables. At least one would reside and act in every county of the state. And at least twenty, including the chief, would operate in Suffolk. They would enforce all the laws, and "especially use their utmost endeavors to repress and prevent crime by the suppression of liquor shops, gambling places, and houses of 'ill-fame.'" The more ardent prohibitionists opposed the bill, but the great majority of the General Court preferred it to the original metropolitan police measure, and it passed overwhelmingly.[61]

Governor Andrew approved the bill also and appointed Colonel William S. King to head the force, which began operations in July. But the colonel's position was difficult. His constables, by several decades the first state police force in the United States, were regarded with no enthusiasm anywhere, as the second choice of both friends and opponents of the metropolitan measure. And neither the governor nor the colonel believed in the law which they were primarily supposed to enforce.[62]

The law provided no maximum number of constables, and during 1865 Andrew employed thirty-nine men, very little over the minimum. Colonel King quit at the end of the year, and issued no report on his activities. But Governor Bullock, who succeeded Andrew, was more enthusiastic, and operations really began in 1866, under Major Edward J. Jones.[63]

At the end of 1867 the force numbered 131, exclusive of clerical help. There was no intervening hierarchy between the head of the force and the ordinary constables, but the pay, three dollars a day plus expenses and witness fees, made the job highly attractive. The great majority of the men were veterans, most of them former officers. Only five had been privates; twenty-four were ex-captains. And the rolls also included an impressive list of former state officials: one adjutant-general, two brigadier-generals, two mayors, one member of the governor's council, one state treasurer, fourteen legislators, twelve justices of the peace, and four police chiefs.[64]

Outside of Boston and the other cities, the men had a variety of useful functions. Sometimes they were the only peace officers available, responsible for all law enforcement. As the men gained detective experience, and the populace became used to the idea that they were provided at public expense, they were increasingly called upon to deal with rural murders and robberies. At fairs, militia encampments, and other country gatherings they were detailed to prevent disorder and watch for pickpockets.[65]

Even in Suffolk County, the constables supplemented the municipal police in ordinary law enforcement, making arrests in several dozen categories. But here and in the Boston suburbs, they were less often entrusted by businessmen with detective jobs, and they did not approach the local officers in the variety of their functions. No one was allowed to forget that their principal job was the suppression of vice, as the military flavor of the force found dramatic expression in frequent raids, searches, and seizures, described in terms of "troops," "assaults," and "skirmish lines."[66]

The two years 1866 and 1867 were the high point of the attempt to enforce prohibition in Massachusetts. The proportion of constables to the population was as great as that of the 1960's. In 1866, the officers made 3,307 arrests for "Liquor Nuisances," 2,240 for "Common Selling," 134 for "Single Sales," and 56 for "Keeping, Intent to Sell." In 1867, the force seized nearly 100,000 gallons of spirits by 630 raids in Suffolk alone. And in the fall of that year the chief reported that "there was not one open bar known to us in the entire state."[67]

All this activity, despite the claims of Major Jones, did not eradicate vice. The constables still had to run their cases through the courts and past unsympathetic juries. Both Colonel King and Major Jones later testified that they had been called in by Governor Andrew and had agreed to approach the problem from the bottom, attacking only the worst places. This was the most acceptable tactic, but it did not live up to the reform ideal. Major Jones publicly stated his belief that there could be no material abatement of prostitution, and noted in 1869 that "the three hundred and fifty-one houses of ill-fame prosecuted by us during the three years are mostly of a character below the average for good order." The constabulary picked its own objectives; it seized spirits in transit, but did not disturb wholesalers. Indeed the commonwealth had no authority to prohibit the possession of liquor in large amounts, which might be used in interstate or foreign commerce. When the force once interfered with the transport of beer the outcry was so great that all of it was returned to the owner.[68]

The most damaging attacks on the constables came from the supporters of license. The state police were perfect targets for abuse by those who heatedly resented the attempt to revive a dead law. The constables were expensive and perhaps unconstitutional; and they received witness fees, although the Supreme Judicial Court in 1857 had denounced payments to salaried peace officers, as "against public policy." One of them shot and killed a man during a raid in 1867, apparently the first such incident in the history of the commonwealth; the case was further aggravated by the fact that the men were not officially authorized to carry guns. The evidence that the force was not seriously enforcing total prohibition merely left it open to the charge of hypocrisy.[69]

During 1867, in fact, it became clear that the activities of the state constabulary were hurting rather than helping the cause of prohibition. On the demand of over thirty-five thousand petitioners, the legislature appointed a joint special committee to consider a license law. For the first time, the opponents of the more restrictive policy took the offensive. Ex-Governor Andrew testified that alcohol was a food and not a poison; Louis Agassiz described the happy condition of wine-drinking Swiss peasants. The city of Boston reviewed its case again, backed this time by clergymen as well as police and court officials. Much testimony centered on the fact that intemperance had increased since the early 1850's, under the prohibitory law. The remonstrants found it hard to deny this. They could still accuse the Boston police of laxity, but Chief John Kurtz merely replied that he had been asked by the governor to leave the problem to the constables. And the core of the petitioners' case was that even the most obnoxious attempts could not effect a prohibition.[70]

The five signers of the majority report agreed. The prohibitionists had been given every chance. The state had tightened its law, and made fixed and uniform sentences mandatory. The Supreme Judicial Court had upheld the great majority of convictions appealed to it. Even a system of state constabulary "until that time unknown in this country and other republics, and borrowed from monarchical countries," had not saved the law from failure.[71]

The committee's "majority" was tenuous. Four prohibitionists compared license to the sale of indulgences by the Church of Rome and two others filed dissenting reports agreeing with neither of the major positions. The General Court, elected in a strongly Republican congressional year, failed to act. But the report did anticipate public reactions. The liquor issue dominated the off-year elections of 1867, and a majority of those elected at that time favored repeal.[72]

Major Jones correctly interpreted the returns as a rebuke to his activities and a threat to his job, and stopped all complaints against liquor violators. His annual report, in January 1868, was the first of a curiously defensive series. It was, he wrote, a "well-known fact" that the prohibitionists had opposed the establishment of a state constabulary. Governor Andrew, in his valedictory address, had cited the advantages, quite apart from the vice laws, of having a civil force at his command. Furthermore, during 1866-67, the constabulary had turned a profit for the commonwealth. It had spent $204,584.33, but successful prosecutions had brought in a total of $278,313.80 in fines and costs.[73]

The major's tone was justified. The first bill presented in the state Senate during the 1868 session called for the abolition of the state constables. Both branches approved the proposal, although Governor Bullock vetoed it. The House overrode the veto; the Senate could not quite muster the two-thirds vote needed, and the constables were barely saved.[74]

Despite this setback the General Court repealed prohibition and passed a license act. The new law freed cider and native wines from any restriction when sold by their makers. The sale of other liquors was subject to local option. If the voters permitted, licenses might be granted in six categories, costing fifty to one hundred dollars each, with a 2 per cent tax on all sales. The maximum penalty for violation was five hundred dollars and/or six months in jail, just half that provided in the Act of 1855.[75]

The bill, moreover, gave the local authorities the right to determine who could inspect licensed premises. In Suffolk County, this right was denied to the state constables. The effect was further to frustrate the force; of the eleven hundred complaints they instigated, only thirty were entertained by the license commissioners, who held that the evidence in the rest was illegally obtained. Meanwhile the General Court continued to insult the officers, eliminating their right to witness fees, demanding monthly accountings, and cutting their number by more than half, back to the minimum of sixty-four.[76]

The reaction to prohibition, however, went too far and generated a counterrevolt. The swift changeover created administrative difficulties, while the high price of the licenses made it impossible for most places to expect them. The Democrats again made the liquor question their most important local issue in the 1868 elections. But the nomination of General Grant assured a large Republican victory. The returns in November completely reversed those of the previous year, and license was doomed as obviously as prohibition had been.[77]

The General Court did as expected, in 1869, by repealing license and reverting to the law of 1855. It followed this by again repealing Ben Butler's statute on drunkenness, reaffirming that voluntary intoxication was still a crime in Massachusetts.[78]

At the same time it turned again to the problem of enforcement. The state constables were not enough. Major Jones, in his report to the governor, stressed this time his belief in prohibition, and there was no move to abolish or cut the force. But the major had shown himself a false champion of the law, and his men had never been adequate to the job.[79]

Most important, the mere continuance of a separate state police organization was not enough to satisfy the anti-urban bias of many reformers and taxpayers; the City of Boston, under this arrangement, was still allowed to manage an independent and expensive force of its own. Municipal expenditures had not quite doubled between 1860 and 1865. With release from enforced economies, they more than doubled between 1865 and 1869, to reach nearly thirteen millions. The progress of a long-delayed political revolution heightened suspicion of this rise; that there were nearly forty Irish police officers in 1869, compared with none at all in 1861, was a measure of increased Irish participation in city affairs. Annexation of neighboring Roxbury, in 1867, and moves to annex Dorchester made it more difficult to escape. Those unwilling or unable to participate in local politics continued to seek some more radical means of achieving their ends.[80]

CHAPTER EIGHT

Crime and Scandal, 1869-1870

In March 1869, the General Court resolved to hold hearings on the question of a metropolitan police for Boston. The proposed bill had been tested several times, and twice come close to passage. There was nothing to indicate that the hearings, the third set in eight years, would differ from their predecessors.

The earlier conventions were observed. Again Boston brought out its most politically distinguished citizens to testify in favor of local control. The petitioners on their part had forgotten little. Observers had grown familiar with their debates about democracy and the city, tradition and the constitution, law and public opinion.

But this time the hearings had a new point, and a new pungency. During the 1860's professional criminality in America had come of age, set in patterns which would last through the nineteenth century and into the twentieth. No acceptable response to this criminality had been worked out, so that the conduct of detective work was more than usually vulnerable to attack. For twenty years the city government and police had been trying to avoid discussion of this issue. Once in the open, it could not be met by appeals to constitutional principles or local opinion. And this set of hearings, with their aftermath, managed to stir up not only the general public but the local authorities as well.

The problem was not confined to Boston. Professional criminals in the nineteenth century did not belong to any syndicate or organization, but there was a kind of loose fraternity which was national and even international in scope. English pickpockets moved regularly from London to Paris or New York with the seasons. Other professionals ranged about the United States and Canada, and the more successful often crossed the Atlantic for refuge or on criminal errands. Common associations and experiences helped acquaint them with

142

each other, and they were usually marked by the common habits imposed by quick money and uncertainty. A large proportion, at mid-century, were Englishmen legally or by birth, and although there was an increasing number of second-generation Americans of English or Irish descent, there were few recent immigrants of other background. Part of their sense of identity was shaped by use of a specialized argot, remarkably stable through the decades, possibly because it was so often transmitted through men in prisons. English professionals in the 1860's used terms still familiar, "stretch" for prison term, "frisk" for search, "queer" for counterfeit, "wire" for pickpocket, "fence" for receiver. Americans in the same decade were "sent up the river" for "pulling heists."[1]

The world of professional criminals was divided into classes according to activity. All involved training and often apprenticeship, but the rewards, skill, and nerve required distinguished them clearly. Some accounts describe a rigidity of specialization hardly credible, with burglars, for example, concentrating exclusively on banks, or stores, or hotels, without venturing into other fields. But there was considerable flexibility in practice. Some forms of criminality tended to die out as measures of protection were taken; the "panel thieving" so prevalent in Marshal Tukey's day was described in the 1880's as "almost historical." Pickpocketing, similarly, appears to have flourished in the mid-century decades and then declined. And the techniques of burglary changed rapidly in response to improvements in security devices. At the top of the criminal profession, men accustomed to dealing plausibly with bankers and businessmen might turn their talents to swindling, the passing of counterfeit, or the planning of burglary. At the bottom, desperation drove men to anything at hand.[2]

Estimates of the size of the professional fraternity are rough, and rare, but not badly inconsistent. The most definite was made by Edwin Crapsey, author of a number of articles on criminality in New York during the 1860's. Crapsey's figure for that city, derived from a survey of its police captains, was twenty-five hundred true professionals, a total further broken into classes.[3]

One hundred men, the captains told him, were in business as illegal receivers. One hundred more operated confidence games such as the "Spanish Prisoner" racket. Perhaps eight hundred were "sneaks" of miscellaneous kinds, the lowest class of criminal, men who operated without plan and grabbed at anything in reach. Two hundred were professional shoplifters, distinguished from "sneaks" largely by their sex; doubly unusual among thieves, these were always women and usually recent immigrants from continental Europe. The one hundred and fifty "bedchamber sneaks" and "second-story sneaks" in the city were specialists in the robbery of private homes and hotel rooms, and experts in the use of keys.[4]

The city's truly professional forgers, twenty-five of them, hardly amounted to a distinct class. Many of them joined forces, for the purpose of cashing paper, with some of the fifty "bank sneaks" or the one hundred "damper sneaks" of the business district. These posed as businessmen, and either engaged in elaborate negotiations or simply loitered about business premises, waiting a chance to grab unprotected bonds or money. Tightened security measures later made such operations rare, but "bank sneaking" in the 1860's was still a respected criminal occupation, capable of yielding hundreds of thousands in paper all at once.[5]

A large "take," proportionally, went to professional pickpockets, estimated at three hundred. Although they seldom stole much at any one time, they were able to work all day and every day. Their skills made them more difficult to catch and identify than most criminals, and the small items they took were easily hidden or disposed of.[6]

Crapsey used the term "burglar," as distinct from "sneak," to describe specialists in the robbery of safes; there were perhaps three hundred and fifty of them. Two hundred were "safe breakers," who with little advance planning broke into buildings and safes with main force, hammers, and jimmies. The seventy-five "safe blowers" were quicker and more skillful, using measured amounts of gunpowder in carefully drilled holes to blow open the doors. More artistic still were the seventy-five "safebursters," experts in the use of elaborate tools, drills, screwjacks, and levers, which could open safes without noise and the consequent danger of detection.[7]

All of these absolute figures are hazardous, but some relative judgments are possible. Considerable evidence suggests that the 1860's, and possibly the 1870's, were the halcyon years for the most spectacular of professional crimes: large-scale bank robbery and burglary by stealth. During the later nineteenth century, the artful burglar held, in the East, the same place in romantic popular imagination as the highwayman and pirate of the eighteenth. At the top of the profession, men like Adam Worth, Spence Pettis, and Langdon Moore were famous characters, well known to the newspaper-reading public as well as to the fraternity. And several conditions combined to make the decade of the Civil War especially favorable for their operations.[8]

One of these advantages was technological. During the nineteenth century, outside of the Wild West, major robbery was ordinarily accomplished through skill rather than force. The competition between those seeking to protect valuables and those trying to steal them was marked by an ascending spiral of improvements in the methods of both attack and defense. Later in the century, burglars replaced gunpowder with nitroglycerin, and developed ever more complex equipment to deal with the increasingly intricate combinations, the layers of alloyed metals and compartments devised by the makers of locks and safes. But during the 1860's, the attack was well ahead of the defense. Until the invention of the Yale lock in 1869, these devices differed chiefly in size and not in intrinsic complexity. And safes, while of various weights and thicknesses, were almost always of brittle iron. In the proper hands, a forty-dollar set of the best English-made burglar's tools was capable of solving any problem.[9]

These technical conditions had existed earlier; what distinguished the 1860's was the availability of large rewards. The nation had never been richer. And the demands of war made these riches available in especially negotiable form. It was much easier to dispose of United States greenbacks in quantity than the distinctive notes of country banks. And government bonds, impersonal and nearly equivalent to cash, multiplied with the national debt. The burgeoning demand for capital required the concentration of money. Skillful men, patient enough to spend months in planning, often found hundreds of thousands of dollars or bonds in a single safe. Several robberies in the 1860's were reported in the million-dollar class.[10]

This increase in large-scale robbery called forth an increase in detective work. Major urban police departments annually published lists of the amounts of money reported stolen and the amounts recovered. The former figure was almost never detailed; neither the victims nor the police had any stake in making it accurate, and no one else was able to verify it. But the amounts recovered were sometimes recorded specifically, and the police were proud of them. In Boston, before the war, the largest total reported stolen was $92,704 in 1859, and the largest recovered was $62,415 in 1860. The annual average for the 1850's was $53,905 stolen, $45,141 recovered. Between 1861 and 1870, the *smallest* amount reported stolen was $109,085 in 1861, the smallest recovered $107,125 in 1868. The most stolen was $983,702 in 1864, and the most recovered $520,227 in 1866; the averages for these years were $274,174 stolen and $145,604 recovered.[11]

In several years the amount of money recovered approached or even exceeded that reported taken. These figures reflected the nature of the detective network, necessarily as widespread as that of professional thieves. A burglar like Langdon Moore specialized in the robbery of small banks in New England or New York State. He might hide anywhere. But the banks would call on detectives from one of the metropolitan centers, where the stolen money would necessarily be disposed.

By the 1860's, the character and methods of detectives were set almost as firmly as those of professional criminals. These men differed from other policemen. In Boston, they did not fit into the organizational hierarchy within which others were normally promoted up the line from night patrolman to captain. Detectives worked at the same salary as lieutenants, two dollars and a half to two dollars and seventy-five cents a day. But they were often appointed directly, without intervening service as patrolmen or sergeants, and had no desire for a captaincy. Theirs was in some ways an enviable job, with a free-ranging independence, the constant attention of reporters, and the promise of extra money for out-of-town "expenses" and rewards. The one quality needed was familiarity with criminals; one detective had served ten years as turnkey of the Charlestown State Prison, another had been previously indicted for burglary, a third convicted as a youth for passing counterfeit money.[12]

The story of George S. Chapman, a member of the Boston detective squad, is in many ways archetypal. Chapman served until 1867, when he was arrested in Hartford for picking pockets; after resigning from the force, he went on to set up his own private agency. He had been called to Hartford to watch for the congregation of pickpockets expected to cover a visit by President Johnson. Such service was frequently performed, on payment of expenses, and gave detectives from various cities a chance to exchange notes and widen their experience. Detectives were jealous and criminals vengeful, and Chapman may well have been innocent of the specific charges against him. But until he was convicted, considerably later, of several Boston burglaries, the incident did not cloud his relations with the force, and he continued to work with his former associates on many cases.[13]

As constant travel made it sometimes difficult or irrelevant to distinguish between the detectives of different cities, so the means and objects of detective work made it difficult to distinguish between those on the public payroll and private detectives, or even those temporarily employed on a single job. Private agencies, often organized by ex-policemen, were common in all large cities, where they shadowed errant wives and checked on suspicious employees. But often the public-private line was blurred. Many, employed by railroads to supervise the honesty of conductors, held warrants as special policemen. The state of Massachusetts, during the 1860's, granted an annual subsidy of fifteen hundred dollars to the New England Society for the Suppression of Counterfeiting. In major cases of robbery, private and public detectives often worked together. The autobiography of Langdon Moore, the burglar, never distinguished between them; a "Boston detective" might be either a policeman or private agent. The city of Boston itself, when robbed by one of its own employees, in 1870, found it convenient to hire James Donahue, alias "John Bull," Marshal Tukey's former office boy and allegedly the leading professional gambler in the city.[14]

Some degree of mutual cooperation involving protection in return for information was essential to the system. But within the limits imposed by this need there was a spectrum of behavior. Individual men or departments, and most notably the always efficient and highly paid employees of the Pinkerton Agency, worked faithfully for their employers and made only the most necessary compromises. Other detectives simply worked for themselves, making arrangements with criminals at the expense of the victims, the law, or both. In the venal atmosphere of the 1860's, this kind of bargaining was especially prevalent. But it rarely happened that the entire machinery of justice was so deeply corrupt that thieves, as distinguished from those who dealt in vice, enjoyed any real security.[15]

Professional criminals often had arrangements with one or more cooperative policemen, but these arrangements could not extend to the whole of the intensely competitive detective fraternity. At best, the relations between detectives and thieves were full of tensions. The man who accomplished a successful crime, difficult to detect and involving easily disposable property, had no need of protection or deals. Conversely, his pursuer had first to identify the criminal before he could profit from the crime. And when any relationship proved embarrassing, the detective could end it with prosecution, either himself or through a colleague.[16]

The best protection for the thief was the victim who neglected either to cause trouble or to press charges. At one end of the scale persons victimized by pickpockets seldom lost enough to be insistent in following up the case. If the person robbed was important, or his watch valuable—gold watches were hard to dispose of—a return could be arranged. The matter was treated as a kind of professional courtesy, with no questions asked. As Chief Kurtz testified in 1869, "When watches have been lost I have written to some half-dozen well-known thieves requiring the return of the watches by some express, and in many cases the watches have been sent."[17]

The use of detectives as intermediaries was even more frequent at the other end of the scale of robbery, and it was often the thieves who asked them to approach the victims. In practice the primary object of detective work was still to recover stolen property rather than to prosecute. The most profitable theft of the decade was the $1,700,000 Lord Bond Robbery, committed on Wall Street in 1866. The case was never brought to trial, although the thieves were known and much of the money recovered, some of it in Boston. The usual split was about half and half, with the detectives taking up to 10 per cent. But it often varied with the strength of the evidence and the nature of the property. In one case reported at the time the police hearings were in progress, a Philadelphia bank was robbed of an amount set at one million dollars. Between $400,000 and $500,000 was recovered in Boston; the amount corresponded to the value taken in railroad, city, and government-registered bonds. The coupon bonds and cash were not returned. Many victims of robbery encouraged this system of detective work. Some criminals benefited from it, and others were forced to acquiesce in it. But it was principally profitable for detectives themselves.[18]

Several other reasons made it not wholly satisfactory. It was in the first place almost exclusively designed to deal with professionals. The detectives were also able to find other badly wanted persons if their identities were known. They used the telegraph and daguerreotype and checked with conductors, hack drivers, and hotel clerks; in the days before the automobile, it was relatively easy to watch the railroad terminals. But the situation was different with unknown persons. Kurtz testified that "in all cases of robbery we arrest any person who is on that 'lay,' as a suspicious person, and keep him until we are satisfied he is not the party wanted." But this kind of dragnet operation did not suit all crimes. Immediately after the Civil War, Boston and other cities began to be visited by a number of "vagrants" of a new type, many of them ex-soldiers or men otherwise uprooted and desperate. In 1865, the city was frightened by an apparent increase in "garroting," or muggings, holdups of a kind not usual among professionals. The chief's only recourse was to arrest "all suspicious persons found in the street, who could give no proper account of themselves." That year 2,532 were arrested in this way, a total which revealed the hopelessness of any attempt to identify individuals.[19]

The great amateur crime was homicide. It is significant that Marshal Tukey's detectives played only a minor and inept role in the most famous case in Boston history, the Parkman-Webster murder of 1849. Many killings resolved into the familiar business of finding a known suspect, but a degree of uncertainty was often enough to baffle the police. And the problem was aggravated by a rising murder rate. In most years before the middle of the 1850's, no homicides at all were reported for Suffolk County. But seventy were recorded between 1860 and 1869. There were, in the same period, eighty-three arrests for murder, a figure which reflects the same kind of hopeless indiscrimination shown in the garroting scare. Only seventeen resulted in indictments, and ten in convictions, all but three for manslaughter.[20]

In part this inefficiency resulted from a lack of technical tools. Some of the achievements of mid-century technology, such as the telegraph, were used in pursuing wanted persons. And in 1862 the Boston police chief instituted a rogues' gallery of several hundred daguerreotypes, to supplement the handbills, verbal descriptions, and mnemonic powers of his detectives. But there was still little which could be used in establishing the identities of persons unknown. It was possible, in the 1860's, for men with microscopes to match and identify hairs and threads and other items. The blood of human beings could be distinguished from that of other mammals. But the use of such evidence was just beginning in Germany and England. In Boston, even medical testimony was seldom used except to establish cause of death, and the coroners were laymen.[21]

Developments later in the century, notably the introduction of state medical examiners, demonstrated the importance of expert help. But it is easily possible to exaggerate the extent to which even modern police forces rely on such aids. The police in the 1860's were capable of using much physical evidence. The better detectives were careful observers, with an experienced knowledge of human motivations. And although Boston did not impose the kind of treatment given New York suspects in "Captain Jourdan's Sweat Box," the men were skilled at extracting confessions. The main barrier to successful detection of amateur crime was not technical but institutional or conceptual.[22]

Early in 1870, after no detectives had been assigned for a full week to work on a back alley murder case, the Boston *Herald* was moved to ask, "What are detectives paid for?" Were they "simply to be detailed for when there is money on a job?" These were significant questions. The relation between the state, the public interest, and detective work was still unclear. Since publicly employed detectives were still relatively new to Anglo-American experience, there were no traditional rules governing their obligations. A British writer noted in 1860 that the detection of crime "according to the practice of English law—for there was never any theory upon the subject—is the province of the injured party, his surviving friends, or any one else who likes to take the trouble." American detectives were still essentially servants of private interests, made generally available by the city. Boston's seven headquarters detectives had all been chosen for their single ability to recognize professional thieves. None specialized in anything else. They did in fact do other kinds of work, and in well-publicized murder cases worked jealously against the state constables. But they were busy men, ordinarily working on several cases at one time. And it had not been established that the patient effort required in crime detection was justified in cases lacking either notoriety or reward. No one had complained in the case which excited the *Herald*, and justice was not an employer.[23]

One of the problems of hiring detectives at public expense was that justice and the public interest could not be entirely ignored. The proponents of a metropolitan police were not primarily interested in this question alone. But in seeking the widest popular support, they chose to focus almost exclusively on the issue with the most dramatic appeal. Their counsel this time was not an impassioned reformer but a criminal lawyer, George Sennott, who functioned as prosecutor. And his carefully gathered evidence inspired grave doubts in many otherwise satisfied with the police of Boston.

The central question aired was whether the detectives were in fact working for the citizens, or for private interests, or for themselves. The old rule about the need for permission to accept rewards was clearly a dead letter. Testimony at the hearings indicated that in one case alone, the Lord Bond Robbery, Detective George Heath had earned eight thousand dollars in rewards, a sum more than eight times his salary. Most rewards were not so well publicized, but their size always created disciplinary problems. The favoritism shown in assigning Officers Heath and William K. Jones to the most productive cases created jealousies; some men quit the force, and others were rebellious. It was difficult for the city to control its own men, who were seldom actually working for their two dollars and seventy-five cents a day.[24]

This last circumstance led several members of the city government itself to question the system and join the petitioners. In addition to a number of smaller cases, Counsel Sennott had two major charges to bring against the chief and detectives. Both of them had been aired before, without losing their savor. And one of them was brought in by an alderman.

The first case involved the 1866 robbery of ten thousand dollars from a safe belonging to George H. Gooding, a Boston broker. Although Gooding was himself well acquainted with a number of criminal contacts, the team of Heath and Jones aided his pursuit of the stolen funds. After two years of a search which extended north to Canada and west to Kansas, the broker was convinced not only that the two detectives were diddling him for expenses but that they were sheltering the thieves, and along with Chief Kurtz had split the money with them. In fact Gooding had been able to capture two suspects of his own, and although his testimony about the Boston police was disallowed in Superior Court, the two were convicted over the pro-testations of Heath and Jones. The detectives and Chief Kurtz were represented by their own counsel in the police hearings, and steadily denied any wrongdoing. But both sides took the committee on a verbal tour of an underworld populated by such characters as "Fatty Norton," and the sordid impression left was damaging to all involved.[25]

The second major case was based on the testimony of Alderman Thomas Gaffield. In 1867 Gaffield had learned, through criminal sources, of an incident which in his opinion discredited the chief. Thomas Hedge, a businessman from Iowa, had been robbed in 1865 of ten one-thousand-dollar bonds at the Providence Railroad depot. Chief Kurtz had written to him, promising to return five of the bonds if he would sent a receipt for them all, and also allow the two-thousand-dollar reward. The matter was arranged through Benjamin Russell, a criminal lawyer acting for Hedge, who apparently kept one-half of the reward himself. When Gaffield heard of the affair, he brought it before the other aldermen, and in a secret eight-hour hearing the facts were brought out. What disturbed him especially was that although others voiced doubts, he was the only one of nine members of the board who did not vote to exonerate the chief of wrongdoing.[26]

Later in the hearing Colonel Kurtz was summoned to answer these accusations. His defense was essentially the same as Marshal Tukey's, seventeen years before, that "abetting with rogues" and the compounding of felony were the very essence of the detective business. Charles B. Hall, Secretary of the New England Association Against Counterfeiting, and Major Jones of the state constabulary, brother of one accused detective, made the same point. While all three insisted that the business could be conducted honorably, their testimony suffered from certain liabilities.[27]

The public during the 1860's was more than ever fascinated by detectives. But knowledge of their activities was imperfect. The police had valid reasons for concealing their methods and sources, and usually answered questions with winks, lies, and Delphic statements. Some popular newspapers gave reasonably accurate accounts of the detective business, and serious magazines on both sides of the Atlantic published articles about it. But curiosity was more satisfactorily met by the romantic detective legend.

Accounts of the kind of roguery chronicled in the Newgate Calendars had a long history in English. And while the detective story was much more recent, and borrowed from the French, it found a quick response. The seminal source was Eugene Francois Vidocq, organizer in 1817 of the first official detective bureau in France. Vidocq's memoirs, originally published in 1828-29, were immediately translated and went through several editions both in England and the United States. With other books by the same author, they inspired a varied detective literature in two languages. The genre had still not reached its peak in the 1860's, but it was flourishing, and readers were already familiar with the deductive brilliance of Dupin, the disguises of Hawkshaw, the adventures of LeCoq and Père Tabaret.[28]

The line between pure fiction and reality was hard to draw. One of the secrets of Vidocq's popularity was that his romances were presented as genuine, and inevitably life was made to resemble art. Vidocq had stressed the ingenious use of physical clues: "Here is a pair of rubbers—go find your man." And as early as 1841, one Boston paper, in reporting the Davis and Palmer jewel robbery, at first ascribed the solution to Officer Clapp's brilliant matching of boots and boot prints. The stream of memoirs by English and American detectives was begun significantly later, in the late 1850's and 1860's, a generation after Vidocq and several years behind the fiction. The officers by then were able to draw on a number of models, including the drama; and their accounts were heavily inclined to romance, to disguises, deduction, lost heiresses, and missing jewels.[29]

One result of these literary legends, and of the willingness of detectives to pander to them, was that increasingly in the later nineteenth century descriptions of actual detective work were treated as exposés, and often received with shock. This was already apparent during the police hearings in 1869. Chief Kurtz and others testified to practices which they accepted as normal. But for many who followed the hearings they were sordid to a degree for which they had not been prepared. The evidence presented in defense, as well as the accusations of the petitioners, precipitated a demand for reform.

These misgivings were not allayed by the argument of C. H. Hill, the city solicitor, who made the case for the *status quo*. In reviewing the evidence against the city, Hill often quoted De Tocqueville on the virtues of New England self-government. His argument for leaving things as they were was essentially Burkean: "All change in itself is an evil." He had equally eminent authority to cite in defense of the detective system. The counsel for the accused policemen, former Judge Foster of the Superior Court, had already testified that the compounding of felony was a knotty legal problem. It was difficult to show at what point it was illegal, if recovery was not specifically made a condition of failure to prosecute. In cases like that of the Concord Bank burglary of 1867, which had been handled by the Boston police, the whole community had a stake in recovery. With so many people involved it was often difficult to show that compounding was not in the public interest. And in answer to misgivings about justice and morality, Hill replied by citing the utilitarian legal reformers, who argued that reimbursement was more important than punishment, following Bentham's dictum that "everything which can be repaired is nothing."[30]

Hill himself later repudiated this line of defense. He was on firmer ground in pointing out that nothing in the negative attacks of the petitioners had proved that a change in control was the answer. The testimony of Major Jones had shown that the state constabulary did not operate in any different way. Of the four aldermen and former aldermen who complained about existing methods, only two believed that metropolitan control would be an improvement. The most rigorous solution was offered by Alderman Jonas Fitch, who suggested that the question of the public interest could be obviated simply by returning to a system of purely private enterprise.[31]

When the hearings were complete, the majority of the investigating committee, as in 1863, recommended a metropolitan police bill. Again the majority expressed its opinion that vice and crime held the political balance in Boston, that the police were used for political purposes, that the liquor laws were ignored. There were differences between this report and its predecessor; the majority did not criticize the personal character of the police, and there was no mention of slavery. In reflection of the bulk of the testimony, the especial stress was on official tolerance of detective corruption. In Boston, the committee concluded, "the will and ability to repress crime, all crime, does not represent the average will and ability of the Commonwealth." But ultimately the metropolitan bill in 1869 met the same fate as it had earlier, this time defeated more resoundingly than in 1861.[32]

The bill failed because the legislature was unwilling to antagonize Boston. The political division between city and state in Massachusetts was never as sharp as in New York. After the early war years Boston had joined the rest of the commonwealth in voting for Governors Andrew and Bullock, Presidents Lincoln and Grant. Party lines in municipal contests were still unclear, and the voters in 1869 faced a total of nine separate tickets. But Mayor Lincoln's successor, Otis Norcross, was also a Republican. Nathaniel Shurtleff, elected as a Democrat in 1867, was repudiated by that party and became a "Citizen" in 1869. Chief Kurtz served under all of them.[33]

The internal problems of the police department, also, were being worked out acceptably. Even Henry D. Cushing, the fiercest of prohibitionists, publicly declared that the officers were a picked group, "second to none in the world," and doing a fine job of enforcing the ordinances. In 1867 the city had revised the departmental rules adopted in 1863. Shortly thereafter, two of the oldest points in controversy, job security and the fee system, found an apparent solution together. The aldermen established an official police relief fund in 1869, with money from the witness fees, which were no longer paid out to individual officers.[34]

A general satisfaction was symbolized, a few months after the hearings, by the first annual policemen's ball, held on February 9, 1870, in order to benefit the relief fund. Police and public danced together under a great banner reading "CHARITY—BOSTON POLICE—FRATERNITY." "The attendance was positively immense," according to the *Herald,* and the affair was counted "without exception, the most successful gathering of the kind this season."[35]

But discontent remained. The exposures of the metropolitan police committee had not been treated lightly; and on November 22, 1869, the burglary of the Boylston Bank, the biggest in the history of the city, dramatized the problem. The thieves were obviously experienced professionals; after renting an office, six months earlier, in a building adjoining the bank, they had carefully made a passage through the walls into the vault. They netted what was first announced as half a million dollars, later reduced to $200,000 in coupon bonds. The detectives had not been able to prevent this, and confidence was not increased by the revelation that George Heath had been in the building on another errand on the night of the robbery. Three days later the *Herald* announced that the bank directors had voted to "compound," offering one-quarter to the police. On November 28, Chief Kurtz sent out a circular to "the chief of every police force in North and South America and Europe," describing the thieves and the bonds and setting a reward of 20 per cent.[36]

No solution was in sight as the new city administration was organized in 1870. On February 15, five days after the policemen's ball, Chief Kurtz resigned. The aldermen issued a report denouncing "the present detective system," which "more than anything else, has tended to bring the department into disrepute." The major recommendation of the report was voted the same day. In a move without clear precedent in any other city, the aldermen abolished the detective bureau entirely, and served notice that they would institute a system which would better meet the demands of law and justice.[37]

The dramatic abolition of the detective bureau was an appropriate end for the most difficult decade in the history of Boston's police. The socially disruptive effects of immigration, earlier, were as important as those of the Civil War. But they had not led to so searching an attack on the practices and principles which governed the force.

Eight years of intermittent probing and constant complaint had not fully prepared the city for the revelations of 1869, and the hearings of that year produced a more immediate effect than those earlier. An attempt to suppress professional thievery, unlike an attempt to suppress vice, did not violate any popular interest. In this matter, where the interests of police and politicians did not coincide, the authorities were capable of vigorous action.

It is true that in most areas the realities of the situation had been only exposed rather than changed. The police business was still subject to attack. Specific concessions could never satisfy that hard core of opponents motivated by hostility to the very character of the city. And the ultimate decision of the General Court rested only in part on the nature of the issues debated.

But it was clear, after the last hearing, that the metropolitan police issue would not soon be raised again. The city was still able to beat down the challenge to its authority. And as it moved into a new period, less disorderly and less defiant, its officials were in a confident mood. In the moment of triumph, few caught the unconscious threat voiced in Solicitor Hill's summation: "You must remember, gentlemen, that all of these arguments against the . . . police tell equally against all self-government in Boston."[38]

CHAPTER NINE

Chief Savage and Readjustment, 1870-1878

By contrast to the preceding decade, the 1870's were relatively quiet. The commercial depression of 1873 was a serious blow to municipal finance. But the basic economic health of the city enabled it to rebound from the Great Fire of 1872. The growth of population was comparatively slow, but Boston continued to expand through the annexation of neighboring communities—West Roxbury, Brighton, and Charlestown—attracted by the advantages of the metropolis.[1]

Several issues which had earlier troubled the police department and the community at large were successfully resolved by changes in policy or in social conditions and attitudes. The liquor laws were modified in line with the demands of the local authorities, and the city no longer denied its responsibility for enforcement. Most police business, as a result, was conducted in an atmosphere of quiet and even neglect.

After the "volcanic eruption" of February 1870, in which the board of aldermen simultaneously fired the chief of police and abolished the detective bureau, the government faced the immediate problem of finding replacements for both. The board had reacted in haste to the widespread suspicion of detective work, and the members had at first no alternatives to offer.[2]

The initial problem was solved with the help of the police themselves. There were a number of candidates for the post of chief, but the divisional captains unanimously supported Deputy Chief Edward Hartwell Savage, who was confirmed without a dissenting vote in mid-March. The choice proved fortunate. Unlike most earlier heads of the department, Savage was a career policeman with long experience, having first joined the night squad under Marshal Tukey in 1851.

Three years later, he became captain of station one, the most difficult in the city. In 1861 he was promoted to deputy chief, a position he held through three changes in political administration, under two superiors and four mayors.[3]

The new chief's first job was to help the aldermen settle the detective problem. The committee on police, in drawing up a new set of rules, made three recommendations. No compromises of any kind should be made with criminals, and no rewards accepted for the return of stolen money; the task of the police was to enforce the laws by arresting the guilty. In place of regular detectives, the committee authorized the chief to give special and temporary detective assignments to ordinary members of the force. And to assure compliance, it suggested a law requiring that all stolen goods be impounded by the state until the thieves were brought to justice. This last proposal was only tentative, and was not adopted. But it did indicate a real seriousness of purpose. The other recommendations were fully approved by Chief Savage, who had his own ideas about the proper conduct of detective work.[4]

Savage noted that the traditional system required the chief, as head of the detective bureau, to "associate with thieves, eat with thieves, and sleep with thieves," a job for which he had no appetite. And the system had two major weaknesses. The almost exclusive use of criminal informers resulted in recoveries but no arrests and thus no prevention of further robberies; and the existence of a specialized detective squad, composed of men experienced in spotting thieves, also enabled thieves to spot detectives. But the chief insisted that there were remedies. By rotating regular patrolmen on plain-clothes duty, and encouraging all men off duty to look out for known offenders, the problem of recognition could be avoided. As deputy chief, Savage had been responsible for founding the rogues' gallery and a descriptive list of arrested felons; through the increased use of these records the men could make up for any lack of personal acquaintance with criminals. The prevention of thievery could be assured simply by driving offenders out of Boston once they were identified.[5]

During his eight years as head of the department, Savage carried his "preventive" plans into operation. In practice, the system did not entirely eliminate the use of specialists. Temporary assignments to headquarters tended to become permanent, and several "special officers" worked in all but name as full-time detectives. But there was some rotation, and the officers were generally chosen from among the regular members of the force. The services of detectives from out of town, traditionally used to cover major celebrations and events, were consistently refused. The members of the old detective squad, fired with Chief Kurtz in 1870, were not invited back, and while there was still some jealousy and corruption, the new men successfully avoided major scandal.[6]

More important, the Savage system was strikingly successful in reducing criminal profits. The chief attributed this result primarily to the use of the whole force as an anonymous "secret service." He could not so publicize the policy, both incomplete and illegal, of warning major professionals out of the city. But this action, combined with a determined resistance to compounding and reward-hunting, proved the more effective.[7]

As soon as the abolition of the old detective bureau was announced, Savage wrote, "They said, 'the fly cops are out in the cold, and Boston is a clean field', and within twenty days delegations of their fraternity, from almost every city in the union, were seen in our streets." But the police were ready to repel this invasion, and the record of money stolen and recovered in 1870 was quite light. One important device was a modification of Marshal Tukey's old "show-up of rogues." Known criminals who appeared in the city were arrested as suspicious persons, and escorted to headquarters, where their pictures and descriptions were taken in public. Traveling thieves learned to avoid the brisk atmosphere of Boston. The first two years after Savage took office there were six major celebrations which would earlier have called out scores of detectives and pickpockets; the chief reported only four incidents of such thievery, two of which resulted in arrest and conviction. The popular press, usually eager for evidence of roguery, reported on several occasions not only that "panel thievery" had become unknown, and pickpockets rare, but that Boston was entirely free of professional burglars of all kinds.[8]

Between 1870 and 1878 there was a marked decline in property stolen and recovered. The nine-year average for stolen property was $92,405, compared with $274,174 for the decade of the 1860's; Savage reckoned that the annual toll was 1/36 of 1 per cent of assessed valuation, contrasted with 1/6 of 1 per cent in the earlier period. The more accurate report of property recovered was $82,138 a year, down an average of $63,000 from the 1860's. During the police hearings of 1869 the Association of New England Bankers had supported the older detective system. But during Savage's tenure there were no bank robberies of any kind in Boston, a circumstance which perhaps accounts for the handsome contributions Kidder, Peabody, and Company made each year to the policemen's ball.[9]

The lessened incidence of thievery made "special officers" more available for other work. Although the chief was indignant at the suggestion that his men be used for such purposes as recovering lost pets, private citizens could expect to receive police assistance, at public expense, in a wide variety of cases. And with other rewards reduced in importance, detectives found special satisfaction in investigating homicides.

This work was eased by a slight decline in the murder rate. But equally important was an increased willingness to take pains. The handling of the torso murder of Abijah Ellis in the fall of 1872 dramatized the careful use of new methods. After the body was found in a barrel recovered from the Charles, the site of the murder was determined by matching wood shavings with debris on the floor of one of the numerous properties owned by the victim; and the police, apparently for the first time, employed a chemist to analyze what proved to be human bloodstains on the underclothing of the accused. Chief Savage, in 1875, claimed that no unsolved murders or manslaughters had been committed in his jurisdiction during the previous four years. In fact, during the 1870's as a whole, 107 homicides were reported, and some 46 indictments, of which 22 resulted in convictions of one degree or another. This left a considerable number "unsolved," but the record was a dramatic improvement over that of the previous decade. Few if any cases went uninvestigated, and the public was not excited by any neglect of the demands of justice.[10]

Under Savage also one of the oldest and most persistent criticisms of the police department eased. The problems of drunkenness and the liquor traffic were less alarming than previously, and changes in the political situation helped to narrow the difference between state and city. As the issues were moderated, it was possible to work out an acceptable relationship between the law and the police force.

Neither state nor city had discovered any satisfactory treatment for drunkenness. The probation officer, John Cluer, left the police force late in the 1860's; the commonwealth stopped contributing to the

Washingtonian Home in 1873; and after the new law of 1869, almost all cases of drunkenness were prosecuted in a manner which reformers had been decrying since Josiah Quincy. About three-quarters of the guilty, unable to pay their fines, were sent to the House of Industry for ten to thirty days. This was a period universally admitted to be too short for reformation and a procedure which smacked of imprisonment for debt. The more confirmed drunkards were sent up for longer terms in the House of Correction; reformers complained that the police rarely charged individuals with common drunkenness, and again the hope of reform was blunted.[11]

But the significance of the newly tightened policy of prosecution was that it showed that the police were finally on top of the problem; it was now physically possible to prosecute all those taken in. Although there was no change in standards, the force throughout the 1870's made a steadily decreasing number of arrests for drunkenness and other forms of disorderly behavior.[12]

The statistics literally reflected the progress of civilization; as the pace of expansion slowed the citizens of Boston adjusted to the demands of life in the metropolis. The census figures indicated that the city was still growing at the rate maintained before mid-century. There were 177,840 inhabitants in 1860, 256,526 in 1870, and 362,839 in 1880. But more than half of the increase was provided by the settled populations of neighboring communities, as Roxbury was annexed in 1867, Dorchester in 1869, and Brighton, Charlestown, and West Roxbury in 1873. Moreover, the character of new arrivals was considerably different from that of earlier generations. European immigration, still largely Irish, was only enough to keep constant the proportion of the foreign born. The newcomers were not so desperate as their predecessors of the 1840's and 1850's. Along with the continuing stream of migrants from rural New England, they were relatively well informed, not so shocked by their transfer to an urban setting.[13]

The city, too, was more ready to receive them. The Irish had developed nearly the full range of community institutions and by the 1870's were participating actively in political life. The growth of factory manufacturing offered more opportunities for unskilled labor, even in time of depression, than had the earlier commercial order. After a generation of experience, the demands of this new organization of work had become familiar and had accustomed men to the rhythms of hours on and off, of workdays and holidays, of periods of sobriety and periods of release. There was mass misery in the city but less insecurity, and desperation was less often expressed in violently disruptive behavior.[14]

The settling process eroded the urgency of appeals for a tightened liquor policy, especially as the political influence of the prohibitionists diminished. The easing of liquor controls had already begun, in 1867, with the reaction to enforcement by the state constabulary. Despite their rebound in the 1868 presidential year, the antiliquor forces lost ground again in 1869. When the 1870 legislature enacted a law enabling "any person" to sell ale or beer without restriction, if the voters in any district so approved, the prohibitionists carried out their threat to secede from the Republican organization. This show of independence proved a decisive mistake. The new group joined the Workingman's or Labor party in nominating Wendell Phillips for governor, with a separate candidate for lieutenant governor. But while labor contributed more than 10,000 votes to the total for Phillips, the prohibitionists added only 6,500. For more than ten years, the ministers and temperance societies had intimidated the managers of the Republican party. After 1870 revealed the hard voting strength of prohibition, no amount of organizational effort was enough to sway the majority of the General Court.[15]

The liquor laws were further relaxed in 1871 through the exemption of all wines. Their enforcement was attacked in the same year through a public investigation of the state constabulary. The opponents of the force charged corruption, offering testimony to show that the constables regularly demanded monthly protection money, five to ten dollars from illegal barrooms and one to two hundred from bawdy houses. One rural witness added that when a constable came to call, "I was there with my stud horse, and besides paying him as above I served his mare." None of the three metropolitan police hearings of the 1860's had been so explicit about bribery as this one, and the emphasis was not accidental. The opponents of the state force were attempting not to strengthen enforcement but to prove that it was impossible, that payments for protection constituted, in effect, a corrupted system of license outside the law.[16]

The General Court responded by reorganizing the constabulary and by reducing the number of men to 70 and the annual appropriation to $60,000. Although Major Jones remained for awhile chief constable, the force was placed under a board of three commissioners. Most important, the law embodying these changes eliminated the special emphasis on vice control. The state police still prosecuted for liquor and especially for gambling offenses. But they were increasingly concerned with their functions as rural detectives and as guardians of order. The commissioners complained that the most important obstacle to efficient operation of the force was its continuing notoriety as the muscular arm of the prohibitory movement.[17]

This notoriety persisted also in the General Court. In 1874, both branches passed a bill to abolish the constabulary in favor of a small state detective force, with no general police duties at all. This was vetoed by the Republican governor. But the veto was unpopular and enabled the Democrats to make the most of the liquor issue. In November, William Gaston was elected as the first Democratic governor in a generation. Both prohibition and the means of enforcing it were toppled at last in the wake of the returns.[18]

The legislature of 1875 again enacted a bill to abolish the constables in favor of a state detective squad, this time without opposition. The business of drafting an acceptable license law was more complex, and occupied most of the session. The formula finally decided upon was one tested in other states, a "high license" act to reduce the number of disreputable sellers. Licenses of fifty to two hundred dollars were required for those selling ales or wines to be drunk on the premises. The sale of spirits was subject to charges of between one hundred and one thousand dollars when sold to be drunk on the premises, and fifty to five hundred dollars when sold to be taken away.[19]

Enforcement was aided by the already apparent decrease in intemperance. According to police estimates there had been since the 1860's a rather ragged decline in the number of liquor shops in Boston. Although the annexations had brought the total up to 3,090 on the eve of the license law, the average for the previous five years was only 2,764. And changes in law and drinking habits made the real decrease larger than was numerically apparent; distillers complained that the heavier use of malt beverages had caused a 40 to 60 per cent drop in their business.[20]

This abatement in the objective problem also eased the pressures for any more material reduction in the number of sellers. The Boston common council normally contained more liquor dealers than any other single occupational group. They comprised 10 or 15 per cent of the total and they spoke for some three thousand proprietors at a time when twenty thousand votes was usually enough to elect a mayor. As in the 1820's they were backed by a powerful group of wholesalers, brewers, and distillers. For half a century, the business of selling liquor in Massachusetts had entailed some degree of risk, and the need for capital and credit bound retailers closely to their distributors. Although not so well publicized as the prohibitionists, the liquor industry had been openly engaged in politics since the election of 1868, and while supporting the Democrats and license in public, they were willing to deal with anyone in power.[21]

In this situation, the license law of 1875 was a real challenge to the city government. The majority of politicians were dissatisfied because of the high fees required. But the local authorities had been urging for twenty years that the city could enforce a license law; it was necessary to enforce this one with enough vigor to show its superiority to the prohibitory system.

The difficulties in balancing political requirements were clearly shown during the first two years of trial. The act provided that the mayor and aldermen of any city might delegate the issuance and supervision of licenses to an appointive board. The city council was willing to avoid this difficult responsibility, and the provision was adopted by a voice vote. None of the three commissioners chosen by the "nonpartisan" Mayor Cobb were politicians, and they were at first exempt from criticism. All three shared the common objection to the high fees and agitated publicly for a more liberal act. But their efforts to follow the spirit of the existing law at first provoked resentments unheard for a generation.[22]

The licenses granted druggists and package dealers were not often in controversy. But the law of 1875 followed precedent two hundred and fifty years old in requiring that the right to sell liquor by the glass should be granted only to those who also served meals; the term "public bar" was still an epithet akin to "free rum." The commissioners chose to apply the relevant clause literally. A police lieutenant and fifteen men were assigned to take orders from the board, and sent to investigate all requests for licenses. Despite the fees required, 3,403 applicants made an effort to comply. But only 2,277 permits were granted. The other places were rejected as unsuitable, largely because the police reported that they were, in fact, mere barrooms.[23]

During the second half of 1875 the entire police force joined the men assigned to the license board in pursuing those who remained outside the law. The board in July employed a special attorney to prosecute these cases. By the end of the year Chief Savage reported that his men had served 971 warrants against unlicensed operators and 153 against those who had violated the terms of their licenses. This left 2,411 dealers still in business, 1,769 legally. The next year, both the commissioners and the police further tightened the restrictive policy. This time there were over 2,403 applicants, but the board issued only 1,386 permits. And the police engaged in a drive which matched the operations of the state constabulary in 1867. Some 2,191 prosecutions were instituted. There were 1,355 successful cases of raid, search, and liquor confiscation, and 474 more in which places were raided without uncovering evidence. A total of 440 were driven out of business, so that only 1,971 remained.[24]

Despite this reduction, the work of the license commissioners during 1875 and 1876 did not result in increased compliance with the law. At the end of the latter year there were more unlicensed places than there had been at the end of the former. Although the number driven out of business indicated that the local police could be more intimidating than the state constabulary, the actual number of prosecutions did not rise over the figures reached earlier in the decade. Many dealers who had begun with the intention of legitimizing their operations found that they could ignore the law in practice. The time and money spent on an annual court appearance was no more than that required in getting a license. Those with licenses, conversely, complained that they were getting no advantage, and indeed that they were legally subject to routine inspection, as unlicensed proprietors were not. And the juries were sympathetic. The law was complex, and in some cases appeared unfair. Many men pleaded that they had tried to obey it and were not only rejected but raided when they revealed themselves. While during the first five years of the decade the allegedly balky Suffolk County juries had reached guilty verdicts in nearly 80 per cent of the liquor cases brought before them, the proportion was reversed in 1875 and 1876, with only 20 per cent declared guilty, and most cases resulting in disagreement or abandonment.[25]

Dissatisfaction was expressed also in politics, through an aroused Democratic party. The license commissioners were Republican, and

Boston since the Civil War was normally a Republican city. But 1876 was an exciting presidential year, in which Boston went for Tilden. The Democratic mayoralty candidate, the courtly, Harvard-educated Frederick Octavius Prince, was secretary of his party's national committee. Prince outraged the press by running as an avowed "partisan." The candidate himself was mainly concerned with national problems, but the liquor issue inflamed his supporters, and the December election resulted in a Democratic sweep of unprecedented proportions, as Prince won 26,000 votes and brought with him nine Democratic aldermen out of twelve.[26]

Early in 1877 the Democrats replaced the existing board of license commissioners with three men of their own. The new board made several major changes in policy, all designed to win better acceptance of the law. They did not propose to reduce the total volume of the liquor trade, a work which was already being accomplished by voluntary means and by the prevalent hard times, but they were concerned with Sunday sales, adulteration, and the disorders which brought complaints from the neighbors. The best way to cure these abuses was to bring as many dealers as possible under the law, through license. The unlicensed dealers would then be branded a disreputable remnant, condemned by competitors, the public and juries, and the legal sellers would genuinely fear the loss of their permits.[27]

During their first year the commissioners licensed the great majority of dealers simply by ignoring the "victualling" requirement. Through arrangement with the courts, illegal sellers were "sentenced" to take out licenses. By April of 1878, the board reported that 2,353 permits were in force, and less than 200 places were in business without them.[28]

For the first time in over thirty-five years, a clear majority of dealers were at least nominally operating under the law, an important first step in establishing compliance as normal. The commissioners were then able to begin the long task of reducing violations. They surveyed but did not interfere with the adulteration of liquor, and they made no important attempt to limit hours or sales to minors. But they chose the Sunday laws as a test, and were able to report a degree of compliance unknown for years.[29]

The board was equally concerned with the changing functions of the police department, and the effects of its new role on public opinion and attitudes toward the law. Before the enactment of license it had not seriously been considered that the job of the local police was to suppress illegalities. But after the abolition of the state force there was no one else to do it. While the fifteen plain-clothesmen assigned to the board were regarded as spies, the ordinary patrolmen were open to criticism as responsible for all the bars along their beats. As a result, the new commissioners noted, "the character and standing of the police force . . . had suffered."[30]

The solution was a simple compromise. The new Democratic board followed its predecessor in using a special group, or vice squad, under its sole orders. But it was considered more manly to leave them in uniform; with the majority of places licensed, they could not legally be refused admittance. At the same time, except for thirty extra men on Sundays, the commissioners explicitly freed the rest of the department from responsibility. The board had already relieved the city council of political embarrassment; it proposed to do the same for the police. Beginning in May of 1877 the chief and captains were no longer required to hear complaints either of laxity or overzealousness.[31]

The abatement of the older police problems, during the 1870's, was the most important condition which sheltered the department from controversy. But the abilities of the chief were also responsible for the lack of any heated criticism. Chief Savage not only handled the detective and liquor problems with tact, but maintained smooth relations between police and public.

Much of his strength within the department was the result of common origins and experience. Together with five of the eleven divisional captains serving in 1870, and nearly half the patrolmen, Savage was a Yankee from upper New England. Born in Alstead, New Hampshire, in 1812, he had worked first as a farm boy and then as a storekeeper in the village of Marlow. After failing in this business he had moved to Boston, while still a young man, to spend some time in paying off his debts. Now a distinguished greying widower, living at home with a spinster daughter, after more than twenty years of service he was regarded as the patriarch of the force.[32]

The chief shared a bond also with other members of the government whose participation in the current affairs of the city inspired an interest in its past. Together with Mayor Shurtleff and City Clerk James Bugbee, his hobby was local history, and he spent much of his adult life in collecting the material for a book eventually published as *Boston Events*. The research involved in this project also contributed, in 1866, to the more successful *Chronological History of the Boston Watch and Police,* which went through three editions in seven years. Both works enhanced the author's reputation as a gentleman of more refinement than usual in his position.[33]

His articulate and forceful views also earned Savage the respect of the city's organized reformers. He did state his belief in the impracticality under existing conditions of suppressing the liquor trade. But at the same time he expressed an admiration for the temperance ideal, and suggested that national legislation to limit the manufacture of alcohol might prove effective. His expert knowledge enabled him, like earlier police chiefs, to serve as guide to the nether world of poverty and crime. And his respectability made him welcome further as an advisor and even lecturer to such groups as the Industrial Aid Society.[34]

The chief's reputation for a kindly generosity was the most important element in his popularity. His books, with their sympathetic tales of pauper children and benevolent policemen, helped to further this reputation. So did the activities of the force under his command. While still a captain Savage had pioneered in giving holiday donations to the families of the North End, and during the 1870's this became a regular departmental charity. The official reports, too, were filled with accounts of aid given the Massachusetts Society for the Prevention of Cruelty to Animals and with suggestions for the better treatment of the insane.[35]

For the newspapers and the public, the most dramatic expression of Savage's humanitarianism was his treatment of "the social evil." Since the days of John Augustus no individual or society in Boston had been so concerned with prostitution. The legislation dealing with the problem, unlike that relating to liquor and other vices, was not subject to constant attention and review. Indeed, as the secretary of the state board of charities observed, no statute explicitly defined prostitution as a crime. The law against keeping houses of ill fame was often inoperative, for these older establishments were steadily giving way to houses of assignation. The owners, pleading ignorance of the use to which their property was put, were difficult to prosecute. The women themselves were subject to arrest only under the common law governing "lewd and lascivious behavior," or as "nightwalkers."

Much like common drunkards, many of them spent their lives shuttling in and out of the House of Correction.[36]

But if the legislature was indifferent, and private reformers were embarrassed, Chief Savage was neither. He had been concerned with the problem since his earliest days on the force, and his reports returned to it frequently. Prostitution was licensed in some American cities as well as in Europe, and there was some newspaper discussion of this alternative in Boston. But despite his belief that its occurrence was inevitable, Savage would not sanction prostitution in this way, by condemning any class of women to a permanent legally degraded status.[37]

His thinking in most ways was entirely conventional. Prostitutes, he believed, were the victims of some individual act of sin. Like most policemen the chief hated pimps and denounced the treacherous seducer in the traditional Victorian terms. But while his reports were filled with appeals to family life and parental discipline, he also made suggestions more radical than those of any other official in the city. The problem of personal guilt should be met by eliminating the double standard in sexual matters; the public and the legislature should condemn the male accomplice equally with the prostitute. After forty years of watching girls arriving in the city, alternately hopeful and desperate, Savage knew that their basic problem was economic. A Young Women's Christian Association was more badly needed than one for young men, in order to provide a wholesome and inexpensive alternative to the boardinghouse. Above all, the newcomers needed higher wages, equal to those earned by men doing similar work. Finally, in order to win their personal and economic rights, women needed political equality through the vote.[38]

Meanwhile, the chief did what he could, along the lines that he and other policemen had followed for a generation. He believed, when first appointed, that the force had been neglecting some if its responsibilities. One of his first acts was to organize a "descent" similar to those of the 1850's. On the night of May 7, 1870, the police in plain clothes raided not one but all the districts in the central city, arresting a total of 350 persons, half of them men. Twenty were charged with keeping brothels, and the rest with nightwalking, "idling," and other blanket moral offenses. Seven-eighths of the women were less than twenty-one years old. While 113 pleaded guilty, only a handful, as hardened offenders, were sent to prison. The police arranged probation for the rest. Some were given jobs. Others, with the help of contributions from interested citizens, were sent home, the majority to country towns in New England.[39]

The chief invited two observers to this "descent," one a member of the Prison Discipline Society and the other a representative of Boston's Catholic charities. Both approved his policy. But no organized group undertook the reformation of adult prostitutes as they did with alcoholics and juveniles; the matter was left to the police. The department no longer employed a special probation officer, but all of the patrolmen, in bringing individuals to court, were free to recommend leniency. Throughout the Savage regime this was the practice in the case of newly recruited young women. Few actions won more unmixed approval for the force and its head.[40]

Despite the wide publicity attending the police, the Boston city council, during the 1870's, was not usually concerned with those affairs which occupied the newspapers or the chief. Except for the first few months of 1870, there was no general discussion of the detectives. The problems of prostitution and gambling were never mentioned; nor was liquor, apart from the debate over licensing. The work of the department offered little opportunity for the discussion of contracts and supplies which occupied much of the time spent in council; except for the building and repair of station houses, almost all of the police expenditures went to wages. As a result, the government was content to leave most matters to the chief and to the three-man aldermanic committee on police.

As in earlier years, the force continued to lose functions to newer and more specialized agencies. The investigation of truancy, always done in close cooperation with the school committee, was already separate by 1870, as the truant officers moved out of the police department in 1866. Only a tangential supervision over the problem remained through the licensing of minors. The employment of children was economically important in Boston, and despite the objections of the school committee and various charitable groups the state made attendance laws less rigorous in the city than elsewhere. The licensing of children in outdoor occupations was not given over to the schools or truant officers but handled by the captains, until in 1871 it was turned over to a separate superintendent of newsboys at headquarters.[41]

A more typical cycle was the changing manner of issuing building permits. This was a task traditionally handled by the marshal and later the headquarters police. In 1870 a police superintendent of building permits was granted a separate title. In his first year, this officer granted 1,442 permits, canceling 1,151 upon completion, revoking 11, and prosecuting two builders for violations. For the next several years a summary of new building construction, by nature, cost, and police division, was included in the annual reports of the chief. But in 1871 the city council established a new department for the survey and inspection of buildings. In 1877 the head of this agency convinced the aldermen that he ought to superintend construction as well as make later inspections. The board accordingly transferred the issuance of permits out of the police department.[42]

But the functions lost by the police were more than balanced by the increasing magnitude of those which remained. Although new duties acquired during the 1860's and 1870's were largely extensions of those assigned earlier, the size of the headquarters staff reflected the growth of the city. By 1871 this comprised the chief and deputy, a clerk and assistant clerk, a messenger, six license superintendents, and two assistant license superintendents, as well as the special officers assigned to detective work, the men on guard at City Hall, and a police constable to serve notices and warnings.[43]

Despite constant changes in the traffic code and in rates of fare, the duties of the superintendents of hackney carriages and wagons were largely the same as they had been in the 1850's. The first licensed 520 hacks, the latter 2,794 trucks and wagons. Both heard complaints from the public about lost articles and unseemly behavior, and, rather rarely, revoked permits when indicated. The police on November 12, 1870 conducted the city's first detailed traffic survey, which counted 51,708 persons entering the city: 10,074 arrived on foot, the rest in some 86 steam trains, 443 horse cars, 1,279 pleasure carriages, and 2,004 merchandising vans.[44]

The superindent of pawnbrokers and junk shops continued to work as a detective as well as a licensing agent. In the course of inspecting the operations of some 54 pawnbrokers and 202 junk dealers in 1870, the officer recovered stolen property worth $1,522, and prosecuted 30 persons for theft.[45]

The legislature and city council continually added to the responsibilities of the superintendent of intelligence offices by bringing new establishments under license. In addition to regular theaters, by 1870 bowling alleys, billiard halls, sippio parlors, and itinerant musicians were included. In that year also, the officer was especially active in investigating ninety-six complaints against intelligence offices. Twenty-five of them were directed against "one-dollar" concerns, many of which were driven out of the city. Forty charged fraud against more established businesses, and resulted in fifteen civil or criminal suits, and the return of $6,448 in fees to cheated patrons.[46]

Renewed objections to special police had the effect, during the late 1860's, of extending the functions of regular patrolmen, especially during the summer, when men were taken from their beats and assigned to do guard duty and even menial labor under the supervision of other departments. Chief Savage was indignant about this practice, not only because it weakened patrol coverage but because the wages involved were charged to the police appropriation. Some 314 man-days, he counted, were spent in "taking care of flowers in the parks." A total of 435 days was spent at the ferry slips, 73 at the public library, 123 at vaccination stations, 281 "on sanitary examination." The demands of the public bath department, rapidly growing since its establishment in 1861, were especially heavy; 1,345 days were spent there.[47]

The city council never discussed the administrative work performed by the various superintendents, but the increase in guard duty reflected its major concern. Most debates assumed that the function of the police was simply to "keep order." Although this term was never defined, its meaning may be inferred from the distribution and disposition of the patrolmen.[48]

The men in 1870 were still divided into three divisions or watches, with the day men serving from 8:00 A.M. to 6:00 P.M., and the two night divisions from 6:00 P.M. to 1:00 A.M. and from 1:00 A.M. to 8:00 A.M. The night men still rotated as station house reserves, also, ready for any emergency and especially for riot. In fact, since the Burns case of 1854, the Draft Riot of 1863 was the only disturbance large enough to call out the whole force, and for a period during the late 1860's and early 1870's the interstation telegraph fell into disrepair. But the reserves were used locally; and the whole force was summoned, and performed well, during the Great Fire of November 1872 and its successor in May of 1873. The city meanwhile never fully lost its fear of mass popular uprising, and "defensibility" was still a major consideration in the construction of station houses.[49]

Within the three-division system the most striking change was the increase in the proportion of day police. Between the union in 1854 and the end of 1870, the number of men had increased from 228 to 500, and the ratio of divisional police to inhabitants from 1 for every 738 to 1 for every 524. In 1854, only about one patrolman in seven had worked in the daytime; by 1870, the three divisions were almost equal in size, so that one-third of the force was on day patrol. The change reflected a significant change in purpose and in social standards. The middle and upper classes of Boston, since the incorporation of the city, had been developing a more sensitive code of propriety. They were at the same time moving farther away, both physically and emotionally, from the rougher texture of life as it was lived in the rest of the city. The night police, in addition to making by far the greater proportion of arrests, especially for drunkenness, had always furnished protection from real physical danger. It was their job to rescue citizens from assault in the dark, and to guard unwatched property from fire and theft. But the day police dealt largely with less violent problems. Those called to work in the library or natural history rooms were assigned simply to quiet noise and subdue high spirits. The men demanded for patrol of the expanding park system were called to prevent assaults not on the person but on the senses, in the form of indelicate behavior or "insult." In 1878 new legislation permitted policemen to make arrests for loitering on the sidewalk or uttering profanity. A man in the daytime might still guard himself or a companion from injury, but the police were required to deal with the less dangerous coarseness of strangers and corner boys.[50]

With the exception of this growing insistence on propriety, the definition of "order" did not change much between the 1850's and 1870's. Nor was there a clear trend in the geographical disposition of the police patrol. Some adjustments were made as the expansion of the city created the need for new divisions. Stations nine and ten were established to cover Roxbury in 1867, station eleven to cover Dorchester in 1869. Division twelve was split off from division six, in 1872, to cover the growing outer fringes of South Boston. West Roxbury, Brighton, and Charlestown became for police purposes divisions thirteen, fourteen, and fifteen, respectively, when they were annexed in 1873. But this growth involved no basic change in the unwritten and rather erratic policy of assigning police first to the business district and second to the vice districts, and third to the purely residential districts.[51]

In terms of its area and population, division two—downtown—was even more heavily covered by police in 1870 than it had been in 1854. The increase was due to the addition of fifteen traffic officers, unique to this division, who no longer patrolled the streets but stood on the corners, ready to unsnarl traffic or help pedestrians across it. But even without these men the total of 75 was disproportionate for a small division with only about 6,805 inhabitants. The beats, averaging only three-quarters of a mile, were the shortest in the city, and the number of inhabitants per beat, 404, was the smallest. The men at this station were clearly there to protect business property and daytime visitors. If the police could not eliminate vice, they could at least set some geographical bounds; according to the chief, there were no houses of prostitution or assignation in the division, and no professional streetwalkers worked it regularly. The 243 places selling liquor were fewer and quieter than those in any other area of the central city. The figure for arrests by division, first issued for the year 1878, indicate similarly that the total of 1,333 for division two was the smallest in Boston proper. By that year, with only 70 men, the downtown area was brought more nearly into line with the other districts.[52]

In 1870 the North End division, number one, was still in second place in terms of the length of beats, but it had not grown proportionately as fast as several others. In contrast to the 35 men of 1854, 45 were assigned in 1870 to cover a relatively slow-rising population of 23,798. Each beat, a little over one mile long, had an average of 1,830 inhabitants. There had been a general decrease in the traditional houses of ill fame, or "ranches," in favor of houses of assignation. But the crowded, gaslit streets of the North End were still the stronghold of the former type, with thirty-three. After the Great Descent of 1870, the 108 full-time prostitutes left in division one accounted for nearly half of the city's total of 242. The district, too, led the city with 457 places selling liquor. And in 1878, with the number of police increased to 53, it led in the total of arrests, with 4,834.

Division three, in the West End, contained 31,813 inhabitants in 1870. Still third in terms of the length of beats, since 1854 it had grown more than division one. Part of the increase, from 27 to 47 patrolmen, was due to the encroachment of buildings onto the Back Bay, a narrow strip of which, along Beacon Street, was covered from this station. Some of the rest resulted during the late 1860's and 1870's from a new influx of Negroes, who helped to maintain the district's old importance as a center of vice. Although the total number of professional prostitutes, 97, was less than in the North End, division three did contain fully 39 houses of ill fame and 14 of assignation, together with 281 liquor dealers. The beats in 1870 averaged one and one-half miles long, with 2,273 residents. And in 1878 the 54 policemen from this station made 3,378 arrests.

The police coverage of division four did not change between 1854 and 1870, with an increase of men from 44 to 63. But it was well provided for, with beats averaging one and two-thirds of a mile long; in part because it included the Common and Public Garden, there were only 1,731 inhabitants per beat. And during the 1870's number four grew faster than any other division, to match the general southward movement of population. If the West End had contrasts, between the back end of Beacon Hill and Beacon Street, division four had variety. Much of it was given over to business; it included four railroad stations, and by 1870 thirty hotels, more than any other division. A new vice center, around South Cove, was swelling faster than the old ones in the north and west. The growth of this new district was clearly of some concern; it had 18 houses of ill fame and 15 of assignation, but only 11 prostitutes, apparently because Chief Savage concentrated much of his effort there. In 1870 the division also contained 383 liquor sellers. The demand for protection in the parks helped to swell the number of police, and so did the growth of the residential Back Bay. By 1878, with 79 policemen, number four led the city in this respect, and was in second place with 4,347 arrests.

Between 1854 and 1870 the city doubled the number of police assigned to the South End division, number five, from 24 to 50 men. But this move did not increase the ratio of police to population. Number five was in area the largest police division in the central city, and by 1870 it contained the most inhabitants, 41,356. But it still presented no acute police problems. Prostitutes resorted to a number of places among its numerous boardinghouses; Chief Savage listed 24 houses of ill fame and 16 of assignation. But as in division four this development was not accepted as permanent, and by the end of the 1870 campaign only 26 girls were counted. The total of 249 liquor dealers noted in the same year was markedly less than that for all central divisions but station two. The beats, well over two miles and covering 2,757 inhabitants, were the longest in the city proper. The increase of men between 1870 and 1879, from 50 to 60, was apparently less than the population warranted; in the latter year, the arrest total of 1,639 was the second smallest in the central city.

South and East Boston, divisions six and seven, both suffered an absolute decrease between 1854 and 1870 in the ratio of divisional policemen to population. East Boston, with a population of 15,433 in 1855, had 21 police; in 1870 the figures were 23,816 and 30. The beats in the latter year were four and one-half miles long, with 3,196 residents per beat. South Boston in 1855 had 23 policemen for a population of 39,215, with beats two and three-quarters miles long and 2,902 residents per beat. Both areas were filled with working-class immigrants, and had relatively few shops and stores. East Boston, in particular, an island with but one hotel, was not visited by strangers seeking excitement, and neither was listed as having any places given to prostitution. Neighborhood bars and liquor shops, however, were common enough; Chief Savage listed 180 for East Boston and fully 393 for South Boston.

Boston's first Irish alderman, Christopher Connor, elected from South Boston in 1869, was the only member of the board who made any public and persistent demand for more police in his particular neighborhood. He was rewarded, in 1872, with the creation of station twelve, and by 1878 there were 75 policemen in South Boston, still not proportionately as many as in 1855, but an improvement. The number of arrests that year was 2,161. East Boston, in contrast, was granted only 4 additional men between 1870 and 1878, and continued to fall behind the rest of the city. The 34 men there made only 1,102 arrests in 1878.[53]

A few patterns are apparent in these figures. Between 1854 and 1878 there was a continuing, somewhat lessening emphasis on the protection of the business districts, and a continuing vigilance over the vice areas. There was an increasing concern for quiet at times and places already quiet, as in the parks and the Back Bay. As a complement, there was a contrary trend away from those working-class districts less troubled by vice and visitors.

The pattern of distribution in the annexed suburbs was roughly consistent with that of the older city. The towns annexed to Boston differed greatly in character and had rather varied police systems. But only Charlestown was a port, and none was troubled by traffic or commuters. With central Boston within easy reach, none furnished any commercial vice but drink. By contrast with the central city all of them, whether given to slums or mansions, were treated as residential. Police were simply provided, without much regard for area, in roughly the same proportion to population as those in comparable districts in the older city.

Roxbury, on the eve of its annexation in 1867, had a police department consisting of a marshal and assistant marshal, 28 "constables, police, and watch," and 18 special policemen and night watchmen. By 1870, divided into divisions nine and ten, it was given 64 policemen to cover a population of 34,553. There was then one divisional policeman for every 540 inhabitants, as compared with one per 510 in the central city. The beats, however, were considerably more extensive than those in downtown Boston, averaging nearly four miles and a quarter.[54]

Dorchester, annexed in 1869, had 13 policemen and 8 watchmen during its last year as a separate town. In 1870, as division eleven, it received 20 policemen, one to every 613 of its 12,261 residents. This ratio, however, was achieved only by extending the beats to lengths of over ten miles each. In 1870 the problem was eased by putting the men on horseback; soon 28 mounted police patrolled Dorchester and other sparsely settled areas.[55]

After 1873 some of these mounties were detailed to West Roxbury, which, as a town, had had only 10 policemen, day and night. As part of Boston it received 26, or one to every 451 members of its population of 11,787. Much of this generous ratio resulted from the placement of men in the extensive parks and excursion areas of this most wooded and attractive part of the city.[56]

Charlestown, before its annexation, supported a captain of police, a lieutenant, and a truant officer, with 31 regular patrolmen. By 1878 the number of police increased to 38, but the ratio to the 28,233 inhabitants was only one to 768, the highest in the city. In contrast, tiny Brighton, a much richer area annexed in the same year, was given far more favorable coverage. Only 4 policemen, working exclusively at night except for market days, had sufficed for Brighton as a town. But they had made the handsome total of 502 arrests in 1872-73, proportionately more than any others in any division of the city. By 1875, with a population of 6,200, division fourteen was provided with 21 men, one for every 209 inhabitants, a ratio lower than that of any but the harbor division. One of the more notable results of the influx of seasoned Boston patrolmen, however, was a dramatic decrease in the workload, as the arrest total dropped to 296 in 1878.[57]

The favoritism shown Brighton and the other richer suburbs was real, but not so great as the simple ratio of police to population suggests. The introduction of area, or length of beats, into the equation helps to even it considerably. Moreover, after the original distributions, some of the inequalities were reduced with time. In 1875, the suburbs as a whole were provided one divisional policeman for every 538 inhabitants, as compared with one for every 422 in the far more compact central city. By 1880 the figures were one to 592 in the suburbs, one to 400 in the central city. At the extremes, by that time Brighton had suffered a proportionate loss of policemen, and Charlestown had registered a slight gain. West Roxbury, with its park system, held firm. Roxbury and Dorchester, both losing some desirability as residential areas, each suffered some loss.

Thus within the two clear patterns, the preference given the wealthier suburbs and the increasing preference given the central city over all suburbs, there were considerable and sometimes contradictory movements. Changes were made by consultation among the captains, the chief, and the police committee. Members of the city council as a whole, reflecting the wishes of petitioning citizens, sometimes called for policemen at this park or at that crossing. But only Alderman Connor made any demand for increase over any wide district. The rest, in public, were concerned only with the more general problem of the number and expenses of the department as a whole. The police force simply developed in response to immediate needs, without comprehensive plan or debate.

The uneventful growth of the 1870's was reflected in the unique popularity of Chief Savage, whose tenure of more than eight years was the longest enjoyed by any head of the department since Marshal Pollard. There were no dramatic incidents, scandals, or investigations. The principle of law enforcement was accepted, while the pacification of the city was measured by declining rates of intemperance and of homicide, and by the passing of riot as a normal form of political expression. These developments helped to ease permanently the task of police. But not all older problems were fully solved, and even in a time of quiet, changes in the nature of local government prompted several groups to reopen the question of the proper relation of police to politics.

CHAPTER TEN

Political Uncertainty: The Commission Movement, 1870-1878

Between 1870 and 1878, while the conduct of the Boston police force was generally satisfactory, that of the local government was not. The difficulties of incorporating new areas into the city, and demands for new services and higher standards of efficiency, created problems that could not be met simply through expansion, as earlier; the rise in municipal spending, after the Panic, came virtually to a halt.[1]

These objective conditions aggravated distrust of the traditional political process, already evident in the 1860's. While the police department was not the main target of this distrust, it was included in the general demand for revision of the machinery of government. The movement reached into the city council itself, where many members were troubled by the management of the force. By the end of the period, as local politics hardened along new lines, the call for change was irresistible.

For the city council, the responsibility of managing the police department was especially heavy during the 1870's. Political power was demanding as well as rewarding, and it involved difficult choices. The men on the force wanted more pay and pensions; supporters wanted jobs; citizens wanted more police and lower taxes. With the onset of depression, it was necessary to arbitrate among all of these pressures in the face of a growing population, declining values, and the accepted imperative of retrenchment. Neither aldermen nor common councillors were paid for their services, but both were required not only to legislate and pass taxes but to serve through committees as executive officers. Many shared a growing belief that these executive functions were embarrassing as well as burdensome, and that the business of governing the city was slipping away from them.

Debates over the interrelated issues of the efficiency, pay, and numerical strength of the police department illustrated some of the aldermen's problems. Boston's patrolmen, at three dollars a day or $1,095 per annum, received an average of $100 more than those of other leading cities; only New York and Brooklyn, at $1,200, did better. But this condition supported two contradictory arguments, as did the more general fact that Boston's per capita spending for government, nearly $41 in 1868-71, was always among the highest in the nation. While some councillors declared that the city was doing more than enough, others countered with an appeal to municipal pride and the fact that Boston enjoyed higher standards and more services than those of sister cities.[2]

Three arguments entered into the typical debate of the spring of 1872, when the police and their supporters presented the council with a pay raise petition signed by citizens worth $1,000,000 in property. One concerned the relative quality of the men and the nature of the work. Alderman Clark, a Republican, noted that "The pay of laboring classes as competent as are the police officers is not over $12 or $15 a week." His Democratic ally, Leonard Cutter, added that the policemen's lot was not especially demanding; the firemen held positions just as responsible, and employees of the health department did work more disagreeable, and neither class was paid as well. There were nearly two thousand applicants for jobs on the police force, all willing to work at the given rate. As a businessman, he would be tempted to fire those who complained in favor of those eager to replace them.[3]

Supporters of the pay raise replied that comparison of patrolmen with common laborers was entirely unfair. Unusual qualities of judgment and tact as well as unusual physical condition were required of the police, who were burdened with special expenses to maintain their uniforms and to support their families, for marriage and fatherhood were virtually "prerequisites" for the job. There was admittedly a crush of applicants, but the great majority could not meet these standards; and the same surplus was available for almost every other job in the government, including unpaid positions on the board of aldermen.[4]

The more important issue centered about the fact that with a given amount of money available the alternative to a raise in pay was an increase in number. Over the years the public, the politicians, and the police themselves combined to create more pressure for the latter than the former. The basic attraction of a policeman's job was not the per diem wage but the total made possible by job security. Security was enhanced by the fact that the total number of policemen was rarely cut and frequently increased. The men could gather signatures for any petition, but citizens were more sincerely concerned with having more men available than with providing the existing force with better pay. And while many politicians were interested in courting favor within the department, they were also interested in opportunities for supporters to join it.

Policemen's wages were not often raised, and it was in fact sometimes possible to cut them. This happened in limited form in 1877 when the base pay for patrolmen was graded between $2.50 and $3.00 a day according to seniority. But a cut in the size of the force occurred only once in the nineteenth century, in 1852-53, during the excitement over Marshal Tukey.[5]

The supremacy of the issue of numbers over that of wages was perfectly illustrated by the outcome of the 1872 debates. Both branches of the city council agreed to raise the police appropriation by $60,000. The aldermen, eight to four, determined to use this sum for more patrolmen. The common council, forty-seven to fifteen, preferred to apply it to a pay raise. In the end, the common councillors surrendered, ignored the great petition and increased the force to 550.[6]

The councillors were nagged by many of the same difficulties in deciding the related problem of pensions. Since all members of the police department had become full-time professionals in the 1850's, with a normal expectancy of permanent employment, the government had been bothered by the question of what to do with the superannuated. It had been twenty years since the watchmen had surrendered their daytime jobs, and many of them, still serving, were in their late sixties and seventies. Simply to fire these men was both politically and humanly painful. Yet the few thousand dollars from witness fees paid annually into the police relief fund was not adequate to provide for them. The sole alternative under existing law, which allowed payment only for current services rendered, was to keep the men on the rolls. The council voted two men full pay for life although they did no work at all; one was a crippled victim of the Draft Riot of 1863, the other had been disabled in equally heroic circumstances during 1866. A few others, also unfit, were carried for shorter periods at full pay. Still others received desk jobs. But the majority remained out on the beats, limping after youthful vandals in the parks, or strolling through long stretches of the suburbs.[7]

The principal problem in retaining the unfit was that it countered the continual demand for a better patrol system. After 1875, the annual addresses of Mayors Cobb, Pierce, and Prince were all critical of the discipline or management of the police, and their complaints were echoed in the city council. Chief Savage, highly popular and not easily replaced, was himself in his sixties, and regarded as a lax disciplinarian, clearly not the man to undertake any major reorganization. Yet the city council was not only reluctant to reform the department but, because of the very nature of local politics, incapable of it.[8]

There was still a flavor of amateurism in Boston's government. Leading citizens, according to the old ideal, were still called for brief periods to participate. The professionals or near professionals, in a situation without party discipline or single "boss" rule, were frequent victims of factionalism and local revolt. Others used municipal office only as a step toward the legislature or Congress. As a result, the city had a large pool of men who had dabbled in municipal affairs, but few with any long experience. The average alderman during the 1870's served less than two years. The three members of the all-important police committee, between 1870 and 1878, averaged one and one-half years, experience; one January, when they organized, all three were new to the job.[9]

The committee met as often as it was called to deal with some specific complaint or petition but only once a year to pass on questions of policy. The general debates over police matters made clear the factual ignorance of the councillors. Members were unsure about the number and functions of the superintendents and special police, about the distinction between the day and night divisions. The police committee itself was sometimes unable to furnish the answers off-hand.[10]

The department was also a difficult source of patronage because no politician could be sure that he could place any given individual on the force. Applicants petitioned the mayor, who sent two nominations for every place available to the police committee, which selected the candidates after checks of qualifications and a physical examination. The names of the finalists were posted publicly for a week so that citizens might register objections. Only then did the full board of aldermen vote approval, and it occasionally vetoed some. Far more were disappointed than accepted.[11]

The price of aldermanic responsibility was heavy. While Savage took credit for improvements, and individual patrolmen for acts of heroism, deficiencies in the police department were always laid to "politics." It was true that "three-headed control" subverted discipline. The mayor and aldermen shared the appointive power, guided by the recommendations of police investigators headed by the chief. Savage complained that the various license superintendents, created and appointed directly by the mayor and aldermen, were not really subject to his authority. The delicate business of transfers between stations was handled entirely by the police committee. Before 1869, the men had generally wanted to serve in stations one and three, which had short beats and long opportunities for the collection of witness fees. Station two rose in popularity after the witness fees were denied to individuals, since it had short beats and few arrests, and its citizens, as in all the central districts, had the habit of presenting watches and other presents to their favorites. In order to win special duty at headquarters, it was necessary for patrolmen to curry favor with the chief. The position of the captains was anomalous, and departmental jealousies generated constant complaint.[12]

The problems of aldermanic control created a demand for an alternative system, about the form of which there was never any doubt. Massachusetts was moving away from a localized and democratic system of administration. The General Court in 1870 began the movement by creating an elective three-man board of street commissioners, with three-year terms, to which the city council surrendered not only the technical duty of planning new streets and altering old ones, but also the power of abating taxes, a provision which suggested suspicion of the council's fiscal responsibility. In 1872, following an investigation of impure meats in the city markets, Mayor Gaston recommended that the aldermen give up their supervision of the health department in favor of another three-man commission appointed by him. An outbreak of smallpox won him support; the health commission, created that year, left the council only the old functions of the city marshal important for patronage, the cleaning of streets and cesspools and the collection of refuse. A third three-man three-year commission, again appointed by the mayor, was established the next year, after the Great Fire, to take charge of the fire department. In 1875 a fourth, the park commission, was given the power of taking lands and making rules for the city's recreational areas. In the same year a fifth, the Boston Water Board, undertook the management of all matters relating to the water supply. Although the creation of all of these commissions violated in some degree the old concept of representative amateur government, the council eventually approved.[13]

But that was not the end of the move to diminish the councillors' functions. In 1875 the legislature passed an act, inspired by depression and taxpayers' complaints, which limited the fiscal authority of all towns and cities in the commonwealth. An absolute ceiling of 3 per cent of valuation, or 1 additional per cent if the debt already exceeded 2 per cent, was set for all indebtedness not contracted for sewers and water supply. Although this act did not immediately affect the finances of Boston, it was a striking expression of distrust.[14]

Distrust, too, in 1873, led the mayor to appoint a three-man commission to recommend changes in the Boston city charter, a task assigned in the past to joint committees of the council. In 1875, the report of the commissioners, in addition to calling for three-year terms for elected officials, strongly criticized government by conciliar committees. Executive business could not properly be handled by "persons who render gratuitous services only, or who are chosen to office not for their experience in the duties they may be called to perform."[15] The police force was the last important department still ruled directly by the aldermen, and the commission recommended the correction of this anomaly by the creation of a new board of police commissioners.[16]

The city council rejected most of the recommendations, but the proposed police commission was not directly voted down. The increasing tendency to rely upon specialists was viewed with relief as well as resentment. Members of both major parties agreed that a commission would be more economical and more efficient than the existing system, and their arguments were bolstered by developments which dramatized the difficulties of political control.[17]

The city government had done nothing to resist the steady growth in both the legal and physical powers of policemen, and often encouraged it. But those who felt it resented it and threatened to break the traditionally united front of authority. During the 1860's and 1870's the General Court continued to extend the powers of policemen under the law. Several new offenses were added to those for which peace officers were allowed to arrest without written warrant: fast driving in 1865, cruelty to animals and presence at gaming in 1869, willful trespass in 1876. There was a similar development in the number of cases in which search warrants might be issued: immature calve's meat in 1866, exhibitions of fighting animals in 1869, all tainted foods in 1876, drugs and instruments of contraception and abortion in 1879.[18]

In practice, the effect of the new laws was slight. Already able, under the common law, to apprehend anyone committing a misdemeanor in their presence, officers were protected from possible legal retaliation in the enumerated cases, when the courts judged the parties innocent. Extension of the use of search warrants was more obviously governed by specific topical concerns: the activities of the Massachusetts Society for the Prevention of Cruelty to Animals during the 1860's, an investigation of the Boston markets toward the end of the decade, public outrage at the practices of organized abortionists in the 1870's. But both sets of laws illustrated the fact that outside of the sensitive areas of slavery and liquor control the state was prepared always to increase and never to abridge the duties, powers, and protection granted its peace officers in criminal cases.[19]

The Supreme Judicial Court also moved in the same direction. There were instances in which the actions of officers in civil cases were declared illegal and in which they were held civilly liable for their actions in criminal cases. But the great majority of all decisions favored the policemen, and no case ever upheld the criminal conviction of a policeman for assault or similar offense.[20]

The two new cases which introduced untested principles were both victories for the police. *Conway* v. *Perkins* narrowed the grounds for false imprisonment established nearly twenty years before in *Tubbs* v. *Tukey*. In the earlier case, the Boston city marshal had been held liable for failing to bring a complaint in person against a man he had arrested. But in *Conway* v. *Perkins* such failure was held legitimate as long as the arresting officer appeared later to testify. The one other case was criminal; in *Commonwealth* v. *Reynolds,* the court cleared up some of the ambiguities in *Commonwealth* v. *Irwin* relating to forcible entry. The Reynolds case established that there was no need to show a warrant for a misdemeanor, committed by a third person, to a homeowner who objected to having his house searched for the miscreant. The door might be broken over the owner's resistance if there were reasonable grounds to suspect that the offender was inside.[21]

But, as in the 1850's, it was difficult to make these official rulings understood or accepted. More significant than the relatively few cases which created precedents were the common ones which reaffirmed settled principles and which indicated the nature of popular doubts and resentments. Liquor legislation was still resisted in the courts as well as in practice. In Boston, too, the law of arrest was subject to some doubt. In these matters, the state and the courts provided local authority with more power than it wished. The rules governing arrest were summarized in the police handbook of 1867; less official accounts were recorded in the Boston *Herald,* and in a fatherly essay of "Advice to Young Policemen," by the chief. All these sources were more cautious in their approach to the arrested citizen than either the courts or the legislature.[22]

This conservatism helped keep Boston policemen out of the higher courts. There were discrepancies between law and practice. The police routinely exceeded their rights in arrests for petty larceny, in the confiscation of valuables after arrest, and in the treatment given suspected professional criminals. But doubts about these practices, which excited no controversy, remained academic. The improper use of force was sometimes an issue at law. The courts in such cases did not hesitate to decide in favor of the symbols of order and established authority. But the matter was not so easy for politicians, for whom the test was not law but opinion.[23]

Policemen were restrained from committing brutal acts by the prior warnings of their superiors, by their own good judgment, and by fear of physical retaliation. The official sanctions were slight. The desire to uphold authority was powerful, and if he committed a negligent or vicious action, any member of the department could count on his fellows, the courts, and the government to clear him of wrongdoing. But an arrest was still often a matter of mutual assault, and in many neighborhoods a sadistic policeman was subject to dangerous abuse.

After the Civil War, the fact that most policemen carried revolvers tipped the physical balance in their favor, making them more formidable but also increasing the danger of brutality on their part. On the other hand, the usual victims of police assault were less helpless and better able to make their complaints heard. Both guns and organized protest figured in the few major incidents reported, typified by the killing of Timothy Lynch in April of 1871.

Lynch was a teamster from East Boston, an area supplied with few policemen. In such neighborhoods as the Irish district around Porter Street, isolated patrolmen were often in conflict with the people on their beats. Serious trouble began on Sunday night, April 2, when two young men, Lynch and Michael Ryan, attempted to rescue an arrested prisoner. Both had been involved with the police before, on charges of assault and drunkenness, and warrants were issued for their arrest the next day. On Monday night five men went out to serve the warrants, and met a hostile crowd; the captain at station seven first sent out the twenty reserves and then called for reinforcements from across the water at the North End. According to police reports, the crowd by that time had become a mob of two thousand persons. Ryan was arrested, but Lynch, in a fury, grabbed at the officers in trying to free him. Three policemen used their clubs on him, not heavily, they claimed, but enough to subdue him; the others held back the crowd while the captives were taken on to the station house and locked up. The next morning, Lynch was found on the floor of his cell in a coma; he was taken to City Hospital and died that afternoon.[24]

At the inquest there were serious differences about the facts. Lynch's neighbors testified that he had been temperate for a year, that the crowd was neither large nor menacing, and that the police had freely brandished their revolvers. According to several accounts Lynch had been dragged to the station by his feet, over the cobblestones, and beaten on the head while shouting, "they have murdered me" or "this is my death blow." Fellow prisoners heard noises from his cell all night, bumps and moans, but no doctor was called until the routine morning inspection.[25]

The coroner's jury preferred the official police version. The attending physician said that except for bruises Lynch did not outwardly appear to have been in desperate condition; it was suggested that the fatal head wound might have been caused by a fall from his bunk. And if in fact it was the result of a clubbing—the officers admitted hitting him twice—the jurors declared that the police had acted only in self-defense.[26]

But the citizens of the district would not let the matter end with this verdict. The veteran lawyer George Sennott helped Lynch's mother to draft a dramatic open letter to Mayor Gaston, copies of which were sent to the newspapers:

Dear Sir:

I am a poor widow, and the mother of nine children. The third eldest, Timothy Lynch, aged eighteen years, was beaten upon the head with clubs a week ago tonight, and died of the beating the next day. He was small for his age, weighing only ninety pounds . . . He was in liquor at the time, and I suppose they took him for that. Oh, Mr. Mayor, why should my boy be killed with so little cause?

I cannot believe that three stout men had to beat a boy to death to get his body to the station house.[27]

No one was apparently startled by the cruel fact, never contradicted, that an Irish teamster in the East Boston of 1871 should be so slight. But the letter from Honora Lynch did persuade the Boston *Herald* to question the police account. Mayor Gaston promised that the committee on police would hear the case. And in a series of mass meetings the neighbors of the dead man elected officers and formed an organization to conduct an investigation, the results to be referred to the aldermen.[28]

The promised hearings ran for two weeks, as both sides repeated and embellished their earlier testimony. One officer declared that Lynch had been " 'the toughest customer' he ever got hold of in his twelve years experience as a policeman." Other witnesses accused the police of pointing cocked revolvers at a crowd largely consisting of curious women and children, and of wantonly beating such bystanders as Mrs. Sarah McCarthy, who was only pleading the case of a neighbor's boy in trouble. But in the end the police committee, like the coroner's jury, decided in favor of the accused patrolmen. There were no further avenues of publicity or appeal, and the case dropped out of the papers.[29]

The Lynch affair attracted more attention than any similar controversy. This was apparently the first time that members of the Boston police department had been accused of homicide. But except for the magnitude of the charges, the incident followed a familiar course and arrived at a familiar conclusion. Other occasions, when careless shots ricocheted and hit bystanders, or when men died unattended in cells, also prompted investigation by the aldermen. Ordinary civil suits were sometimes instituted against allegedly brutal policemen; the attention surrounding the Lynch case inspired enough so that a municipal judge called in the fall of 1871 for some kind of Supreme Court ruling on the definition of "reasonable force." George Sennott, who could hardly have expected a fee from Mrs. Lynch, figured in a number of other affairs in which his primary aim appeared to be the exposure of malpractice. Sennott's associate in one suit had recently been embarrassed in a "panel house" incident; the relations between policemen and many members of the criminal bar were tense. The newspapers, also, pursued incidents of "clubbing," and added at least the sanction of publicity.[30]

But there were no channels of political protest. Except in one accidental shooting of two children, no member of the city government publicly furthered a complaint against a policeman guilty of the abuse of force. The Lynch case, despite its ethnic overtones, was ignored alike by the Irish members of the city council and by the Yankee representatives from East Boston. Despite the Buttrick decision of 1861 the patrolmen were still considered agents of the city, the most visible representatives of its authority. Any punishment resulting from the basic right to use force at their discretion would threaten their usefulness. In a matter in which they were intimately concerned, a rejection of the sworn testimony of any member of the force would be a blow to the morale of all. Through the 1870's no investigation of abuse resulted in contrary findings.[31]

There was clearly an unwritten tradition that those in charge of the police force should not attack individual members in public. But for many councillors the practice was difficult to honor. The silence surrounding the Lynch affair was especially unnatural. There was no assurance that a similar incident might not occur again, and in the changing political climate of the period there was no predicting what might happen if it did.[32]

The strain of defending individual policemen from public hostility was eased by the fact that such hostility was not common, and that acts of brutality were normally outweighed by acts of benevolence. But in the 1870's, even benevolence was in controversy. For many citizens, the most popular function of the department was the service of free soup in the station houses. But to those interested in more purposeful charity, this easy providence was a breach of doctrine. The objections of this influential group provided one of the few local issues which threatened easily to translate into class antagonism. Since one side appealed to public sympathy and the other to public fears, the soup problem occupied more political attention than any other function of police.

In 1868 the building of a new, unified headquarters on Chardon Street, together with the reformation of the overseers of the poor, had symbolized again the old desire to coordinate the activities of public and private charity into a common system. But the object was not so easily attained. In theory, all applicants for aid were to be directed to this one set of offices. But the original prohibition against weekday "lodgers" in the police stations could not be followed in practice. The need was often urgent, and there seemed no justice in discriminating against those who had no homes in favor of the drunks who could not find them. There was another, deliberate violation of theory when in 1868 the city council began to appropriate several thousand dollars annually for free soup, distributed, during the winter, not by the overseers of the poor but by the police.[33]

Other official and unofficial practices made the police department a convenient agency for administering outdoor relief, at first without official objection. The soup was prepared by the patrolmen at the stations and given to all who lined up for it. The cost of an average serving of one and one-fifth pints came to about two and a half cents, and the mixture was generally approved as nourishing. Chief Savage claimed that some effort was made, when strangers came in, to check that they were local residents, and "deserving." The patrolmen in such cases made inquiries, but not until after the first visit. The "lodgers" from out of town received only the leftovers, and "if less worthy, were equally grateful."[34]

The soup was quietly given and taken for several years. There were no inquiries or complaints deserving direct reply until the fall of 1873. The financial panic that September severely affected the city government, for its budget traditionally rose and fell in rhythm with the business cycle. It was also apparent that the need for relief would be heavier than it had been for years. With a hard winter ahead, Mayor Pierce wrote to the overseers of the poor for advice. Former

Mayor Lincoln, chairman of the board, took this opportunity to clarify the position of the group. The heavy demand on the city's charitable resources made it necessary to eliminate any unsupervised action. Boston was famous not for "lavish expenditures" in beneficence but for a careful system with which free soup interfered. He further condemned the police kitchens as illegal, for the city was not allowed to appropriate money for the relief of nonresidents. The city solicitor confirmed that view. On November 24, Pierce recommended to the city council that they cancel the soup and leave relief to the overseers.[35]

The aldermen moved to follow the mayor's advice. But reaction in the common council was more spirited. The senior councillor, George Shaw, had personally visited the kitchens and was impressed by their operation. Misery bred crime and soup helped to prevent it. No agency was better equipped to serve it than the police. He had seen the chief give money from his own pocket to those in need—there was no more charitable man in the city. And the patrolmen, who moved daily among the poor, were better qualified than any self-styled body of experts to determine who was "worthy."[36]

Shaw thought his own speech effective enough to have copies printed and passed among his constituents. His colleagues took the opportunity, then and later, to express their hostility to the Benthamite rigidity of the overseers' system. The matter came before the council several times as the cold weather approached and then arrived. Each time it was emphasized that those seeking charity at Chardon Street were investigated, shamed, made to wait, and ultimately had to declare themselves paupers before getting aid. The police in contrast were naturally sympathetic, and trusted by those on their beats. Moved by these arguments, the common council voted to override the problem of legality and continue the soup; there were on the last vote only six dissenters out of a membership of eighty.[37]

The kitchens had champions among the aldermen also, led by Republican chairman John Clark and by Democrat James Power, who echoed a familiar argument: "My lot has been with the poor . . . I am one of them . . . . It seems to me that if anything should enter into our police systems it is charity." But their opponents, while conceding that theirs was not the "popular" side, replied that "police work is one thing and work of charity is another." The board held to its original motion, the last time by a tie vote of six to six.[38]

No soup was served that winter. But those in favor applied successfully for an enabling act from the legislature so that when the debate
began again in the fall of 1874, there was no legal obstacle. Five
thousand dollars was appropriated for 1874-75. For the next several
years the police not only continued to run the kitchens but began to
distribute shoes and medicines, privately contributed for the purpose.[39]

But the soup remained an annual issue in the city council as well
as in the police stations. The overseers, once aroused, continued to
press their objections. Although no councillors undertook a full defense of "scientific" charity, many pointed to the abuses which might
result from carelessness. People traded their pints for liquor, and in
some places the keepers of cheap lodginghouses skimped on meals and
sent boarders to the stations. One other objection touched upon a
recognized social issue with some popular appeal. Free soup attracted
tramps, who not only burdened the charitable resources of the city but
posed a danger to its citizens.[40]

The growing problem of vagrancy was a matter of considerable
contemporary concern. The station house lodgers of the 1850's had
been regarded in most cases as homeless unwillingly, new arrivals,
immigrants, visitors seeking work. By the 1870's there was an increase
in the proportion of nonresidents, from about two-thirds to six-
sevenths, and in native Americans, from less than one-fourth to about
one-third. More immediately important was the total increase. There
had been 17,352 lodgers in 1860; the Civil War years brought a
decline, and there were only 16,721 in 1865. In the five years after
the war, however, the total nearly doubled, to 30,560. And as Chief
Savage noted in his report for 1876, it doubled again between 1870
and 1875, reaching 62,740. By that time the increase had become a
subject of official and popular notice. The General Court, in 1866,
passed the first of a series of laws aimed at vagrants, enabling peace
officers to arrest them on sight, and providing for jail terms of up to
one year. But the vagrants were too numerous, and their offenses were
too vague, for the authorities to deal with them through mass imprisonment.[41]

By the 1890's the bare-toed, grizzled bum would be a stock character on the stage and in popular cartoons. But the public in the
1870's was not yet familiar with the type. In both periods there were
differences of opinion about the kind of problem represented. Observers agreed that tramps were gregarious, widely traveled, white

males, Americans almost always of English or Irish ancestry. As distinct from local beggars they were not usually alcoholic or otherwise crippled. It was clear, too, that some were only temporarily out of work, while others had decisively abandoned the pressures of employment and family life. But there was no agreement about which of these types predominated. While some believed that the tramps were only looking for dry bedding and apple pie, others warned that they belonged to the antisocial world of criminals.[42]

The latter was always the official view, as promoted by the state board of charities. Chief Savage, in 1876, blamed what he called an unprecedented national crime wave on the increase in vagrancy. At about the same time there was a change in common newspaper attitudes. The Boston *Herald,* in a long article on "The Migratory Bummer," was inclined to be tolerant early in 1875. But that summer the *Herald* joined other papers in blaming wild-eyed vagrants for various incidents of rural violence, notably for the famous New Hampshire rape and decapitation of Josie Langmaid. Later in the decade the state police, deprived of their function as agents of vice control, took a special interest in tramps. Several were sent in disguise to travel with and investigate them, and reported that they were capable of any villainy.[43]

The current excitement made the junction of tramps and soup a politically effective tactic for the overseers of the poor. Chief Savage, in 1876, made it policy to give soup to lodgers only in extreme cases, a total that year of ninety-four. But this concession did not for debating purposes break the association already made. A three-man commission appointed in 1877 to investigate public charity reported that the various city institutions mixed their populations indiscriminately. All those not criminal or sick should be moved to the House of Industry, the almshouses, and the schools for neglected children. They were to be under the care not of the directors of public institutions but of the overseers of the poor, who would be able to apply their rigorous methods from the moment of application to that of self-support, or to the grave. Free soup was to be stopped and those seeking free lodgings at the police stations were to be sent instead to some place where they could be made to work and to bathe.[44]

These suggestions were, however, ignored. Debate over the soup problem continued, and it became evident to charitable reformers that the police department might subvert their program so long as it was subject to the common council.[45]

Through the middle of the 1870's, the movement toward a police commission continued to gather support. Three successive mayors—Independent, Democratic, and Republican—endorsed the idea after 1875, citing the need for economy and efficiency. In 1878, when the aldermen voted eight to four to petition the legislature for the necessary authority, it was clear that the measure would pass.[46]

But the vote in the common council, thirty-six to thirty-four against the proposed petition, indicated that the movement was not unanimously approved. The council could not block passage, but the intensity of debate reflected an important, and recent, change in tone. The arguments in favor of a police commission had at first been bipartisan and abstract. By 1878 they had become partisan and specific. The election of Mayor Prince brought the new emphasis into the open, but the situation had been developing for some time.[47]

Boston politics, after the Civil War, had retained much of its older character. The city had reverted to its "nonpartisan" ideal and to the traditional selection of respectable amateurs to the leading posts in government. Mayor Shurtleff, elected as a Democrat in 1867 and 1868, was repudiated by his own party in 1869 and won on the Citizens' and Republican ticket. William Gaston was elected in 1870 and 1871 as the candidate of Democrats and Citizens. Republican Henry Lille Pierce succeeded him for a single term. Samuel Crocker Cobb, chosen in 1873, 1874, and 1875, was nominated the first two times by both Republicans and Democrats, and the last time by the Citizens alone, in defiance of both major parties. All these men were undeniably gentlemen. Shurtleff had been educated at Harvard, and Gaston had a degree from Brown. Neither Cobb nor Pierce had gone to college, but both were successful businessmen; Pierce indeed was on his way to becoming a millionaire chocolate manufacturer.[48]

The four mayors differed in capability, but they all followed the forms of allowing the office to seek them, and all wore their party labels lightly. The Republicans simply followed majority opinion in the state. Democrats like Cobb and Gaston were former Whigs, who had hated slavery less than they feared civil war; others were old-family men with a mercantile bias against high tariffs or a gentleman's distaste for Grantism. Many aldermen were of the same stamp. Most were men of substance; in 1875 the twelve members of the board owned property assessed at $769,000. On the local level Republicans and Democrats differed only on specifics; no general issues officially divided them, and certainly none based on class or ethnicity. There were often several tickets in the field, and some candidates usually ran unopposed.[49]

But beneath this familiar surface there was a politics of another kind. The common council, of more than seventy men, was often turbulent and rarely disposed to nonpartisanship. It was elected on a straight party ticket, with the Republicans, more evenly scattered through the city, usually in control. The eminent names among the members were outnumbered by those of liquor dealers, criminal lawyers, small tradesmen and laborers, who often raised embarrassing questions.[50]

This other politics revealed its face most dramatically in 1875, when Councillor Halsey J. Boardman led a Republican revolt against the renomination of Mayor Cobb on the party ticket. Cobb had angered many professionals by ignoring the interests of the gas, contracting, and horsecar companies which habitually did business with the city. Although Boardman agreed in principle with the policy of economy in depression, he attracted many Democrats with his proposal to hire large numbers of unemployed laborers on city-connected projects. This class issue was carried far enough so that the Boston *Herald*, at first sympathetic, accused Boardman's supporters of using "communistic" appeals. Beyond this brief alarm, set off by a fiery circular written by Thomas Riley of the Democratic city committee, many respectable taxpayers saw the specter of lower-class Irish control of the city.[51]

The Irish had been a long time in asserting a claim to political office in Boston: a common councillor in 1859, a handful during the 1860's, an alderman in 1870. But Irish votes had long been important. By the 1870's leadership was developing quickly. The Irish Democratic ward organizations were entirely local, without city-wide unity, but all shared common aims and practices. Vote fraud was an old story in Boston, but none was so flagrant as in the case of ward two in 1872, which at the last moment elected William Gaston over Henry Pierce until the ballots were recounted. Irish politicians, although they had no coherent program, were more frankly political, more frankly interested in city jobs and in the liquor trade than was considered decent. Their language, if not their actions, was often populistic. And they were beginning to assert themselves within the party, to question the leadership of old-line Whig-Democrats; Riley's revolt against Cobb followed immediately on his replacing a Yankee as chairman of the city's Democratic caucus.[52]

The strength of the Democracy was often muted by "nonpartisan" leadership and by the fact that there were in the city "at least 4000 purchasable Democratic votes, and no one knows better where to lay hands on them than the Republican . . . Wirepullers." But as party lines hardened nationally they tightened locally as well. The plurality given Tilden in 1876, followed by the partisan campaign and victory of Mayor Prince, showed clearly what the Democrats could do when aroused. And Prince, as secretary of the national committee, was plainly interested in building the local organization through patronage, much of which went to the Irish. There had been forty-five Irish-born members of the police force in 1871; by the end of the decade there were an even one hundred, a circumstance which aroused the fears of Republicans, "nonpartisans," and nativists alike.[53]

All of these groups united, after one year of Democratic ascendancy, to recall Henry L. Pierce in opposition to Prince. After one of the most bitter battles in the history of the city, Pierce was elected together with a Republican board of aldermen. There was thus a partisan edge to the mayor's request for a bill creating a board of police commissioners.[54]

The Republican majority in the General Court was ready to welcome the mayor's proposals, incorporated into a bill which, in its final form, went considerably beyond previous suggestions. Chapter 224 of the Acts of 1878 created the usual kind of commission, with members nominated by the mayor and approved by the city council. They might be removed by a two-thirds vote in both branches of the council, or for cause by the mayor alone. The council retained control over appropriations, and could fix the maximum number of policemen at each grade. The mayor might take command of the force in emergencies. Otherwise the commission had full and exclusive control over policy, spending, and personnel.[55]

A pioneering provision of the act also authorized the city, on the recommendation of the commission, to grant police pensions amounting to one-third of pay at retirement. Another section enabled the council to delegate full responsibility for the various licenses already administered by the police superintendents. But the most controversial part of the act was mandatory. The opening section required that the city council surrender control over liquor licensing, formerly delegated to the licensing board, to the board of police. There was some administrative logic to this move. But it also enabled Mayor Pierce to dismiss Mayor Prince's appointees on the licensing board. It was designed to make the new Republican police commissioners among the most powerful men in the city.[56]

One of the most striking features of the new police act was the last sentence, which declared that it "shall take effect upon its passage" on May 15. Unlike earlier reforms of the city charter, this one was not subject either to referendum or to conciliar approval. The conduct of the police during the preceding eight years had not been unpopular. The movement for a police commission had been at first designed only to deal with political and administrative problems which were recognized widely and without emotion. But the legislature clearly wanted no official debate on the act as adopted. The provisions, the timing, and the atmosphere of its passage all raised questions about the nature of local politics which went beyond the matter of police.[57]

CHAPTER ELEVEN

Political Breakdown: Charter Reform, 1878-1885

The commission established in 1878 remained in charge of the Boston police department for seven years, during which it satisfied many of the expectations of its supporters. Full-time supervision facilitated a number of administrative reforms, and the return of prosperity allowed a major increase in the force and further experiment in the pacification of the city. But success was not enough to save the commissioners from attack. Some of their problems were fundamentally insoluble. The law expressed an ideal impossible to realize. And social change was not always an ally; as the standard of achievement rose, so did the standard of expectation.

This ancient difficulty was not in itself the major issue. The gap between law and practice existed in part because it was wanted, and since the Civil War it had been growing steadily narrower. The performance of police had been the subject of political agitation since the incorporation of 1822, and the government had always previously managed to contain the varying demands of the citizens. The distinctive feature of the 1880's was loss of this ability to compromise.

The city had never been able to satisfy that mistrust of local government first evidenced in the 1860's. For many taxpayers, by the middle 1880's, the process of alienation was complete. The division of municipal politics along ethnic lines reached a climax at the same time. As a result partisan conflict often paralyzed the government; its members, alternately jealous and afraid of responsibility, no longer presented a united front to their opponents. By 1885, as sixty-three years earlier, the traditional political forms no longer fit the character of the community.

The first three police commissioners were expected to improve the performance of the department and to keep it free from controversy. None of them had any previous experience with police work, but all brought special assets to the job. Colonel Henry S. Russell of Milton, a Democrat, provided the chairmanship with "nonpartisan" respectability. Samuel Spinney of East Boston was a veteran politician, expected to assure Republican influence on the board. James M. Bugbee had served as clerk of committees under several administrations; a prolific member of the Massachusetts Historical Society, he knew as much about the city as any man in the government.[1]

Since the previous license commissioners had already issued the yearly liquor permits, all three new members applied themselves first to the reorganization of the force. The board was free to set rules and practice, and the city council was initially cooperative in passing needed ordinances. Acting together, they began immediately to reclassify offices and to clarify lines of authority in the interest of efficiency.

At headquarters, the chief of police was renamed "superintendent" in the London fashion and ordered to report daily to the board. The deputy superintendent was given immediate control over the former license superintendents, now "inspectors," and their assistants. One new man, at sergeant's rank, was responsible for the newly instituted licensing of street railway employees. In accordance with chapter 98 of the Acts of 1878, the mayor assigned a probation officer to the staff, the first since John Cluer in the 1860's. A third new man was required to investigate all damage claims against the city. The commissioners themselves reinstituted a detective bureau of six "inspectors of police," headed by a chief immediately responsible to the superintendent. A general increase in the number and weight of the departmental rules called for further expansion of headquarters personnel: in addition to five men provided for duty in the corridors, there were two messengers, three clerks at sergeant's rank, a civilian clerk for the commission, and another for the superintendent, the latter two responsible for a total of forty books of records.[2]

Outside of headquarters several classes of policemen appointed by the commissioners actually worked for other officials. A man in each division was assigned to one of the two new state medical examiners, to investigate all suspicious or violent deaths. Eleven worked as guards or watchmen for the school committee, the library, the probate offices, and the county storehouse for confiscated liquors. An ordinance classified these men as "departmental police" and made permanent what had often been temporary duty given regular patrolmen; the commission graded them as "house watchmen," entitled to only two dollars and fifty cents a day. The board also approved one-year warrants for a total of 259 men who worked for private employers. Fully 218, in the year after the Great Strike, were appointed as railroad police, and 41 as specials of other kinds.[3]

The board made only one attempt to reclassify the officers at divisional level; the city council rejected their plan to eliminate the lieutenants and appoint "desk sergeants" at reduced pay. But this defeat was overshadowed by the general personnel shake-up announced on October 21. On that date the two senior captains, Samuel Adams and Cyrus Small, became superintendent and deputy superintendent of the force. Chief Savage was made probation officer, in accordance with his known interests and reputation. Deputy Quinn became a captain, while two captains were demoted, four others retired, and four transferred to other stations. Lieutenants and sergeants were reshuffled in similar fashion. All men below captain's rank had already been given physical examinations; those who failed were pensioned, fired, retired, or given jobs as house watchmen. In all, during its first six months at work, the board of police commissioners promoted 29 men, demoted 21, fired 22, encouraged 11 to resign, transferred 18, and pensioned 31.[4]

New rules were designed to assure that standards were met in the future. Applicants were forbidden to offer petitions or otherwise attempt to use political influence. Promotions were granted only after examination. Prospective sergeants were tested on the police rules and infantry drill; lieutenants and captains were required in addition to answer questions on infantry tactics, state law, city ordinances, and police reports and records. No promotions would be granted, except in extraordinary circumstances, until at least two years after the previous appointment. And in an effort to instill a greater sense of discipline and dignity, all men were ordered to greet their officers with the military salute.[5]

Much of this first year's activity resulted in real improvement. The police department was still an unnecessarily complex organization, but most of the complexity resulted from the council's insistence that some men be paid from the police appropriation without being responsible to or appointed by the board. The commissioners were able to reduce the previous number of departmental police from twenty-eight to eleven, and after the first year they cut the number of railroad police drastically; only five, indeed, were appointed in 1879. In general, the board was interested in simplicity and definition, in eliminating special officers and temporary duty. The great October shake-up, the first manifestation in Boston of what became a traditional device among new heads of police, clearly took courage. "Nonpartisan" personnel policies were not followed to the letter, especially those which concerned the desirable jobs at headquarters. But no alderman denied that within two years "no matter what political backing a man may have, it is impossible for him to get on the force unless he is a first-class man."[6]

Thereafter the commissioners continued to work for improved standards. In 1879 they opened a school for rookie patrolmen; the two weeks of instruction included two daily hours of classroom work, together with regular tours with experienced patrolmen. All men were trained in methods of reviving persons rescued from fire or water; the Massachusetts Hygiene Association, beginning in 1884, taught first-aid techniques. Promotional examinations, in 1883, were made competitive instead of merely qualifying. A state civil service law in 1884 required all applicants to pass tests which demanded competence in reading, writing, and arithmetic through long division. With major additions in 1880 and 1882, the force, thus improved, reached 789 men by 1885.[7]

The desire for economy had been one of the motives for establishing the police commission, and the board was relatively careful with its money. The department was less expensive during 1878-79 than it had been in any year since the annexations of 1873. Thereafter costs rose with the number of men, to approach one million dollars by 1885. Most of the increase went unchallenged, although there were certain embarrassments. The board's own clerk, Francis Goldethwaite, ran off with $775.75 in dog-license receipts in 1882. His successor, Harvey N. Follansbee, followed this example the next year in a defalcation of some importance. Follansbee, a crippled ex-policeman, embezzled nearly $28,000 from the police relief fund, and lost it all in stock speculation before surrendering. The police association vote to absolve his aged father-in-law from his responsibility as bondsman left the fund in ruins. It had been inadequate in any case, and thereafter almost all pensions had to be drawn on the treasury. The commissioners approved them only in the case of the fully disabled or deserving; "routine" service for the required fifteen years was not enough. But the yearly total still exceeded $28,000 in 1885, and demands were increasing.[8]

In such matters, the board often acted against the interests of the men under its authority. But in its other relations, with the public and the government, the commissioners inevitably identified with the force. At least one chairman made it policy to defend all policemen under civil suit, in person and without fee. In recognition of the fact that the men were often called to court during their off-duty hours, the new rules drawn up in 1878 allowed them each a maximum of one witness fee a day. Like the police chiefs before them, board members constantly petitioned the city council for better living quarters in the station houses and suggested other improvements of all kinds, with a success limited only by the government's willingness to act.[9]

Several technical improvements originated with the new board. The department acquired three police ambulances, which proved their worth in carrying several hundred cases to the city hospital each year. A new police station in the growing Back Bay was set up to protect the women and children left unattended all day. The station, number sixteen, was built according to the board's own specifications; solid and defensible, it was considered a model of beauty as well as utility.[10]

One major suggestion, carried over from Chief Savage, was effected finally in 1884. The city council, with the utter lack of debate which had always marked the issue, voted finally to provide the department with sidearms at public expense. The commissioners purchased and distributed eight hundred numbered Smith & Wesson .38 revolvers, and for the first time every member of the patrol force went routinely armed about his beat.[11]

The one major proposal rejected was potentially the most important. The commissioners, having examined its workings in detail, suggested that Boston should adopt a police signal system, pioneered in Chicago, and by 1883 already in use in several other cities. A series of patrol or alarm boxes along the beats had proved the most valuable technical aid to police yet developed. By requiring that patrolmen call the stations at regular intervals, the officers might be sure that the men were actually making the rounds, and at some reasonable pace. Combined with a system of call-wagons, the boxes could revolutionize the process of arrest. Those taking persons in custody might ring for transportation instead of wrestling their prisoners all the way back to the stations. Information about accident, riot, and disaster could be relayed from the beats to the stations, as the logical extension of the existing system of relay from the stations to each other.[12]

The adoption of the alarm system posed a number of problems. Several companies with different models competed for the right of installation, and one of them, as yet untried, was based in Boston. The expense was considerable: over one hundred thousand dollars for installation, and operating costs in the tens of thousands each year. A majority of the special committee appointed to investigate the signals in 1883 reported in favor of immediate adoption, at least on trial, but the aldermen decided to wait.[13]

Rejection of the boxes was a serious rebuff to the commissioners and to the mayor who had favored them. But there was some consolation in the stated grounds for refusal. The four-man minority of the investigating committee pointed out that wicked Chicago had only one patrolman for every thirteen hundred citizens. In contrast,

We have the most efficient and largest police force of any city in the country. Property is well-protected. Riots that call for a large number of police at any point have not occurred in years. There is no section of the city that cannot be travelled at all hours of the night in perfect safety; and we believe that it is good policy to let well enough alone.

Their report, in effect, was endorsed by the full board of aldermen; it was still official opinion that Boston had the finest police in the Union.[14]

The board of police between 1878 and 1885 avoided damaging controversy over most matters outside of the critical areas of vice and politics. While abandoning the forms, it continued the policies by which Chief Savage had quieted the potentially dangerous issue of professional criminality and detective corruption. Six men were named detective "inspectors," and like house watchmen and special police exempted from the physical requirements demanded of the regular force. Three of the six had been "special officers" under Savage; the other three, drawn from the patrol force, replaced a like number who were demoted or fired. An acute new rule declared that frequent changes in detective personnel were to be expected, and that demotions were not reflections on the individuals involved.[15]

The chief inspector, Alfred R. Drew, had a history typical of the experienced hands. He and his brother Alvin had joined the watch in 1849, when they were running an illegal lottery in East Boston, with the help of young Langdon Moore, later the noted burglar. Both brothers became policemen in 1854. Although Alvin was fired in 1857 for reasons the aldermen refused to disclose, Alfred was made a "special officer" in 1870 and had served as a headquarters detective ever since.[16]

But the detectives continued to operate under the stiffer standards set in 1870. It was still policy to arrest, photograph, and "run out" professional criminals upon discovery. Under this system, Boston maintained its immunity from the great robberies of the 1860's. Follansbee's defalcation was apparently the single largest larceny reported; in several years, as previously, more money was listed recovered than stolen.[17]

The official statistics of homicide dropped even more sharply during the 1880's than they had during the previous decade, and the methods of investigation were markedly improved. Only forty-eight cases were reported between 1879 and 1885, as compared with ninety-five between 1871 and 1878. Chapter 200 of the Acts of 1878 required that violent or suspicious deaths be investigated by state medical examiners, professionals who replaced the coroners and could call in scientific help when needed. Policemen were detailed to assist, and when murder was indicated, the courts, district attorney, and regular detectives were called in. The whole procedure, pioneered in Massachusetts, was widely praised and copied elsewhere.[18]

The detective bureau was subject only to the criticism that it had too little to do. The commissioners, barred by ordinance from employing more than six inspectors, circumvented this regulation by using three patrolmen to share the work. In 1884 they petitioned to give these extra men official status at three dollars and fifty cents a day. The city council's police committee approved the measure, and only Democrat J. W. Fraser objected. The whole squad, he charged, had made only 475 arrests the previous year, fewer than any other ten men on the force. These ranged "all the way from suspicion of stealing by boys to stealing property worth two or three hundred dollars." David Barry, in reply, reminded his fellow aldermen that "Today the City of Boston stands the hottest city in the union for a thief . . . the members of the government know that full well." "Laughter" was the only recorded rejoinder to this defense, and the raise went through.[19]

The commissioners had an even easier time in dealing with the hostility of organized charity to the distribution of free soup. The plans already suggested for the treatment of vagrant lodgers went into effect in February 1878. At a cost of four thousand dollars, a place was fitted up to provide both work and sanitary facilities for applicants. Those seeking lodgings were reported to the overseers of the poor, and were required to bathe and to work for two hours before being given space and a meal. With the work test, the number of "lodgers" dropped dramatically, from 63,000 in 1877 to a total of only 1,775 in 1879-80. The threat of a tramp invasion vanished and the political opposition to free soup faded. Despite an antisoup petition in 1884, signed by representatives of virtually every charity in the city, the appropriation passed routinely each year.[20]

The relations between police and labor unions raised a more explosive issue. The police committee, in December of 1878, was asked to allow extra pay to members "who performed extra service in protecting life and property in the recent strike of laborers on Grand Junction Wharf." But members of both parties objected that there were no clear precedents. The only previous antilabor activity had occurred nearly twenty years earlier. In February of 1860, the Lynn authorities had asked for a carload of Boston patrolmen to "preserve order" during a shoemakers' strike because the local militia was untrustworthy. The mayor and the police committee sent the men, but were later rebuked by the board of aldermen on the ground that such free service to other cities was illegal and expensive. Since then the Boston police had never been used in number to deal with strikes either in or out of Suffolk County. But there was a logic to such use. In strikes as in riots, the militia might indeed be "untrustworthy," either out of sympathy or because of the danger of armed violence. Elsewhere the state or district police were beginning to cover labor disturbances, and their example was suggestive.[21]

It was common practice for private employers, such as theater owners, to hire off-duty patrolmen for guard duty, paying them through the city treasury. The members of the city council in 1878-

79 could not recall any case of such employment during a strike, but the police commissioners assured them that there had been several earlier instances. The question had arisen only because an employer attempted to establish a different practice. T. H. Warren & Co., the firm which owned the wharf, had put in a request at station seven, and the captain had sent out a number of patrolmen in the usual way. But the company afterward refused to pay for them, claiming that the protection of property during strikes was or should be an ordinary public duty.[22]

The police committee in effect endorsed this argument by refusing the men extra pay. But the city council was not so easily convinced. Acceptance of the principle involved might lead to an expensive drain on resources. Moreover, the councillors were not willing to antagonize the strikers by comparing their protest to a riot. Wendell Phillips' Labor Party had met some success in the municipal elections of 1869; since then a "People's Ticket," representing many of the same interests, had been one of those sporadically entered in local campaigns, and during the 1870's the government always contained a few men of both parties who were proud to speak for the workingman. Democrat Patrick McGaragle of ward eight denied that the longshoremen had misbehaved or that there was any need for extra protection. Republican Alderman Curtis Guild, editor of the *Commercial Bulletin* and later lieutenant governor of the commonwealth, significantly made the same point. The police commissioners promised that similar cases would not occur again, and for the next several years spent no public money on behalf of strike bound employers.[23]

This debate over the labor issue was unique and quickly settled. The more typical conflicts between the board and the city council were petty, with one struggling to maintain independence, the other trying to assert authority. The most revealing was the faintly comic struggle over amusement licenses. The city marshal, and later the police, had always been part of the licensing process. In an effort to simplify matters the aldermen in 1878 followed the enabling provision of the new police act by surrendering all of their licensing authority to the commissioners. But the business of issuing permits for theatrical and other public exhibitions entailed privileges which were soon missed.[24]

Most members of the city council, serving without pay, were jealous of the minor perquisites of office. Despite traditional criticisms the common councillors regularly voted to issue police badges to each other. The aldermen held dinners and went on excursions, and members of both branches took junketing trips to examine the conduct of public business in New York and other points of interest. So long as they had the licensing power, too, the aldermen were entitled to free passes to all public shows, in order to see that the conditions of license were being observed. It had not been anticipated that this practice might end when the function passed to the board of police.[25]

Alderman Flynn raised the question in October of 1879. He had heard complaints from the mothers of newsboys and bootblacks that their children were wasting their wages on the immodest offerings of the Howard Athaneum, although minors were legally forbidden to attend. Upon going on Saturday night to investigate, he had been refused free admittance, and complained to the board of police. The commissioners retaliated by relaying his protest to the newspapers, which made derogatory remarks about "deadheads" and parasites. This news aroused the entire board of aldermen, and the two other Irish Democrats backed Flynn. On November 3 an order required the police commissioners to enforce the law and apologize. But the commission was defiant; on November 10 it replied that the law was enforced and that there was no need to apologize.[26]

The issue continued to simmer for several years. In 1881, over the objections of the corporation counsel, the aldermen reasserted their control over amusement licensing, despite the charge that they intended merely to blackmail the commissioners into granting free tickets. The next year the ordinance was repealed because it seemed to entail a dangerous responsibility; the aldermen might be held accountable for such disasters as the recent conflagration at the Ring Theater in Vienna. But a new board of aldermen in 1883, as the memory of the Vienna fire faded, passed the ordinance once more, and was again able to inspect places of amusement free of charge.[27]

The affair illustrated the relationship between the city council and the police commission. The councillors were willing to surrender responsibilities but not influence. They had no desire to involve themselves in the muddy business of criminality, but still wished to set policy in such matters as strikes and soup. That left a standing threat of conflict with the board of police, not only over free tickets, but also over affairs of greater political significance.

The three most politically sensitive concerns of local government involved contracts, hiring, and the grant of special privileges. The police signal systems, in the early 1880's, made the department for the first time a major source of contracting profits. The jobs at its disposal had always been among the most coveted in the city, however difficult their use as patronage. No privileges exceeded liquor licenses in importance. While the city council, through the power of appropriation, retained control over major new contracts, the legislature had given the board of police the exclusive right to hire, fire, and grant liquor permits. When the board took an independent stand, there were no quiet channels of protest; the councillors could control the commissioners only through the ultimate power of appointment and removal.

In fact the membership of the board was constantly changed. Former Mayor F. O. Prince returned for three terms between 1879 and 1881 and was able to replace entirely the board appointed by his Republican predecessor. When Bugbee's term ran out in 1879 Prince named Henry Walker, who had served him as license commissioner in 1877. Spinney, whose appointment expired in 1880, and Russell, who resigned at the same time, were succeeded by T. J. Gargan, another of Prince's license commissioners and a former overseer of the poor, and by E. J. Jones, former head of the state constabulary. Mayor Prince retired in 1881, to be followed by a Republican, City Physician Samuel Abbott Green, who fired the entire board of police. In their stead he named Brigadier Nathaniel Wales of the state militia, T. L. Jenks, a former alderman and director of the city's East Boston Ferry, and Benjamin D. Burley, former superintendent of intelligence offices at police headquarters. The next mayor, Democrat Albert Palmer, replaced Burley with Michael Curran, who had had no previous experience in public office. Palmer was defeated in the 1883 election by Republican Augustus P. Martin, but Martin was unable to get his nominations approved by the city council, so that the commission achieved a brief and precarious stability.[28]

Usually the board was balanced among men with military or police experience, lawyers, and politicians. While most of the commissioners were competent and respected, none was really distinguished. Only Russell was a gentleman by Back Bay standards, and he suffered the most difficulty in winning approval from the council. Resented by both parties as an outsider, he was confirmed by a bare two-vote margin. The council wanted pliability in certain matters of importance even more than nominal party allegiance; and its demands were difficult to meet. Significantly, no men were reappointed, and only three ever achieved any other city office after their service on the commission.[29]

The battle over the signal system helped to shorten the official life of the board members. When the commissioners reported in 1883 that the system should be introduced into Boston, they in effect endorsed the tested Gamewell devices, which the majority of the conciliar finance committee also favored, perhaps in response to outside pressures. But resistance developed along party lines. The minority Democrats urged a trial of competitive devices; and one of them, Felix Strange, claimed to have personally inspired the invention of the rival Wilson System.[30]

Much of this difficulty, in 1883 and 1884, resulted from divided authority. Republicans controlled the board of police during this period; Democrats, for the first time in history, dominated both branches of the city council. The commission pressed for immediate adoption of the signal devices, which only Gamewell was ready to supply, and refused any other system. But the council would not provide the necessary appropriation, and it prevented Mayor Martin, in 1884, from choosing a new Republican commissioner. The result was three years of deadlock and inaction.[31]

The police commissioners took the initiative in the political battles over appointments. The board's rules were strict, but left free play in the matters of transfers, headquarters jobs, and promotions for those qualified. But the law, which reserved personnel policy entirely to the commission, only prevented the city council from interfering regularly or openly. Councillors still had informal means of influencing the board of police. Their power over salaries could win concessions elsewhere. The ability to set the number of appointments at each grade provided the same kind of leverage. The council could abolish posts, thus firing incumbents, just as the commissioners could redefine functions so as to establish jobs. And when the commissioners were especially balky, their actions led not only to angry letters and debate but to well-publicized fisticuffs.[32]

The bitterness involved in liquor licensing overshadowed all other battles. The concentration of authority in the agency in charge of enforcement also focused pressure upon it, and vice control concerned a far greater number of private citizens that the other issues which divided the city council and the board of police.

The decade of the 1880's, like that of the 1870's, was a period of declining intemperance. The figures for drunk arrests in the state as a whole were rising, as smaller places increased their police forces. But the increase of police in Boston had no such effect. Arrest statistics fluctuated rather than moving steadily in one direction. The 17,360 persons charged with drunkenness in the relatively heavy year of 1880-81 represented a lower ratio to population than existed in the 1860's.[33]

The state continued to tinker with its law. In 1880, following the demands of most experts in the field of criminal and charitable work, the General Court moved hesitantly in the direction of reform. Those convicted twice in twelve months might be sentenced to full-year terms while those guilty of rare or single offenses were let off with one-dollar fines and no payments of costs. But the new law was a failure. Few judges actually imposed the one-year terms, which in any case were not long enough to satisfy reformers, who wanted open-ended sentences. The police commissioners complained that the fines were too slight to deter. Perhaps more important, the officers were less hesitant to arrest when the penalty was light, so that arrest totals mounted. The legislature in 1881 added the payment of costs to the fine, thus retreating to the previous pattern of definite but light punishment, without reformation.[34]

There were no important changes in the license laws or their enforcement during the first half of the 1880's. Successive boards of police followed somewhat different policies, especially in the vigor with which they pursued unlicensed places. There were above 700 arrests in 1878-79 and in 1884-85, but only 90 in 1880-81. More important than these variations was the policy, inaugurated by the old board of license commissioners in 1877, of granting permits to the majority of applicants. Beginning in 1878-79, when 2,126 places were given licenses, the total mounted steadily, usually by about 200 a year. Legality was established as normative, and so thoroughly that the commissioners were able to double the fees in 1883 without any drop in demand. The biggest police problems were sales on Sunday or to minors by those already licensed. On the average, slightly more than one hundred hearings a year were held as a result of complaints about such violations, which private citizens reported more frequently than unlicensed sales.[35]

The official figures do not indicate that vice was increasing. But they were not enough to silence criticism. The popular attitude toward the liquor trade was more resentful than that of most local politicians. State elections indicated that only a small minority of citizens were interested principally in prohibition and attendant reforms. But the annual votes under the local option section of the license law showed that a substantial minority of citizens, when not asked to abandon other political interests, were willing to prohibit sales in Boston. Some 13,850 of 37,230 voters favored prohibition in 1883. The number who wished a stringent licensing policy must have been greater. Both groups were too large for Republican politicians to ignore.[36]

Republican resentment of the policies of the board of police was most acute between 1879 and 1881, under the commissioners chosen by Mayor Prince. The crucial political issue was who received the permits and under what obligations. In 1881, in control of both branches of the city council, the Republican party managers determined at least to exercise their power of investigation.

Jesse Gove, the party boss and alderman of East Boston, in May called for the removal of two of the three board members. Major Jones, he pointed out, was the largest bail-bond commissioner in the city, a circumstance which created a possible conflict of interest, for police officers might recommend his services. T. J. Gargan had been absent from his post for sixty days because of illness, and the law demanded full-time service. A majority of aldermen agreed and appointed a committee to investigate the conduct of the board generally.[37]

A series of eight hearings stretched over as many months; since publicity was Gove's only purpose at first he had no reason to hurry, and he found that Chairman Henry Walker was a perfect witness, frank and defiant. It was true, Walker stated, that he had issued no special orders to enforce the liquor laws; reverting to the older theory of indirect administration, he merely waited for citizens to complain. He admitted also that, because of a belief in the inevitability of vice, he was personally in favor of licensed prostitution and gambling, a conclusion never before voiced by a public official in Boston. As to the charge that he had licensed the resorts of criminals, Walker asserted simply that these, too, had a right to some quiet place of refuge, and that "they cannot go to Parker's."[38]

This was sensational testimony. Every organized charity in Boston responded with petitions calling for the removal of Walker and his colleagues. The strategy of delay was rewarded in December when Republican Samuel Abbott Green defeated Democrat Albert Palmer in the contest for mayor. Green's victory threatened the commissioners with more than embarrassment. Formal ouster proceedings had never before been instituted against the members of any Boston commission. But the majority of the aldermanic investigating committee issued a report in late December, just in time for action by the new administration, which called for the firing of the entire board of police.[39]

The Democrats responded with a storm of objections. The aldermen had known about Major Jones's bonding business at the time of his appointment, and he was ready to give it up if necessary. Mr. Gargan had recovered his health. And the charges against Chairman Walker proved only that he was "a liberal gentleman"; the board could not be held responsible for the inevitable. The minority attacked the procedures of the committee, pointing to the testimony of obvious malcontents and the lack of opportunity for rebuttal. Most significant, also, Mayor Green was warned that the removal of Gargan from the highest post ever held by an Irishman in Boston would be considered "an insult to every Catholic . . . in the city."[40]

These arguments did not move the mayor, who replaced the three commissioners with a Republican board. But the victory for the party, and for the reformers who had backed it, was short-lived. The drastic means employed left political scars, and under existing law there was no way of assuring that the Republicans could permanently control the police, or that their interests were in fact compatible with those of their allies.[41]

The most potent political threat to the board of police was not in fact the city council or even the local party out of power, but that influential class of citizens which had felt left out of politics for at least a generation, which could hope for satisfaction only in the General Court. Their temptation to appeal to the legislature, as for the Republicans, was heightened by the fact that Boston by 1885 was a two-party city, in which the majority of voters were Democrats and the majority of Democrats were Irish.

Part of the mounting criticism of the police commission was paradoxically the result of improved conditions. The establishment of license as normative meant that many disreputable places received the stamp of official approval. And while the statistics indicated a relative decline in intemperance, there were many citizens more interested in absolutes. If drunkenness was less worrisome than formerly, it was still a major problem; and to the extent that it was being controlled, there was more time to work in areas previously overlooked.

The New England Society for the Suppression of Vice, formed in 1878 as a branch of Anthony Comstock's New York organization, was at first interested primarily in indecent publications, and had police support not only in pursuing distributors but in securing a new law to make prosecution easier. But very shortly it began to concentrate more heavily on gambling, which had not earlier aroused much local concern. This new effort in an area for which the police were officially responsible criticized by implication the entire machinery of local law enforcement. An unusually impressive list of officers gave the society weight; the leading philanthropist Robert Treat Paine was a member, as were Boston's most respected ministers, E. E. Hale and Phillips Brooks, together with the presidents of Dartmouth, Yale, Amherst, and other colleges.[42]

The newspapers were also beginning to express an interest in gambling. The Boston *Herald* occasionally printed articles about gilded vice, featuring faro palaces with liveried Negro attendants much like those described in the 1850's. More alarming was the apparent increase in betting among the lower and especially the middle classes. The Louisiana Lottery was regularly advertised in Boston. There were flourishing pools on horse racing and baseball games, together with "policy shops" run largely by West End Negroes. The society warned businessmen that other places, with complex games and tables modeled after the more expensive resorts, were patronized by their clerks and other white-collar employees. "Betting has only been tolerated," the *Herald* wrote in 1878, "because heretofore it has not been carried to excess by those who can ill afford to lose wages." And after that year the agitation against it was focused more clearly than ever on the board of police. Since gambling rooms always provided liquor as well as betting facilities, the new police control over licensing made the commissioners doubly responsible.[43]

Early in 1882 a second reform organization, the Citizens' Law and Order League of Massachusetts, joined the New England Society for the Suppression of Vice. The league was designed to supplement official enforcement of the vice laws, especially the license act. The prosecution of liquor offenders had been a problem for a generation and more because of a notable gap in procedure. Individual policemen brought cases to the lower courts and conducted them in person. But when these were appealed, and legal problems arose, the police, unready to pursue them, dropped the charges or placed them "on file." Some of these cases were turned over to the district attorney of Suffolk County, but his office was not organized for independent or aggressive action and was unwilling or unable to handle large numbers of liquor cases. As a result, when the state constabulary stopped prosecuting in the middle of the 1870's, there was a great drop not in cases initiated but in cases brought to verdicts. The league's own paid agents and lawyers, in the first months of 1882, prosecuted sixty cases on their own, in and near Boston, and obtained verdicts in forty.[44]

Both the league and the society were at first enthusiastic about the police commissioners appointed by Mayor Green. The first annual report of League Secretary Edwin L. Dudley, in 1882, boasted that after one year of activity, partly because of police cooperation, sales to minors had been cut by fully 90 per cent, and Sunday sales by over a third. The society, with only one paid agent, was more dependent on the commissioners and acted simply by bringing suspected places and practices to their attention. Its annual report noted in the same year that the board at its suggestion had conducted a notable crackdown on gambling.[45]

But both groups were soon disillusioned. The society in 1884 reported the need for "a radical and thorough reform of our police system." During the previous year its agent had collected a list of forty gambling and policy shops, and one hundred rooms or places used for other immoral purposes. The commissioners had largely ignored the lists, and the few places raided had been shut down for one day only. Without official cooperation the agent had been reduced to pleading with the owners of the real estate involved, a procedure which resulted in a total of five shutdowns or evictions. The Law and Order League, less dependent, was more successful in 1883, conducting 421 prosecutions and winning 259 convictions. But in 1884 the league's agents were harassed by denunciation in the city council and by a series of inconclusive actions for perjury. The number of prosecutions and guilty verdicts dropped markedly, to 177 and 131, respectively. Crippled for lack of official help, the league, too, by late 1884, was calling for a major change in the management of police.[46]

During the same brief period in which local reformers passed through this cycle of hope and disillusion, the local Republicans were also concerned about the future of the board of police. Mayor Green served only a single term, in 1882. That November the hated renegade Benjamin Butler was elected governor, running this time as a Democrat opposed to the liquor laws. In December Albert Palmer, a Butler protégé, defeated Green. The entire Democratic slate of aldermen was swept in with Palmer, and for the first time that party controlled the common council. Palmer appointed an Irish Democrat to the police commission, leaving it in Republican control, but by only two to one. The Republicans aroused themselves in 1883 to defeat Butler on the state level, and in a record turnout elected businessman Augustus P. Martin to the mayoralty. But the common council prevented Martin from appointing a member of the Law and Order League to the police commission. The significant change in the conciliar majority clearly indicated that it would be only a matter of time before the Democrats again controlled the police as well as the rest of the government.[47]

The intransigence of the city council gave point to the complaints of a third group. Eighteen eighty-four was the year of the Mugwump, the one in which Massachusetts passed its first civil service law, a measure which included the police. The same interest in governmental efficiency demanded reforms in the city charter which would increase the power of the mayor at the expense of the council. Mayor Martin, in June, appointed a three-man commission to draft comprehensive revisions.[48]

The December elections of 1884 provided the final impetus to this gathering movement for change. During the 1870's Boston's Democrats had been divided into two wings, Irish and Yankee. The balance, already tipping, was decisively upset by Governor Butler's appointment of Irishmen to all eight Suffolk County seats on the Democratic state committee. The Democratic candidate for mayor in 1883 was Alderman Hugh O'Brien. And in 1884 O'Brien was elected, together with the now usual majorities in both branches of the city council. While the new city administration prepared to take office in January and the rising boss P. J. Maguire moved to solidify Irish control of the local Democracy, the General Court undertook to strengthen Yankee supervision of the city itself.[49]

The first of three bills designed to limit the powers of the council was aimed at its fiscal authority. With the recovery from depression Boston had begun in the 1880's to boost its spending and tax rates; the latter, in 1884, jumped $3.50 to a record $17 per $1,000. Chapter 178 of the Acts of 1885 limited the Boston tax rate to $9 per $1,000 for current expenses, exclusive of the payments on the debt and the state tax. This was discriminatory legislation, applying to Boston alone. And it was stringent enough so that all new proposals in practice would require special exemptions, making the legislature an appropriating agency more important than the city council.[50]

A new city charter met the suggestions of Mayor Martin's commission and of virtually all municipal reformers by providing for a clear separation of powers at the expense of the council. Chapter 266 gave the mayor the right to veto separate items in appropriation bills, and made him solely responsible for all executive departments. Chapter 178 had already limited the council's power *over* taxation and appropriations; chapter 266 virtually limited its authority *to* taxation and appropriations, as the councillors were forbidden to send orders and instructions to administrative officers.[51]

This new charter passed the House by a nearly unanimous vote. No one denied the need for economy. And it was widely recognized that a mayor like O'Brien, who lacked the personal and social authority of his predecessors some generations before, needed the ex officio power to govern. The most bitter resistance was offered not to these more sweeping provisions but to a bill which transferred the appointment of police commissioners from the mayor to the governor and allowed them to pay for ordinary expenses through direct requisitions on the city treasury. For more than twenty years the police had been symbols on the one hand of local corruption and on the other of local independence, and Boston was unwilling to surrender them.[52]

While the Law and Order League and the Society for the Suppression of Vice had suggested the new metropolitan police bill, passage depended ultimately on the Republican majority. Yet only three Boston newspapers supported the bill and even Jesse Gove opposed it, backed by at least one-third of the Republicans as well as the Democrats in the city council. The legislature, as in the 1860's, was not inclined to flaunt lightly the opinion of the city. The battle, in consequence, stretched not only through the usual weeks of hearings but through an unusual four-month floor fight.[53]

The proponents of the bill agreed, as they had since 1863, that the officers themselves were "the finest." Even ex-Mayor Martin, who had been shocked on first visiting the policemen's ball to observe the men waltzing with cigars in their teeth, agreed that they were a well-chosen group. Representative Chamberlain suggested that "Nine out of ten of the Boston Police want this bill passed." In any case, since the Civil Service Act of 1884, the issue of political appointments was less stressed in public than violation of the vice laws, blamed on pressures from the common council.[54]

The opponents of the bill, marshaled by Representative Murphy of Boston, also relied upon traditional arguments, quoting De Tocqueville, denouncing utopians, and citing the deficiencies of the state constabulary and the old New York Police Commission. The appeal to localism and democracy had sufficed in the past, and experienced reporters expected Murphy to block passage in the House. Their opinion was apparently confirmed when the majority of the committee conducting hearings on the bill reported against it in March.[55]

But conditions had changed since the 1860's. The city council had been denounced before, but the city council had not before been Irish or Democratic. The state Republicans had coveted the power of the police before, but the police had not before been the liquor-licensing authority for the city. No legislator, in debate, spoke simply in terms of partisan advantage. But there were appeals to fear and bigotry on the floor, and there was no masking of ethnic and political jealousies in the corridors. Pat Maguire, in public and apparently in liquor, continued his purge of Yankee members by reading long-time Common Council President Edward Jenkins out of the Democratic party. Mayor O'Brien appointed an Irishman to the police commission, tipping the political balance. And on April 16, as the common council engaged in its worst name-calling row in memory, the House of Representatives surprised observers by voting 108 to 81 in favor of considering the police bill.[56]

Although three-quarters of Boston's representatives were opposed, this first vote was a clear sign of defeat. Murphy continued to lead a desperate parliamentary resistance through every possible maneuver including a filibuster. But the House passed a gag rule on June 9. The Senate passed the bill on June 11. And with the governor's signature the metropolitan police measure became chapter 338 of the Acts of 1885.[57]

In 1885 as in 1822, dissatisfaction with "the government of the police" sparked a movement to change the traditional form of the city government as a whole. The new act, together with the tax limit and charter, created a new relationship among the city, the state, and the citizens, the meaning of which was not at once understood. Part of the confusion resulted from the mixture of motives responsible for the reform. Boston had been incorporated on a positive note, in order to increase efficiency, to stimulate achievement, and to recognize the fact that it was already a city. Some of the same sentiments were involved in the Acts of 1885, but they were clouded by bitterness and bigotry. The new charter was the work of a minority; it was not clear whether it would fit the needs of reformers, Republicans, or the rest of the inhabitants.

After a few years of experience it became in fact apparent that the changes were not as radical as either friends or opponents had expected. The tacit division of power between Republicans and Democrats, state and city, was never complete, and it had the advantages of a compromise; it contained chronic tensions not formerly eased within the framework of local politics. While the mayor's new authority was accepted, legal curbs on the city council did not silence the interests it represented, and the legislature was unable to prevent substantial increases in municipal spending. Boston was politically vigorous enough to assert itself regardless of forms: "The nature of things sets limits to theories. In theory the General Court creates cities; in fact cities grow . . . ."[58]

CHAPTER TWELVE

Epilogue and Conclusion

In practice, after 1885, state direction of the Boston police force did not prove an unnatural break with established tradition. The department had never been controlled by any single set of interests. The functions of "police" as defined in the 1820's had been almost entirely local. But the commonwealth had never surrendered its constitutional or practical influence in the affairs of its capital. Throughout the nineteenth century the character of police work was continually revised in response to the experience of other cities, the needs of the municipality, and the requirements of the state. The development of other agencies reduced the originally dominant involvement of the police in municipal administration. At the same time the department assumed the responsibilities of the citizens and other agents for the enforcement of state law. Conflict often accompanied these changes. Some tension was simply inherent in the use of force, and would continue. Some resulted from a gap between ideals and practice. But by the last quarter of the century an equilibrium had been reached. It was already apparent what the police could do and what they could not; after 1885 the department would develop along lines already determined.

The city government's original concept of police involved duties inherited from the selectmen and other town officers. The city marshal, who assumed these functions in 1823, was principally concerned with municipal administration. His office, before and after its incorporation with other agents of police, provided an expedient means of dealing with a variety of urban problems. The widespread duties, reaching into many areas of local government, made it inconceivable that any outside authority should be involved. The enforcement of criminal law, in the early nineteenth century, was still the responsibility of aggrieved citizens, or of the sheriffs, courts, and constables created by the commonwealth. Much of it was in fact ignored, and an attempt to apply it could be politically disruptive as well as physically dangerous.

But the employment of police in municipal administration was governed not by theory but by convenience. Boston was a conservative city, rarely innovating bold projects or new techniques. But it was always well managed, with an unusually high tax rate and proportionally superior services. The police were valued especially for the flexibility which made them adaptable to new demands. But when better machinery was developed the government did not hesitate to transfer their responsibilities. The creation of the sewer, health, street, and building departments all diminished the role of the police in local administration.

The lessening of such uses coincided with an increase in their use to "maintain order." The local authorities never denied their responsibility in this matter. Marshals and watchmen were always charged, in some degree, with keeping the streets clear of human as well as material disorder and obstruction, a task which necessarily called for the invocation of law and force and which became more aggressive as the concept of order itself expanded.

In contrast to the business of municipal administration, in which other agencies progressively assumed the functions of police, the business of maintaining order was one in which the police progressively assumed the functions of the citizens. As long as the community was small there were sanctions more powerful than law, and when the law was invoked, the sheriffs, constables, and courts relied in practice on the initiative of the inhabitants in making complaints and swearing out warrants. Boston was physically compact, with settled traditions, comparatively easy to govern and to police. But as the city developed, problems arose which the community was unable to meet in traditional fashion. The creation of a professional, preventive police was both a result and a cause of the inability of citizens to deal with these matters by themselves.

Riot, one of the first problems recognized as beyond control, dramatized the need for force. The leaders of government were firmly set against popular violence as a means of political and social protest, except in the explosive case of slavery. After the creation of the new police in 1838 only the great Draft Riot of 1863 proved impossible to contain.

The issue of felonious criminality was more complex. Those mad or desperate offenses which accounted for most serious crime were not proportionately on the increase during the nineteenth century. But the citizens were progressively worse equipped to protect themselves from, or to punish, criminals; and there was a rise in sophisticated crimes for profit, with which only a few were able to deal privately. Both conditions contributed to the demand for an aggressive police. So did the growing concept that the state itself had an interest in preventing criminality, greater than that of injured individuals.

A third general social problem was continuously demanding. It is impossible to assess accurately the changing incidence of the disorderly behavior of which drunkenness was the center and symbol. But it is clear that such behavior became ever less tolerable. The demands of an interdependent urban economy made drunkenness more disruptive than it had been under the town. Tighter standards of middle-class behavior, coupled with the reform movements that began in the 1830's, made it more easily condemned. As Boston became a city of strangers, the ineffectiveness of the older sanctions was widely recognized.

A continuing conflict over the proper enforcement of the laws complicated the use of police to arrest for these misdemeanors. Whether drunkenness was regarded as a sin, or later as a disease, reformers never doubted that it was a basic social evil or that morality was properly the concern of legal authority. Before the 1830's the law in many matters was regarded as the expression of an ideal. But the creation of a strong police raised the exciting possibility that the ideal might be realized, that morality could be enforced and the state made an instrument of social regeneration. Local authorities briefly tried and then rejected the experiment. But even after 1850, with conservatives in almost continuous control of Boston, reformers continued to press the issue and to focus their hopes on the legislature. For a brief period in the 1860's the commonwealth repeated the experiment and then discovered that prohibition was tolerable only when evaded.

Conflict over the liquor laws never stopped, but it eased significantly after the Civil War. However they differed with reformers over the existence of vice, the men who governed Boston were always concerned with its social effects. As dominant opinion in the city became more disapproving of public misbehavior, the effort to control disorder involved an increasing intolerance of moral offenses. With the demands of law eased, the city accepted the duty of execution. By 1885 the police were primarily agents of law enforcement, and disputes centered around matters of degree rather than of principle.[1]

Apart from the issue of vice control, and more briefly the reclamation of fugitive slaves, the development of police authority was not usually in controversy. The acts of policemen might be resented individually and specifically, and the marshal or chief was not usually popular: no head of the department from 1822 to 1878 ever held any other office after leaving it. But there was agreement on the need for strength, and no resentment of the general exercise of power.

The agreement in part resulted from the fact that the growth of police was not in itself responsible for any major change in the conception of what the state could do. The criminal and administrative codes expanded enormously; Governor Butler, in 1883, charged with some reason that the manufacture of offenses had become "a state industry." But this multiplication reflected a growth in complexity rather than in severity; the state in the eighteenth century was theoretically more restrictive than in the nineteenth. The real change was in practice and attitudes. The increase of police simply made feasible the expectation that most codes would be enforced, and not indirectly by the citizens but directly by agents of authority.[2]

Furthermore, the development of the department did not add to the powers of peace officers as individuals. There was a notable increase in the number of statutory cases in which the police could make arrests without written warrant. But in some ways these laws limited personal discretion. The old statutes defining the powers of the watch and various other officers were broad enough to fit most cases, at least under the section dealing with "suspicious persons." The judiciary held the key to the exercise of legal force, and it maintained that the discretion given peace officers was broad and ancient under the common law. The arming of patrolmen, together with increased numbers and improved communications, did give the officers a decided physical advantage. But at the same time the democratization of politics and the press opened channels of protest against abuses.

Above all, the police were never a group apart. Only in a few matters, notably detective corruption, did they have a distinct and separate interest. The fee system, which had created resentments earlier, was controlled once the department was professionalized. The police in Boston, unlike those in other countries, and the constables, did not serve directly as agents of the courts, and their efforts as individuals often softened the formal demands of justice. The variety of their functions, most of which were innocuous and some humane, kept them from being identified exclusively with force. And it was the conscious policy of both state and city, through formal requirements of residence and such informal requirements as fatherhood, to keep the officers close to the citizens.

The change from municipal to state control in 1885 made some difference. The new commissioners abandoned such locally popular functions as the distribution of free soup and assumed such unpopular one as the protection of property during strikes. They also broke the political deadlock over such expensive improvements as the signal system. But fundamentally the force remained unchanged, charged with the same duties, recruited from the same classes, subject to the same pressures. There was no diminution in the purely municipal functions, already in essence reduced to two; the department continued to serve as the "eyes and ears" of others, reporting problems when found, and it remained responsible for traffic control, directly and through the licensing power.[3]

Nor was there any important addition to the business of law enforcement. The city had already accepted its responsibility for controlling vice through license and had succeeded in licensing the great majority of liquor dealers. There was no immediate drop in the number of permits granted and no change in the more general policy of arrest. The police were still concerned only with the regulation of public behavior, and not with any more fundamental reform.[4]

The experience of state control merely demonstrated in Boston what other cities had already learned, that political change at the top was not enough either to solve problems built into the structure of American law or to upset the complex relations between police and public. The legislature had intended no such revolution. The officers, and the commissioners, were still citizens of Boston. The city retained formal and informal controls over their actions, and the state, while more remote, was neither oppressive nor unresponsive. The police department was in fact what it was designed to be, simply a useful tool of government. So long as government itself was still regarded as a tool of the people, the citizens remained confident of their ultimate ability to use both as desired.

APPENDIX I

A Note on Criminal Statistics

The criminal statistics of nineteenth-century Boston and Massachusetts are in some cases unreliable and in most, incomplete. But it is possible to make some conclusions on the basis of the available figures, and it may be possible, with further study, to make more.

A. The regularly issued sources include the following.

1. City Doc. no. 5 (1851), *Annual Report of the Police Department of the City of Boston by the City Marshal,* and its successors. Cited in the text by date issued, which usually follows the year covered. Except for a single report issued in 1834 as Common Council Doc. no. 9, and a fragmentary report in 1849, the series begins in 1851, always included in the City Documents until after 1885, when it was published first among the Documents of the House of Representatives and then, beginning in 1894, among the Public Documents. The reports include a full summary of the causes of arrest, with the number of males, females, residents, nonresidents, and often citizens and foreigners arrested. Two of these summaries are appended as Tables A and B, for the years 1856 and 1884-85. In all years, also, the police reports include the figures for money reported stolen and money recovered. The former figure is probably unreliable, as neither the citizens nor the police were interested in making it accurate, and there was no way of checking it. The third set of statistics generally but not always available in the police reports is an estimate of the number of illegal establishments in the city, unlicensed liquor shops, gambling rooms, and houses of ill fame, all reported by the police captains. There are clear reasons for suspecting these figures, but they were never challenged, and were often cited by reformers. The police chiefs rarely boasted of a decrease or covered up an increase, but simply held that they were not responsible for them.

2. House Doc. no. 20 (1868), *Annual Report of the Constables of the Commonwealth for the Year Ending December 31, 1867,* and its successors. Cited in the text by year issued. From 1868 to 1871 these are included in the House Documents, thereafter in the Public Documents. They include arrest statistics and figures for stolen and recovered property, by county.

225

226   APPENDIX I

Unlike the municipal police reports, they do not include estimates of illegal establishments, as the state police were considered responsible for suppressing them.

3. Senate Doc. no. 1 (1833), *Report of the Attorney General to the Legislature of Massachusetts, January 2, 1833,* and its successors. Cited in the text by year covered rather than year issued. Before 1860 these are included sometimes among the House Documents, sometimes among the Senate Documents, except between 1843 and 1848, when the office was abolished. After 1860 they are regularly included among the Public Documents, although in abbreviated form they continue also in the House Documents. The reports include summaries of higher court cases in which the attorney general was involved, including all capital cases. Appendices contain an abstract of the cases handled by the district attorneys, separately compiled by the secretary of the commonwealth during the time when the attorney generalship was abolished. Later appendices include a full abstract of all criminal cases in the lower courts, by county.

4. Senate Doc. no. 1 (1830), *Report of the Inspectors of the State Prison for the Year Ending the 30th of September, 1830,* and its successors. Published in the Senate Documents, and after 1858 in the Public Documents. Includes number, county residence, offenses, and sentences of prisoners.

5. House Doc. no. 12 (1842), *Abstract of Returns of the Keepers of Jails and Overseers of Houses of Correction, for the Year Ending November 1, 1841,* and its successors. Compiled by the secretary of the commonwealth. Published sometimes in the House Documents, sometimes in the Senate Documents, after 1858 in the Public Documents. The abstract contains, in simplified form, the number, offenses, and sex of persons committed to the various reformatory and penal institutions. Some of the same material, before 1843, is included in scattered reports published in the House Documents, beginning with H. R. 50 (no title; 1827), which summarizes the statistics from 1821 to the date of issuance.

6. Common Council Doc. no. 23 (1837), *Report of the Inspectors of Prisons,* and its successors. Included, from 1837 on, in the City Documents, and issued twice yearly, this has an advantage over the abstract above in that it includes a full rather than a simplified list of offenses for those committed to the Boston institutions.

7. *The Annual Registry of Births, Marriages, and Deaths in Massachusetts for the Year Ending December 31, 1850,* and its successors. Cited in the text by year covered rather than by year issued. Published separately each year, in Boston, as are several of the reports above; also included, after 1858, in the Public Documents. The relevant material for criminological purposes, the number of homicides reported, is summarized for the

period before 1850 in Lemuel Shattuck, *Bills of Mortality, 1810-1849* (Boston, 1893). Unfortunately the official statistics are hardly reliable, at least to 1855. For reasons unexplained there is a dramatic and statistically improbable rise in the totals beginning in 1855, and afterwards the registry figures differ somewhat from those of the state medical examiners. There is no way of checking the methods employed, but there is no reason to doubt that the figures after 1855 were compiled in some uniform way, and are fairly accurate at least in relation to each other.

B. In addition to the regular reports, there are several sources which provide otherwise unobtainable material, or evaluate and correlate the official statistics in various ways. *Plain Facts Addressed to the Inhabitants of Boston on the City Expenses for the Support of Pauperism, Vice, and Crime* (Boston, 1834), published by the council of the Massachusetts Temperance Society, contains statistics of the police court and reformatory institutions not officially available. *The Speech of Francis W. Emmons . . . on Regulating the Sale of Alcohol* (Boston, 1848) contains some fragmentary statistics on arrests by the Boston watch. Several quarterly watch reports were published in the Boston *Herald* in 1853, on January 12, April 5, July 7, and October 3. Public Doc. no. 19 (1864), *First Annual Report of the Board of State Charities,* and its successors, deserves special mention. These reports were published in the Public Documents until the board was split into several agencies in 1878. That part of the report numbered separately as the *Report of the Secretary* includes a wealth of tables, historical comparisons, and comments on the law and penal institutions.

C. There are, finally, three secondary sources which deal with late nineteenth-century criminal statistics.

An article by Waldo L. Cook, "Murders in Massachusetts," in the American Statistical Association *Publications,* new series, vol. III (September 1893), pp. 357-378, rather naïvely traces the decline in the murder rate between 1871 and 1891 through a decline in indictments.

Another article by Frederick G. Pettigrove, "Statistics of Crime in Massachusetts," in the American Statistical Association *Publications,* new series, vol. III (March 1892), pp. 1-17, is more sophisticated. Dealing with the 1880's alone, and taking into account the increased numbers and activities of police, Pettigrove concludes, on p. 10, that serious crime was diminishing.

A more scholarly and ambitious undertaking is Sam Bass Warner's *Crime and Criminal Statistics in Boston* (Boston, 1934), the second volume of a survey of crime and criminal justice in Boston conducted by the Harvard Law School. Although the study deals primarily with the 1920's and early

1930's, some comparisons stretch back into the 1880's, and one to the 1860's. And it is doubly useful in providing a guide to the use of criminal statistics and in providing some perspective on the figures for the early and middle years of the nineteenth century.

In general Warner's conclusions are compatible with a projection of trends noted in the text. If the metropolitan region rather than Suffolk County is used for purposes of comparison, a technique not possible but theoretically desirable because of suburban growth, the total number of prosecutions per 100,000 inhabitants decreased considerably between 1883 and 1931 (Warner, *Crime and Criminal Statistics,* p. 19). Even when Suffolk County alone is used, the same pacification is evident in a sharply declining rate of arrests for assault and battery (*ibid.,* pp. 24-25). The homicide rate also probably dropped slightly in the same period (pp. 20-23). Arrests for drunkenness, despite extreme variations, were slightly lower at the end of the period than at the beginning (p. 27), although there was a considerable increase in police. An eightfold increase in prosecutions for gambling, and a marked increase in those for sexual offenses (p. 26), reflect new concerns resulting from heightened standards of propriety. But in general, if drunkenness and motor vehicle offenses are omitted, the figures between 1883 and 1931 (p. 27) held relatively steady, indicating that the police in the former year were already doing about all that was wanted or expected.

Warner's figures re-emphasize that the crucial developments in the character of criminality and in the official effort to control it occurred sometime in the unstudied period before the 1880's. The figures for this period, because of incompleteness, different base years, and different schemes of classification, are difficult to interpret. The statistics alone, except those relating to stolen property, do not, unless used with other sources, indicate such changes as the sophistication of professional crime: "burglary," for example, or "breaking and entering," may be an offense committed by a countryman with an axe or by a master craftsman with a kitful of delicate tools. And all statistics, again excepting the figures for stolen property, relate only to arrests or convictions, and do not pretend to measure the actual incidence of crime or illegal behavior. But there is some relation between the two. And by introducing a variable not usually included, the number of police as well as the number of prosecutions per 100,000 population, it is possible to offer two tentative general conclusions.

First, through the middle of the nineteenth century there was a sharply positive correlation between increases in police and increases in total arrests and prosecutions. The heavy case load of arrests per individual policeman indicates that the officers were straining to keep up with criminality as defined by contemporary social standards, and that the actual incidence of such criminality was much higher than shown. But by the 1870's a plateau was reached in arrests per 100,000 population, although the number of police kept rising, so that the number of arrests per patrolman began to drop, a trend which has continued to the present. After the period in which the plateau was reached and the case load began to drop, the arrest totals in many categories may be regarded as relatively accurate indicators of the changes in criminal patterns year by year.

Second, the statistics of conviction for felony per 100,000 population show a marked and steady drop throughout the period covered. There were often changes in the legal definition of felony, but these offenses were always more clearly recognized than those crimes against public order which account for most arrests and prosecutions. The fact that felony convictions per 100,000 population were dropping while the number of police was rising indicates not only that the actual incidence of felony was decreasing but that it was decreasing even more dramatically than the statistics demonstrate.

TABLE I-A. SUMMARY OF ARRESTS FOR 1856

Summary of totals	
Arrested	17,538
Committed	8,979
Males	13,700
Females	3,878
Foreigners	14,067
Americans	3,471
Nonresidents	3,507
Minors	2,756
Individual complaints	
Assault with intent to kill	27
Assault on officers	74
Assault and battery	1,223
Assault with deadly weapons	34
Aggravated assault	1
Attempt to kill	8
Attempt to rob	4
Assault	22
Adultery	33
Attempt at rescue	57
Attempt to commit rape	2
Arson	7
Burglary	285
Breaking glass	78
Bigamy	3
Bail bond	5
Common drunkards	935
Common beggars	39
Common nuisances	9
Disturbing the peace	761
Drunkards	6,780
Detained as witnesses	249
Dealing in lottery tickets	6
Disturbing public assembly	3
Deserters from shipboard	8
Escaped convicts	11
Embezzlement	10
Extinguishing street lamps	1
Extortion	7
For safekeeping of bonds	61
Fraud	10
Forgery	14
Fornication	52
Fugitives from justice	2
Gambling	240
Gambling on the Lord's Day	18
Having sling shot	2

TABLE I-A. SUMMARY OF ARRESTS FOR 1856 (*continued*)

Having burglar's tools	1
Having worthless money	2
Idle and dissolute persons	139
Indecent exposure of person	10
Interfering with officers	1
Indecent assault	1
Keeping noisy houses	82
Keeping gaming houses	7
Keeping and lending houses of ill fame	99
Lascivious cohabitation	2
Larcenies from persons and buildings	598
Larcenies (simple)	1,252
Lewdness	42
Murder	8
Malicious mischief	110
Making counterfeit money	4
Maiming	1
Manslaughter	1
Night walking	267
Noisy and disorderly persons	2,276
Obstructing railroad tracks	3
Obtaining goods by false pretenses	21
On warrants	165
Pickpockets	92
Passing of counterfeit money	16
Peddling without a license	38
Passing worthless money	14
Perjury	1
Procuring abortion	2
Presuming to be an officer	1
Robbery	63
Receiving stolen goods	21
Rioters	10
Rape	2
Suspicious persons	319
Stubborn children	75
Selling obscene books	1
Stealing a ride	14
Swindling	8
Trespass	1
Truants	59
Violation of the Sunday Law	79
Violation of city ordinances	199
Vagrants	282
Woman in man's apparel	1

Source: Annual Police Report (1857), pp. 6-9.

TABLE I-B. Summary of Arrests for 1884-85

Summary of totals	
Arrested	28,932
On warrants	5,159
Without warrants	23,773
Held for trial	25,321
Discharged on examination	3,611
Males	23,901
Females	5,301
Foreigners	14,402
Nonresidents	9,043
Minors	3,986
Individual complaints	
Abandoning child	2
Abduction	2
Accessory to assault	2
Adultery	41
Arson	9
Assault and battery, simple	2,410
Assault, felonious	266
Assault, indecent	10
Assault on officer	24
Assuming to be an innholder	2
Assuming to be an officer	3
Assuming to be a victualler	1
Attempt to break and enter a building	35
Attempt to break and enter a railroad car	1
Attempt to commit larceny	12
Attempt to murder	3
Attempt to rape	9
Attempt to pick pocket	5
Attempt to rescue prisoner	21
Attempt to obtain property by fraud	2
Attempt to pass counterfeit money	1
Attempt to extort money	6
Attempt to rob	8
Bail bond	5
Bastardy	6
Being present at unlawful game	105
Breaking and entering a building	38
Breaking and entering a railroad car	4
Breaking and entering a vessel	2
Burglary	5
Capias	7
Carrying concealed weapons	9
Common beggars	7
Common brawlers	23
Common drunkards	219
Conspiring to convict of crime	1
Conspiracy to defraud	2

TABLE I-B. SUMMARY OF ARRESTS FOR 1884-85 (*continued*)

Conspiracy to assault	1
Conveying property unlawfully	6
Contempt of court	2
Concealing stolen property	1
Concealing leased property	10
Concealing mortgaged property	4
Criminal libel	1
Cruelty to animals	31
Default warrant	109
Defrauding an innholder	3
Deserters	37
Disorderly	514
Distributing obscene print	1
Disturbing peace	162
Disturbing public meeting	25
Disturbing public school	4
Drunkenness	16,780
Embezzlement	117
Enticing to prostitution	1
Escaped convicts	13
Evading payment of fare	19
Extinguishing street lamps unlawfully	1
Extortion	2
Fast driving	23
Forgery	45
Fornication	53
Fraud	37
Fugitive from justice	10
Gambling	42
Gaming on the Lord's Day	53
Giving false alarm of fire	1
Housebreaking	60
Idle and disorderly	214
Indecent exposure of person	35
Insane	275
Incest	1
Keeping houses of ill fame	43
Keeping an opium resort	1
Keeping gambling houses	13
Keeping noisy and disorderly houses	27
Keeping a liquor nuisance	7
Larceny, simple	1,722
Larceny, felonious	510
Lewd and lascivious conduct	38
Mayhem	1
Malicious mischief	348
Malicious trespass	38
Maintaining a lottery	3
Manslaughter	12

TABLE I-B. Summary of Arrests for 1884-85 (*continued*)

Murder	6
Mutinous conduct	1
Neglected children	16
Nightwalking	168
Obtaining property by fraud	68
Passing counterfeit money	8
Peddling without a license	6
Perjury	9
Polygamy	9
Profanity in a public place	176
Rape	6
Receiving stolen goods	38
Refusing duty as a seaman	1
Robbery	88
Refusing to assist an officer	3
Refusing to send minor children to school	2
Refusing to support a minor child	54
Runaways	121
Rescuing prisoners	10
Selling leased property	5
Selling mortgaged property	3
Shop breaking	218
Stealing ride	37
Stubborn children	114
Suspicion of larceny	255
Smoking opium unlawfully	13
Selling lottery tickets	2
Sodomy	7
Suspicion of forgery	8
Suspicion of breaking and entering	34
Suspicious persons	1,153
Suspicion of robbery	14
Suspicion of murder	3
Suspicion of assault	4
Suspicion of arson	1
Surrender by probation officer	1
Setting fire to building	3
Subornation of perjury	1
Threats	66
Truants	89
Uttering forged order	1
Unlawfully using a team	3
Uttering altered U. S. notes	1
Unlawfully using a boat	3
Vagrancy	250
Violation city ordinance	500
Violation dog law	25
Violation liquor law	138
Violation health law	4

TABLE I-B. SUMMARY OF ARRESTS FOR 1884-85 (*continued*)

Violation railroad law	10
Violation Sunday Law	75
Violation U. S. revenue law	3
Violation of screen law	6
Violation of election law	2
Witnesses	329

Source: Annual Police Report (1885), pp. 5-9.

Police Division Maps

Map A, the central police divisions in 1870, is taken from the description in the *Annual Police Report* (1871), pp. 1-8. The boundaries are the same as those of 1854, when the divisions, all but number eight loosely based on the watch districts, were created.

Map B, the police divisions in 1876, is taken from the description in the *Annual Police Report* (1875), pp. 1-11. Between that date and the 1960's, although the outlines of the peninsula were altered and new territory was added, most of the divisions remained essentially unchanged. Some were consolidated and two new ones were drawn to include Hyde Park and Mattapan, as there were incorporated into the metropolis. See *Annual Police Report* (1961), p. 22.

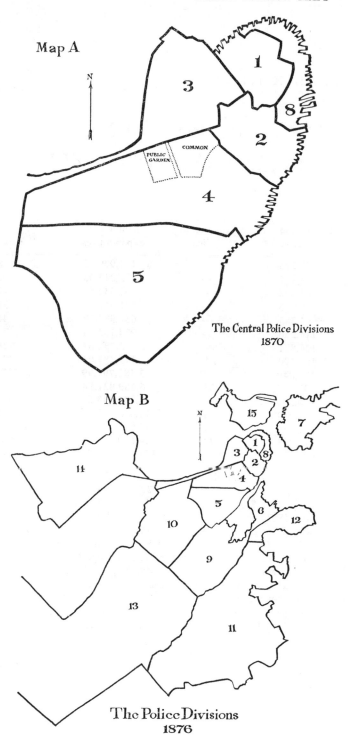

Map A

The Central Police Divisions
1870

Map B

The Police Divisions
1876

Boston Police, Population, and Expenditures, 1820-1885, 1961

Year	Population of Boston	Number of police	Municipal expenditures	Police expenditures
1820	43,298	—	$ 171,979.02	$ 8,768.40
1825	58,277	—	375,214.43	8,898.02
1830	61,392	—	362,334.69	11,333.51
1835	78,603	—	701,611.22	31,887.75
1840	93,383	—	632,984.28	46,434.12
1845	114,366	—	974,102.14	73,361.90
1850	136,881	—	2,395,382.62	124,386.80
1855	160,490	246	2,795,483.63	204,485.73
1860	177,840	297	3,582,791.99	230,337.63
1865	192,318	375	6,389,821.84	432,187.22
1870	250,526	500	12,496,533.61	578,344.96
1875	341,919	661	15,478,979.85	877,643.45
1880	362,839	697	12,995,048.40	881,153.81
1885	390,393	789	14,609,402.97	987,763.99
1961	697,197	2,753	353,079,541.74	18,221,408.09

Source: Population and expenditures through 1885 in Charles P. Huse, *The Financial History of Boston from May 1, 1822 to January 31, 1909* (Cambridge, 1916), pp. 348-351, 376-377; number of police through 1885 in *Annual Police Report* (1885), p. 3, *ibid.* (1861), p. 3, *ibid.* (1866), p. 7, *ibid.* (1871), p. 16, *ibid.* (1876), p. 3, *ibid.* (1880), p. 1, *ibid.* (1885), p. 3; 1961 population and total municipal expenditures in *City of Boston and County of Suffolk: Auditing Department: Annual Report for the Fiscal Year Ending December 31, 1961,* pp. 114, 10; 1961 police and police expenditures in *Annual Police Report* (1961), pp. 70, 52. The police expenditures for all years to 1855 include constables, watchmen, and police, and not the internal health department; the number of these officers is omitted because they are not directly comparable with those of police after 1854. Note that the population figures sometimes differ slightly from those given in the text; different sources give different figures apparently because some attempt to adjust them to a standard date, as January 1, rather than to the actual census date.

Notes on Sources

OFFICIAL DOCUMENTS: THE STATE

A survey and description of the available state documents to 1861 is contained in Oscar Handlin and Mary Flug Handlin, *Commonwealth: Massachusetts 1774-1861: A Study of the Role of Government in the American Economy* (New York, 1947), 288-290. For those dealing with criminal statistics, see Appendix I.

There were, in the period covered, three annotated compilations of the statutes: *The Revised Statutes of the Commonwealth of Massachusetts, Passed November 4, 1835* (Boston, 1836), *The General Statutes of the Commonwealth of Massachusetts . . . Passed December 28, 1859* (Boston, 1860), and the *Public Statutes of the Commonwealth of Massachusetts, Enacted November 1, 1881 . . .* (Boston, 1882). Supplements were frequently issued to keep these volumes up to date, and the annual *Acts and Resolves* were published each year.

The *Journal of the House of Representatives of the Commonwealth of Massachusetts* was first published in 1864, and *Commonwealth of Massachusetts: The Journal of the Senate* began in 1868. The earlier journals are available only in manuscript. There was, in this period, no regular record of the debates and proceedings of either branch, but the running accounts published in the Boston *Advertiser* were bound and collected in 1856, 1857, 1859, and 1862.

The *Massachusetts House Documents* and the *Massachusetts Senate Documents*, both published regularly beginning in 1826, and the *Massachusetts Public Documents*, published irregularly from 1846 to 1858, and regularly thereafter, contain a variety of materials difficult to classify. The legislative documents include the annual adresses of the governor, unpassed acts and resolves, special reports and testimony before legislative committees, and both regular and special reports by executive officers. No logic dictated which of these materials were published by the house and which by the senate, and many were individually bound as well. The Public Documents include only regular executive reports, but the addition of this series did not prevent the continued publication of some of these in the House or Senate Documents. One especially important report is available only in the separately bound edition. House Doc. no. 415, *Reports on the Subject of a License Law by a Joint Committee of the Legislature of Massachusetts, together with a Stenographic Report of the Testimony* (Boston, 1867), comprises, in four reports and 893 pages

239

of testimony, the most important single record of contemporary attitudes toward liquor regulation.

The formal *Reports of Cases Argued and Determined in the Supreme Judicial Court of Massachusetts,* beginning in 1804, are important not only in tracing legal developments but in providing sworn testimony as to the circumstances in many cases, notably those involving riot and the reclamation of fugitive slaves. Contemporary practice, followed in the text and footnotes, was usually to cite the first seventeen volumes in the series by the over-all volume number, for example, "16 Mass." The next eighty volumes, between 1822 and 1868, reported by Octavius Pickering, Luther S. Cushing, Theron Metcalf, Horace Gray, Jr., and Charles Allen, were cited by the volumes of the particular reporter, for example, "1 Allen." Beginning in 1868, with volume 97, citations were again made by over-all volume number, such as "M.R. 100."

OFFICIAL DOCUMENTS: THE CITY

In some respects the documents of the city of Boston provide a record inferior to that kept by the state; in others they are more rationally catalogued and more comprehensive. See Appendix I for those dealing with criminal statistics.

The manuscript minutes of the board of aldermen, officially entitled *Records of the City of Boston: Mayor and Aldermen,* are available beginning in 1822, on microfilm in the Boston Public Library. A *Journal of the Common Council of the City of Boston* was published in 1868, 1869, and 1870. But both series were superseded, beginning in 1869, by the *City Council Minutes,* a verbatim record of the proceedings and debates in both branches.

A number of early reports and official documents were bound together, in 1824, as *City Papers, 1821-1824.* Another overlapping set was collected as *City Documents, 1821-1828.* The regular annually issued *City Documents,* however, did not begin until 1834. For the first few years, this collection, the municipal equivalent of the House, Senate, and Public Documents combined, contained some numbered as "City Documents" and some as "Common Council Documents"; by 1850, reports from all executive departments were included. An *Index to the City Documents, 1834-1891* (Boston, 1891), topically arranged, provides a guide to all of them, including special reports on a number of subjects especially relevant to this study, such as truancy, poor relief, the treatment of criminals, and traffic control.

Many of the materials included in the *City Documents* were also published separately. Three are especially important. The *Inaugural Addresses of the Mayors of Boston, 1822 to 1852* (Boston, 1894), and the *Inaugural Addresses of the Mayors of Boston, 1853 to 1867* (Boston, 1896), were continued, after 1867, in individual pamphlets. The *Annual Report of the Receipts and Expenditures,* cited as the *Auditor's Report,* was issued regularly beginning in 1813. *The Municipal Register, Containing Rules and*

Orders of the City Council, Recent Laws and Ordinances, and a List of the Officers of the City of Boston was first published in 1847; the separate volumes are often more comprehensive than the version bound among the *City Documents,* and in later years contain a variety of statistical and historical material.

The various editions of the city ordinances are in general less satisfactory than those of the statute law, although fully eight of them appeared in the period covered: *The Charter of the City of Boston, and Ordinances Made and Established by the Mayor, Aldermen, and Common Council, with Such Acts of the Legislature of Massachusetts as Relate to the Government of Said City* (Boston, 1827); *The Charter and Ordinances of the City of Boston, together with the Acts of the Legislature Relating to the City* (Boston, 1834); *The Charter and Ordinances of the City of Boston, together with the Acts of the Legislature Relating to the City* (Boston, 1850); *The Charter and Ordinances of the City of Boston, together with the Acts of the Legislature Relating to the City, and an Appendix* (Boston, 1856); *The Charter and Ordinances of the City of Boston, together with the Acts of the Legislature Relating to the City, and other Municipal Laws* (Boston, 1863); *Ordinances and Rules and Orders of the City of Boston, together with the General and Special Statutes of the Massachusetts Legislature Relating to the City* (Boston, 1869); *Ordinances and Rules and Orders of the City of Boston, together with a Digest of the General and Special Statutes of the Massachusetts Legislature Relating to the City* (Boston, 1876); and *The Revised Ordinances of the City of Boston, as Passed Prior to December 31, 1882, Being the Eighth Revision* (Boston, 1882). In addition, *A Supplement to the Laws and Ordinances of the City of Boston* (Boston, 1866) was published to include corporate agreements, the rules and orders of the departments, and a digest of relevant supreme court decisions on the powers of the municipality and its agents. But despite the number of available editions, the state of the ordinances remains confusing. Until 1869, when the city began to publish the *Acts and Ordinances,* equivalent to the *Acts and Resolves,* it is difficult to determine when individual ordinances were passed. In the early editions, they are not chaptered or numbered but simply titled. The edition of 1827, in particular, is incomplete; before the creation of adequate machinery for enforcement, it appears that several ordinances were not merely ignored but forgotten, and the city council sometimes re-enacted rules which were technically still valid.

NEWSPAPERS

Before 1830, newspaper coverage of purely local events is highly superficial and irregular. *Bowen's Boston Newsletter and City Record,* unfortunately published only during 1825 and 1826, includes considerably more than the *Columbian Centinel* and Boston *Courier,* typical of the conservative older press.

Between the 1830's and the 1850's the situation is considerably better, although it is still necessary to check several papers to find complete accounts of elections and other occurrences. Priscilla Hawthorne Fowle's "Boston Daily Newspapers: 1830-1850" (unpublished Ph.D. dissertation, Radcliffe College Archives, 1920) is a useful guide. Among those used in this study, the Boston *Post* was the lively organ of the Democratic party, while the *Daily Atlas* and *Semi-Weekly Atlas* spoke for the Whigs. The Evangelical Boston *Recorder,* the freethinking *Investigator,* the *Semi-Weekly Mercantile Journal,* the *Weekly Messenger,* and the Catholic Boston *Pilot* were all addressed to smaller groups. The *Bunker Hill Aurora,* the Boston *Daily Mail,* and the Boston *Traveller* are all typical of the politically independent popular press.

From the 1850's on there is no shortage of local reporting. The Boston daily *Herald,* beginning in 1851, is the most important source. The largest paper in the city, during most of the period covered, it was consistently independent in politics, skeptical, gossipy, and thorough. The Boston daily *Advertiser,* founded in 1855, was frankly conservative and Republican, the city's newspaper of record, with the fullest accounts of legislative debates and proceedings. Stories in these two may be checked in the *Evening Transcript,* which while Republican was less a party organ than the *Advertiser,* and in the popular Democratic *Globe,* which began publishing in 1872.

CONTEMPORARY PAMPHLETS, REPORTS, SPEECHES, AND SO ON

The pamphlet literature of reform is voluminous, although often redundant; the pieces are generally valuable in proportion to their specificity and their dates of issuance. The publication of Josiah Quincy's influential *Remarks on Some of the Provisions of the Laws of Massachusetts Affecting Poverty, Vice, and Crime* (Cambridge, 1822) was in itself a landmark in reform history. A publication of the Massachusetts Temperance Society, *Plain Facts Addressed to the Inhabitants of Boston on the City Expenses for the Support of Pauperism, Vice, and Crime* (Boston, 1834) is useful for its penal statistics and its early date. *Licensed Houses: An Examination of the License Law of the Commonwealth of Massachusetts* (Boston, 1833), by "M. V. L.," is an acute summary of the legal and political problems involved in liquor legislation. Several temperance groups reprinted legislative testimony or speeches, such as *The Argument of Peleg Sprague, Esq., before the Committee of the Legislature, upon the Memorial of Harrison Grey Otis and Others* (Boston, 1840), or *The Speech of Francis W. Emmons of Sturbridge on Regulating the Sale of Alcohol* (Boston, 1848). Few of the large number of printed sermons, by clergymen and others, are as powerful and revealing as Theodore Parker's "A Sermon on the Moral Condition of Boston, Feb. 11, 1849," in Francis Power Cobbe, ed., *The Collected Works of Theodore Parker,* vol. VII: *Discourses of Social Science* (Boston, 1864), pp. 114-145. Two pamphlets which advocate regulation without prohibition are more specific than most: B. F. Clark's *Prohibition of the Sale of Intoxicating Liquors Impracticable: The Maine Law a Failure* . . . (Lowell, 1864), and Francis F. Bird's *Modification or Absolute Prohibition: Which . . .?* (Boston, 1869).

Several reform-minded groups or individuals, other than temperance societies, reported on their own activities. John Augustus, the pioneer in probation work, was his own publicist, and his *Report on the Labors of John Augustus . . . in Aid of the Unfortunate* (Boston, 1852) is the only important source. A magazine full of progress and comparative statistics, *The Prisoner's Friend,* was the organ of the Prison Discipline Society beginning in March of 1851. The New England Society for the Suppression of Vice, now the Watch and Ward Society, has published its *Annual Report* continuously since 1880. The Citizens' Law and Order League of Massachusetts began issuing its *Proceedings* in 1883.

Both reformers and their opponents were concerned with the metropolitan police question. Wendell Phillips' *Speech on a Metropolitan Police, at the Melodeon, April 5, 1863* (Boston, 1863) was followed by several others. The actual reprinted testimony is more valuable. Reformers published the *Argument of Charles M. Ellis, Esq., in Favor of the Metropolitan Police Bill* (Boston, 1863) and *The Testimony of Augustus P. Martin for a Metropolitan Police Commission for the City of Boston* (Boston, 1885). On the other side, *The Argument of Thomas Coffin Amory Against the Proposed Metropolitan Police Bill* (Boston, 1863) and *The Argument Made Before a Joint Special Committee of the Legislature of Massachusetts by Clement Hugh Hill Against the Establishment of a State Police in the City of Boston* (Boston, 1869) were done by the official city printer.

Relevant contemporary material unrelated to reform is much less common. Sheriff Charles P. Sumner's *A Discourse on Some Points of Difference between the Sheriff's Office in Massachusetts and England* (Boston, 1829) is a revealing personal document as well as a useful historical sketch. Colonel Theodore Lyman, son of the mayor, published a number of eyewitness accounts and recollections in *Papers Relating to the Garrison Mob* (Cambridge, 1870), the most valuable source on that famous incident. *The Resolves of the Boston Ex-Fire Department,* an undated broadside in the Bostonian Society Collection, provides an insight into one of the strongest forces in pre-Civil War local politics. The Bostonian Society also has two untitled reports, dated 1832, of the New England Association Against Counterfeiting. And the same society possesses a collection of nineteenth-century police and watch badges, billies, rattles, and caps, many of them donated by Chief E. H. Savage.

BOOKS AND ARTICLES: ON MASSACHUSETTS AND BOSTON

In most respects the history of state and city has been well recorded, and the secondary sources are easily available. Such older collective works as

Justin Winsor, ed., *The Memorial History of Boston, Including Suffolk County, Massachusetts, 1630-1880* (4 vols., Boston, 1880-1881), and Albert Bushnell Hart, ed., *The Commonwealth History of Massachusetts, Colony, Province, and State* (5 vols., New York, 1927-1930), are still useful. Oscar and Mary Flug Handlin's *Commonwealth: Massachusetts 1774-1861: A Study of the Role of Government in the American Economy* (New York, 1947) and Oscar Handlin's *Boston's Immigrants: A Study in Acculturation* (rev. ed., Cambridge, 1959) are both comprehensive social and economic histories, with extensive guides to the existing literature.

The major scholarly works covering the political history of the state during the nineteenth century are also guides to the other political literature. Samuel Eliot Morison has sketched the framework in *History of the Constitution of Massachusetts* (Boston, 1917), a deliberately dry account prepared for that year's constitutional convention. Arthur Burr Darling's *Political Changes in Massachusetts, 1824-1848* (New Haven, 1925) fits with William Gleason Bean's "Party Transformation in Massachusetts, 1848-1860, with Special Reference to the Antecedents of Republicanism" (unpublished Ph.D. dissertation, Harvard University Archives, 1922), to provide a solid working account of state-wide party issues up to the Civil War. The postwar decades are not so well served. Edith F. Ware's *Political Opinion in Massachusetts During the Civil War and Reconstruction* (New York, 1916) is disappointing and little concerned with local issues. Geoffrey Blodgett's "Massachusetts Democrats in the Cleveland Era" (unpublished Ph.D. dissertation, Harvard University Archives, 1960) is helpful in places, although largely an account of intraparty matters, with emphasis on national affairs.

The various political sources are rarely concerned with the actual workings of the state government, and there is very little in the three most relevant areas: the system of criminal justice, the development of official charity, and the temperance reform. The various biographies of leading jurists contain little on the history of law, and almost nothing on criminal law and procedure. William T. Davis's *History of the Judiciary of Massachusetts Including the Plymouth and Massachusetts Colonies, The Province of Massachusetts Bay, and the Commonwealth* (Boston, 1900) is simply a compendium of biographical data. *The History of Public Poor Relief in Massachusetts, 1620-1920* (Boston, 1922), by Robert Kelso, is disappointing, a plea for the system endorsed in 1920 and largely concerned with its antecedents. For liquor legislation, George Faber Clark's pious *History of the Temperance Reform in Massachusetts, 1813-1883* (Boston, 1888) may be used as a chronicle.

There is somewhat more material on the development of official institutions in Boston. C. W. Ernst's *Constitutional History of Boston, Massachusetts* (Boston, 1891) begins with the settlement; Henry H. Sprague's *City Government in Boston, Its Rise and Development* (Boston, 1890) begins with incorporation. *The Financial History of Boston from May 1,*

1822 to January 31, 1909 (Cambridge, 1916), by Charles Phillips Huse, is a very helpful monograph which necessarily surveys all of the services and projects undertaken by the city. Arthur Wellington Brayley's *Complete History of the Boston Fire Department* (Boston, 1889), largely a membership list, is still useful. The opening chapters of "Private Charities in Boston, 1870-1900: A Social History" (unpublished Ph.D. dissertation, Harvard University Archives, 1962), by Nathan Irving Huggins, deal with a period earlier than the title indicates, and the whole work helps illumine official as well as private charitable work. Chief Edward Hartwell Savage's *Police Records and Recollections: Or, Boston by Daylight and Gaslight* (Boston, 1873) belongs in a special category. The second half of the book is a revealing collection of anecdotes; the first half, a chronicle of events relating to politics and policing, provides numerous clues and starting points for the modern researcher.

The material on Boston's political history varies with the period. The early town meeting has a many-sided appeal at one end of the scale; at the other, twentieth-century battles between Yankees and Irishmen have fascinated novelists and scholars alike. Carl Bridenbaugh's pioneering books, *Cities in the Wilderness: The First Century of Urban Life in America, 1625-1742* (New York, 1938) and *Cities in Revolt: Urban Life in America, 1753-1776* (New York, 1956), are still the most complete on local affairs during the colonial period. The title of John B. Blake's *Public Health in the Town of Boston, 1630-1822* (Cambridge, 1959) conceals the fact that it is incidentally an excellent study of political methods and machinery, which carries the account up to the time of incorporation. Geoffrey Blodgett's study, mentioned above, picks up the thread at the other end, with accounts of the administrations of Mayors Mathews and Quincy during the 1890's, just before the solidification of Irish control.

The great gap is in the middle, and covers most of the nineteenth century. Police Commissioner James Bugbee's often spritely story of "Boston Under the Mayors: 1822 to 1880," the second chapter in volume III of Justin Winsor's history, is the only chronological account. Unlike the scholarly political histories of the state, it has no bibliography, and there are in fact few supplementary materials other than the newspapers. The best remaining approach to the character and methods of local politics is through the study of its participants.

Of all the candidates for mayor of Boston, during the period covered, only the first two have attracted biographers. Samuel Eliot Morison's *Life and Letters of Harrison Grey Otis, Federalist, 1765-1848* (Boston, 1913) unfortunately contains only a few lines on municipal affairs. *The Life of Josiah Quincy of Massachusetts* (Boston, 1868), by his son Edmund, is routine. James Walker's "Memoir of Josiah Quincy," in the Massachusetts Historical Society's *Proceedings,* vol. IX (1866-1867), pp. 83-156, is considerably better. Best yet is Josiah Quincy's own *Municipal History of the Town and City of Boston During Two Centuries* (Boston, 1852), largely a record of his own experiences, recollected in tranquillity.

Mayor John Prescott Bigelow is the only local politician to have left a personal collection, in the Harvard College Library; most of the material, other than a few newspaper clippings, comprises minor items from his years as the Commonwealth's secretary of state. The semi-official *Mayors of Boston* (Boston, 1910), published by the State Street Trust Company, has one-page sketches of all the chief executives. Some local officials belonged to the Massachusetts Historical Society, and among its *Proceedings* are memoirs of James Savage, Nathaniel Shurtleff, Thomas Coffin Amory, Martin Brimmer, Samuel Crocker Cobb, Henry Lille Pierce, Clement Hugh Hill, William Whitmore, Samuel Abbot Green, James McKellar Bugbee, and Arnold A. Rand. A unique pamphlet, *Members of the Common Council of Boston for 1845, With Their Place of Birth, Occupation, Condition of Life, etc.* (Boston, 1845), collects the kind of information that the Boston *Herald*, beginning in the 1850's, published irregularly around election time. The *Index to Obituary Notices in the Boston Transcript* (1875-1899, 2 vols.) covers the last few years of the period, but the many inexplicable omissions include even former mayors of the city. William Travis Davis's *Professional and Industrial History of Suffolk County, Massachusetts* (3 vols., Boston, 1894) contains the names and usually sketches of all men admitted to the bar, and traces the business connections of others. The Boston *Directory,* too, published from 1800 on, lists the occupations as well as addresses of all residents.

BOOKS AND ARTICLES: ON TEMPERANCE, CRIME, AND POLICE

Joseph R. Gusfield's *Symbolic Crusade: Status Politics and the American Temperance Movement* (Urbana, 1963) is an insightful but rarely specific study of the antiliquor agitation. Both D. Leigh Colvin's *Prohibition in the United States* (New York, 1926) and John Allen Krout's disappointing *Origins of Prohibition* (New York, 1925) were written under the shadow of the Eighteenth Amendment; Andrew Sinclair's fine study of *Prohibition, The Era of Excess* (Boston, 1962) has very little on the nineteenth century. The thirteenth chapter of Alice Felt Tyler's *Freedom's Ferment* (Minneapolis, 1940) is still the best introduction to the pre-Civil War movement. Judge Robert C. Pitman's partisan older account of the legal problems, *Alcohol and the State: A Discussion of the Problem of Law as Applied to the Liquor Traffic* (New York, 1877), may be used within the more sophisticated framework outlined in Frederick A. Johnson and Ruth R. Kessler's excellent summary of "The Liquor License System: Its Origin and Constitutional Development," *New York University Law Quarterly Review,* vol. XV (1936), pp. 210-251, 380-424.

There are two general guides to sources on crime and the police. For an American student, Frederick Augustus Kuhlman's *Guide to Material on Crime and Criminal Justice* (New York, 1929) is more helpful than *A*

Contribution Towards a Bibliography Dealing with Crime and Cognate Subjects, 3rd ed. (London, 1935), by Sir John Cumming.

There is no history of professional criminality, but there are a number of useful contemporary accounts. Of special interest because of its early date is James Faxon, ed., *The Record of Crimes in the United States* (Buffalo, 1833), a collection of horror stories. Descriptions of the underworld by reporters and detectives did not generally appear until several decades later. Ball Fenner's *Raising the Veil: Or, Scenes in the Courts* (Boston, 1856), is one of the first of these, a comparison of vice and criminal court procedures in several American cities. British periodicals published a number of accounts such as "Professional Thieves," *Cornhill,* vol. VI (1862), pp. 340-353; "Crime and Its Detection," Dublin *Review,* vol. L (May 1861), pp. 150-197; and "Aids of Science in the Detection of Crime," *Chamber's Edinburgh Journal,* vol. LIII (Feb. 5, 1876), pp. 101-103. Edwin Crapsey was the first to study the fraternity in America, in three very helpful articles in *Galaxy:* "Our Criminal Population," vol. VIII (September 1869), pp. 345-351; "Why Thieves Prosper," vol. VIII (December 1869), pp. 519-527; and "The Nether Side of New York," vol. XI (February 1871), pp. 188-197. The first of our detective reminiscences is *Knots Untied: Or, Ways and By-Ways in the Hidden Life of American Detectives* (Hartford, 1871) by George F. McWatters. It belongs firmly in the romantic tradition, together with the entire output of the prolific Allan Pinkerton, typified by his *Professional Thieves and Detectives* (New York, 1880). A more reliable form is the full-length catalogue of criminal types; an increasingly detailed record is provided by three books, Phil Farley's *Criminals of America, or Tales of the Lives of The Thieves* (New York, 1876), Inspector Thomas Brynes's *Professional Criminals of America* (New York, 1886), and the joint work of two Boston officers, Superintendent Benjamin P. Eldridge and Chief Inspector William P. Watts, *Our Rival the Rascal: A Faithful Portrayal of the Conflict Between The Criminals of This Age and The Defenders of Society—The Police* (Boston, 1897). *Recollections of a New York Chief of Police* (New York, 1897), by George Washington Walling, the first of several memoirs by heads of the New York force, belongs partly in this category. On the other side of the fence is *Langdon W. Moore: His Own Story of His Eventful Life* (Boston, 1893), the detailed autobiography of a famous burglar. There are also several interesting books by Josiah Flynt, or Willard: *Tramping With Tramps* (New York, 1901), *The World of Graft* (New York, 1901), and *My Life* (New York, 1908). Flynt, the black-sheep nephew of Frances Willard, used only his first two names; he spent most of a brief life ended by alcoholism in the company of underworld figures, to whose description he brought a curious combination of iconoclastic sophistication and middle-class conservatism.

For the most important of amateur crimes, Thomas M. McDade, ed., *The Annals of Murder: A Bibliography of Books and Pamphlets on American Murders from Colonial Times to 1900* (Norman, Okla., 1961) contains a wealth of material. This is more than a bibliography; McDade's comments on many cases shed light on the history of detection and the use of evidence.

There are a number of histories of the foreign and especially of the English police. The most scholarly of the latter is Charles Reith's *The Police Idea: Its History and Evolution in the Eighteenth Century and After* (London, 1938), which centers on the founding of the London Metropolitan force in 1829. W. L. Melville Lee's *A History of Police in England* (London, 1901) is the most detailed of the popular works; John Coatman's *Police!* (London, 1959) is a survey of organizations the world over. Erland Fenn Clark's *Truncheons: Their Romance and Reality* (London, 1935) is the definitive work, with one hundred plates and descriptions of five hundred instruments.

The development of the legal powers of peace officers is outlined in Jerome Hall's "Legal and Social Aspects of Arrest without Warrant," *Harvard Law Review,* vol. XLIX (February 1936), pp. 566-592. Two contemporary books are also helpful. Charles W. Hartshorne's guide for *The New England Sheriff: A Digest of the Laws of Massachusetts Relative to Sheriffs, Jailers, Coroners, and Constables, with Forms* (Worcester, 1844) summarizes some of the relevant laws and court decisions to the time of writing. So does Christopher G. Tiedeman's *A Treatise on the Limitations of Police Power in the United States* (St. Louis, 1886); the word "police" is used in its widest sense.

Policeman and Public (New Haven, 1919), by Arthur Wood, and *Our Lawless Police* (New York, 1931), by Ernest Jerome Hopkins, deal with the policeman's lot from two very different points of view. The first is a perceptive set of lectures by a former New York police commissioner. The second, a popular account based on the Wickersham Report, is more limited in aim and imagination.

Studies of departmental administration comprise the largest single category of books about police. They are primarily intended to show how procedures, organization, and equipment may be improved, prescribing the proper length of billy clubs and beats; the London system is usually taken as the model, and efficient law enforcement as the goal. Many also contain brief historical sections, and a few provide some more revealing general observations. The first, most colorful, and in many ways the most insightful is Leonhard Felix Fuld's *Police Administration: A Critical Study of Police Organizations in the United States and Abroad* (New York, 1909). More important for setting the typical pattern are Raymond Fosdick's *European Police Systems* (New York, 1915) and *American Police Systems* (New York, 1920). Most relevant of the local studies is Leonard Vance Harrison's *Police Administration in Boston* (Cambridge, 1934), part of the Harvard Law School's survey of crime and criminal justice in the city. The most recent work in the general field is *Police Systems in the United States,* 2nd rev. ed. (New York, 1960), by Bruce Smith.

Notes

CHAPTER ONE

FROM TOWN TO CITY: THE POLICE IN 1822

1. Josiah Quincy, *A Municipal History of the Town and City of Boston During Two Centuries* (Boston, 1852), p. 40; Henry H. Sprague, *City Government in Boston: Its Rise and Development* (Boston, 1890), pp. 1-31; Quincy, *Municipal History*, p. 23.

2. Noah Webster, *An American Dictionary of the English Language* (New York, 1828), Vol. II. Historical dictionaries differ about the age and immediate origin of the word "police" in English. But there is general agreement that it was introduced, in its wider sense, from France, early in the eighteenth century. Importation to America occurred some time later, in some cases violently. According to Augustine E. Costello, author of *Our Police Protectors: History of the New York Police from the Earliest Period to the Present Times* (New York, 1885), p. 47, the first official use in New York occurred in 1778, when British Major General Daniel Jones appointed a "Superintendent General of the Police," with dictatorial power over "all . . . matters, in which the economy, peace, and good order of the City of New York and its environs are concerned"; the mayor was used only as an assistant. During the 1820's and the 1830's the official records of Boston and Massachusetts use "police" as synonymous with "health," "constables and watchmen," "licenses," and "ordinances." Unofficial use in the same period is often quite confusing, even though the most distinctive American contribution, the definition of "police power," first enunciated by the Supreme Court in 1827, was slow to appear in common speech or writing.

3. The earlier attempts to incorporate the town as a city are described in Sprague, *City Government in Boston,* pp. 1-31; for a modern evaluation of the meeting in operation see Carl Bridenbaugh, *Cities in the Wilderness: The First Century of Urban Life in America, 1642-1742* (New York, 1938), *passim,* and Carl Bridenbaugh, *Cities in Revolt: Urban Life in America, 1743-1776* (New York, 1955), *passim.*

4. Bridenbaugh, *Cities in Revolt,* pp. 116-117; Bridenbaugh, *Cities in the Wilderness, passim.*

5. Earlier attendance in Bridenbaugh, *Cities in the Wilderness,* pp. 6-7; later in Quincy, *Municipal History,* p. 28; ward elections in C. W. Ernst, *Constitutional History of Boston, Massachusetts* (Boston, 1894), p. 86; complaints of new population in Quincy, *Municipal History,* pp. 153-154.

6. The administration of these matters is described in John B. Blake, *Public Health in the Town of Boston, 1630-1822* (Cambridge, 1959), *passim*.

7. *Ibid.,* pp. 162-172, 190-191, 192-206, 238, 217.

8. *Ibid.,* pp. 156-157, 223-224.

9. *Ibid.,* pp. 172, 238.

10. Quincy, *Municipal History,* pp. 65-66; Blake, *Public Health in Boston,* pp. 200-204.

11. Figures on court cases and on the populations of various penal institutions during the 1820's are summarized in Massachusetts Temperance Society, *Plain Facts Addressed to the Inhabitants of Boston on the City Expenses for the Support of Pauperism, Vice, and Crime* (Boston, 1834), pp. 7, 9, 12, 15, 17. See also Appendix I.

12. Criminal convictions in Mass. Temp. Soc., *Plain Facts,* p. 15; character of "Nigger Hill" in Oscar Handlin, *Boston's Immigrants: A Study in Acculturation,* rev. ed. (Cambridge, 1959), p. 96, and Quincy, *Municipal History,* p. 104; sensitivity of citizens in Quincy, *Municipal History,* p. 109.

13. Oscar Handlin and Mary Flug Handlin, *Commonwealth: Massachusetts 1774-1861: A Study of the Role of Government in the American Economy* (New York, 1946), pp. 254-255; *Revised Statutes of the Commonwealth of Massachusetts, Passed November 4, 1835* (Boston, 1836), ch. 14, secs. 93-99. In the lack of direct and reliable materials about the operations of the eighteenth- and early nineteenth-century police, their reliance upon individual complaint is illustrated largely by the changes introduced later. See later, Ch. Three, pp. 34 ff.

14. For resentment of police, see Josiah Quincy, *Remarks on Some of the Provisions of the Laws of Massachusetts Affecting Poverty, Vice, and Crime* (Cambridge, 1822), p. 7.

15. For history of the office, see Charles P. Sumner, *A Discourse on Some Points of Difference Between the Sheriff's Office in Massachusetts and England* (Boston, 1829), pp. 5-6; for duties, see *Revised Statutes* (1835), ch. 14, secs. 55-92; for powers of arrest see C. W. Hartshorne, *New England Sheriff: A Digest of the Laws of Massachusetts Relative to Sheriffs, Jailers, Coroners, and Constables, with Forms* (Worcester, 1844), p. 226, and *Revised Statutes* (1835), ch. 143, sec. 7; for riot, see st. 1784, ch. 34, and st. 1812, ch. 134.

16. Sheriff Sumner estimated that the average official tenure was ten years (*Discourse on the Sheriff's Office,* p. 21); he himself died in office, after a generation of service (*Records of The City of Boston; Mayor and Aldermen,* vol. XVII, June 10, 1839, p. 227); quotations in Sumner, *Discourse on the Sheriff's Office,* pp. 18, 16; fees in *Ninth Annual Report of the Committee on Finance, Appendix: Report of the Committee on the Subject of Fees of Office* (1821), pp. 8-9. The annual records of the committee on finance are hereinafter referred to as *Auditor's Report,* with date.

17. Fees in *Auditor's Report, Appendix* (1821), pp. 8-9; quotation in Sumner, *Discourse on the Sheriff's Office,* p. 18; court decisions summarized in Hartshorne, *New England Sheriff,* p. 31.

18. Sumner, *Discourse on the Sheriff's Office,* p. 5; *Revised Statutes* (1835),

ch. 15, secs. 66-77, ch. 14, secs. 55-92; *Auditor's Report, Appendix* (1821), pp. 8-9.

19. Ernst, *Constitutional History,* pp. 19-20; *Revised Statutes* (1835), ch. 15, secs. 66-70; st. 1802, ch. 7.

20. Functions of constables in *City Records,* I, May 17, 1822, 20-22, and *ibid.,* May 27, 1822, 32; fees in *Auditor's Report, Appendix* (1821), pp. 8-9; institution of complaints in *Revised Statutes* (1835), ch. 15, sec. 76.

21. Names of constables appointed in *City Records,* I, July 29, 1822, 64; previous occupations obtained from *The Boston Directory, Containing the Names of the Inhabitants, etc.* (Boston, 1822 and earlier years); official pay in *Auditor's Report* (1822), pp. 29-30; Constable Reed in the Boston *Herald,* March 13, 1887.

22. Quote on character of watchmen in Costello, *Our Police Protectors,* p. 42; establishment of watch in Ernst, *Constitutional History,* p. 166; watchmen's duties in *Revised Statutes* (1835), ch. 17, secs. 4-5; lighting responsibility in *City Records,* I, May 17, 1822, 20-22.

23. St. 1801, ch. 26; *City Records,* I, May 17, 1822, 20-22; *Revised Statutes* (1835), ch. 17, sec. 3; Edward H. Savage, *Police Records and Recollections: Or, Boston by Daylight and Gaslight* (Boston, 1873), p. 60.

24. Number of watchmen in Quincy, *Municipal History,* p. 272; distribution and functions in *City Records,* I, May 17, 1822, 20-22, and *ibid.,* XII, July 17, 1833, 165; South Boston situation *ibid.,* II, November 25, 1824, 461.

25. Savage, *Police Records,* p. 60; *City Records,* I, October 30, 1823, 450; *ibid.,* I, May 17, 1822, 20-22.

26. Quincy, *Remarks on Poverty, Vice, and Crime,* p. 7.

27. Sumner, *Discourse on the Sheriff's Office,* p. 11; Quincy, *Municipal History,* p. 155; Ernst, *Constitutional History,* pp. 72-74; Quincy, *Municipal History,* pp. 26-27.

28. Sprague, *City Government in Boston,* pp. 1-31.

29. Vote in Quincy, *Municipal History,* p. 40; charter in *The Charter of the City of Boston and Ordinances Made and Established* (Boston, 1827), pp. 3-20. This and later editions are hereinafter referred to as *City Charter and Ordinances,* with date.

CHAPTER TWO

CHANGE AND CONSERVATISM: THE CITY MARSHAL
AND THE GREAT MAYOR, 1822-1829

1. James McKellar Bugbee, "Boston under the Mayors, 1822-1880," *The Memorial History of Boston,* ed. Justin Winsor (Boston, 1881), vol. III, ch. II, p. 224.

2. *Ibid.,* p. 225.

3. James Walker, "Memoir of Josiah Quincy," Massachusetts Historical

Society *Proceedings,* vol. IX (1866-67), pp. 83-166; Josiah Quincy, *A Municipal History of the Town and City of Boston During Two Centuries* (Boston, 1852), p. 56; Bugbee, "Boston under the Mayors," p. 226.

4. *City Charter and Ordinances* (1827), pp. 3-20.

5. Bugbee, "Boston under the Mayors," pp. 226-233.

6. *City Charter and Ordinances* (1827), pp. 208-210.

7. Powers of arrest in, e.g., *Revised Statutes* (1836), ch. 129, sec. 1; superintendent of police, and assistant, in C. W. Ernst, *Constitutional History of Boston, Massachusetts* (Boston, 1894), pp. 81-82; abolition in *City Charter and Ordinances* (1827), p. 208.

8. *City Charter and Ordinances* (1827), pp. 208-210.

9. Pollard's career in James Spear Loring, *The Hundred Boston Orators* (Boston, 1852), pp. 365-367; see also Boston *Daily Atlas,* January 8, 1835, and Josiah Quincy, *Municipal History,* pp. 100-101; importance of office in City Doc. no. 5 (1824), *Report of the Special Committee on the Duties of the City Marshal.*

10. Quincy, *Municipal History,* pp. 147-148; *City Charter and Ordinances* (1827), p. 170.

11. Marshal's health authority in *City Charter and Ordinances* (1827), pp. 158-168, 208-210; prosecutions *ibid.* (1827), p. 209; review by council in, e.g., *City Records,* II, October 11, 1824; "referred to marshal" in, e.g., *ibid.,* V, February 5, 1827, 45.

12. Licensing of dogs in *City Charter and Ordinances* (1827), p. 167; firearms forbidden *ibid.* (1827), p. 132; attendance at fires in Quincy, *Municipal History,* p. 155; processions in *City Records,* X, April 2, 1832, 302; assistance at market in *City Charter and Ordinances* (1827), p. 209; reports building construction in *City Records,* VI, February 18, 1828, 47.

13. Concern in City Doc. no. 5 (1824), *Report on the Duties of the City Marshal;* attempts by common council in *City Records,* IV, February 20, 1826, 60, and *ibid.,* VII, June 29, 1829, 179; marshal's respect in, e.g., *ibid.,* II, October 11, 1824, 395; quotation in Common Council Doc. no. 9 (1834), *Report of City Marshal,* pp. 1-2.

14. Deputies in *City Charter and Ordinances* (1827), p. 208; horse in *City Records,* III, December 26, 1825, 407.

15. Common Council Doc. no. 9 (1834), *Report of City Marshal,* pp. 2, 3, 6-7, 4.

16. *Ibid.,* p. 8.

17. *City Charter and Ordinances* (1827), pp. 208-210.

18. Josiah Quincy, *Remarks on Some of the Provisions of the Laws of Massachusetts Affecting Poverty, Vice, and Crime* (Cambridge, 1822), p. 3; Quincy, *Municipal History,* pp. 35-36; House Doc. no. 46 (1820). For later citations of Quincy's report see, e.g., Public Doc. no. 17 (1872), *Eighth Annual Report of the Board of State Charities of Massachusetts,* p. 54, and City Doc. no. 36 (1878), *Report of Commission on the Treatment of the Poor.*

19. Quincy, *Remarks on Poverty, Vice, and Crime,* p. 6; Quincy, *Municipal History,* pp. 35-40, 48, 103, 106.

20. Quincy, *Remarks on Poverty, Vice, and Crime,* p. 4.

21. Quotation in *City Records,* V, February 26, 1827, 71; pay petitions in, e.g., *ibid.,* V, February 26, 1827, 71, and *ibid.,* II, October 21, 1824, 409; petitions for increase *ibid.,* II, November 25, 1824, 461, and *ibid.,* V, August 6, 1827, 249; expenditures in Charles P. Huse, *The Financial History of Boston from May 1, 1822 to January 31, 1909* (Cambridge, 1916), pp. 348, 354; private watch in *City Records,* V, May 19, 1827, 94, and *ibid.,* I, October 30, 1823, 450; volunteers *ibid.,* I, July 10, 1823, 282.

22. Quotation in House Doc. no. 415 (1867), *Reports on the Subject of a License Law: Appendix,* p. 418; constables in *City Records,* I, July 24, 1823, 294, and *ibid.,* August 21, 1823, 368; captain *ibid.,* II, October 21, 1824, 409-413, and *ibid.,* I, July 23, 1823, 262.

23. Description in Quincy, *Municipal History,* pp. 154-156; quotation in Arthur Wellington Brayley, *A Complete History of The Boston Fire Department* (Boston, 1889), p. 141; dissatisfaction in Quincy, *Municipal History,* p. 155.

24. Quincy, *Municipal History,* pp. 155-157.

25. *Ibid.,* pp. 156, 159, 158.

26. *Ibid.,* pp. 156, 159.

27. Quincy, *Municipal History,* pp. 160-163; Brayley, *History of the Fire Department,* pp. 162, 166.

28. Quincy, *Municipal History,* p. 102.

29. *Ibid.,* p. 104.

30. Licenses in Quincy, *Municipal History,* p. 272; expenses in *Auditor's Report* (1824), p. 14; later patrols in *City Records,* V, December 27, 1827, 377, and Edward H. Savage, *Police Records and Recollections: Or, Boston by Daylight and Gaslight* (Boston, 1873), p. 63.

31. *Columbian Centinel,* July 3, 1825; Savage, *Police Records,* pp. 107-112; Boston *Courier,* July 29, 1825.

32. *Columbian Centinel,* December 24, 1825; Quincy, *Municipal History,* p. 397.

33. Quincy, *Municipal History,* pp. 267, 268, 271, 272.

34. *Ibid.,* p. 273.

CHAPTER THREE

RIOTS AND A NEW POLICE, 1829-1838

1. James McKellar Bugbee, "Boston under the Mayors, 1822-1880," *The Memorial History of Boston,* ed. Justin Winsor (Boston, 1881), vol. III, ch. II, p. 233; "Inaugural Address . . . by Harrison Grey Otis" (1829), in *Inaugural Addresses of the Mayors of Boston* (Boston, 1894), vol. I, pp. 126-129; Samuel Eliot Morison, *The Life and Letters of Harrison Grey Otis, Federalist: 1765-1848* (Boston, 1913), pp. 250-251, 284. Inaugural addresses

are hereinafter referred to by name, date, and page number in the collected addresses.

2. Private gifts in Josiah Quincy, *A Municipal History of The Town and City of Boston During Two Centuries* (Boston, 1852), pp. 28-39, and Bugbee, "Boston under the Mayors," p. 241; Charles P. Huse, *The Financial History of Boston from May 1, 1822 to January 31, 1909* (Cambridge, 1916), p. 78; Otis proposals in *Inaugural Address* (1830), pp. 137-138.

3. Otis, *Inaugural Address* (1830), p. 139; *Auditor's Report* (1831), p. 24; *ibid.*, p. 28.

4. Removal of constables in *Auditor's Report* (1830), p. 28; increase of licenses in Massachusetts Temperance Society, *Plain Facts Addressed to the Inhabitants of Boston on the City Expenses for the Support of Pauperism, Vice, and Crime* (Boston, 1834), p. 21; number of watch in *City Records*, VIII, July 6, 1830, 178.

5. Bugbee, "Boston under the Mayors," p. 236; Boston *Advertiser*, December 3, 1831.

6. Bugbee, "Boston under the Mayors," p. 236; Huse, *Financial History*, p. 349; Wells, *Inaugural Address* (1833), 168-171.

7. *Auditor's Report* (1834), p. 24; Huse, *Financial History*, p. 30; *City Records*, X, August 12, 1832, 320; *ibid.*, X, July 2, 1832, 261; *ibid.*, X, July 9, 1832, 276.

8. Wells, *Inaugural Address* (1833), p. 170.

9. *City Records*, XI, July 17, 1833, 165-166; *ibid.*, XI, June 24, 1833, 178; *ibid.*, XI, July 1, 1833, 178.

10. Huse, *Financial History*, p. 354.

11. Murders are reported in Lemuel Shattuck, *Bills of Mortality, 1810-1849, City of Boston* (Boston, 1894), pp. 27-45; Houghton murder in Edward H. Savage, *Police Records and Recollections: Or, Boston by Daylight and Gaslight* (Boston, 1873), p. 64; riot in Arthur Wellington Brayley, *A Complete History of the Boston Fire Department* (Boston, 1889), p. 185.

12. One of many accounts of this famous incident is in Bugbee, "Boston under the Mayors," pp. 238-240.

13. Boston *Advertiser*, August 13, 1834; *Auditor's Report* (1835), p. 36; Bugbee, "Boston under the Mayors," p. 240.

14. Boston *Advertiser*, August 13, 1834; Bugbee, "Boston under the Mayors," p. 240.

15. *City Records*, XV, September 18, 1837, 304.

16. St. 1786, ch. 38; *Revised Statutes* (1835), ch. 129.

17. *City Records*, XII, August 16, 1834, 241; Huse, *Financial History*, pp. 348-349.

18. Copy of a letter to Mr. Knapp, one of the publishers of the *Liberator*, October 19, 1837, in Theodore Lyman 3rd, ed., *Papers Relating to the Garrison Mob* (Cambridge, 1870), p. 66; account by Mayor Lyman in T. Lyman 3rd, *Garrison Mob*, pp. 15-16.

19. Accounts of the riot by Lyman and Garrison in T. Lyman 3rd, *Garrison Mob*, pp. 14-24, 31-38; for a more recent account, see Lawrence Lader, *The*

Bold Brahmins: New England's War Against Slavery: 1831-1865 (New York, 1961), pp. 17-27.

20. T. Lyman 3rd, *Garrison Mob*, p. 5; Lader, *The Bold Brahmins*, pp. 23-25.

21. Statement by Phillips in T. Lyman 3rd, *Garrison Mob*, p. 6; newspaper opinion summarized in Boston *Recorder*, October 30, 1835.

22. Armstrong, *Inaugural Address* (1836), p. 208; Huse, *Financial History*, pp. 348-349.

23. Bugbee, "Boston under the Mayors," pp. 243-246; *City Records*, XV, June 22, 1837, 212-220.

24. *Ibid.*, 219, 218.

25. Story of Sears in the Boston *Herald*, February 3, 1884.

26. Bugbee, "Boston under the Mayors," p. 246.

27. *City Records*, XV, September 18, 1837, 303, 304, 305.

28. *Ibid.*, XV, September 18, 1837, 305.

29. City Doc. no. 15 (1837), *Report on the Message of the Mayor in relation to the Police, passim.*

30. *Ibid., passim.*

31. *City Records*, XV, September 18, 1837, 303-305; Howard O. Sprogle, *The Philadelphia Police, Past and Present* (Philadelphia, 1887), pp. 75, 99-101; Augustine E. Costello, *Our Police Protectors: History of the New York Police from the Earliest Period to the Present Time* (New York, 1885), p. 81.

32. Material on fire companies in *Resolves of the Boston Ex-Fire Department* (n.p., n.d.), broadside in Bostonian Society Collection; Oscar Handlin, *Boston's Immigrants: A Study in Acculturation*, rev. ed. (Cambridge, 1959), p. 187; the Boston *Herald*, December 16, 1851; approve police in *City Records*, XV, November 20, 1837, 366.

33. Savage, *Police Records*, pp. 63, 79, 93-94.

34. Arrest challenged in the Boston *Herald*, January 18, January 20, 1853; suit in *City Records*, VI, April 11, 1828, 112-113; petitions of watchmen *ibid.*, XI, March 11, 1833, 61; citizen's petition *ibid.*, XV, July 3, 1837, 237-241; assaults on officers in House Doc. no. 18 (1846), *Abstract of District Attorneys' Reports*, p. 8.

35. *Revised Statutes* (1835), ch. 143, ch. 129, and ch. 85; st. 1854, ch. 250; st. 1852, ch. 224.

36. *Commonwealth* v. *Hastings*, 9 Metcalf 259 (1845).

37. Money paid to informers in, e.g., *Auditor's Report* (1825), p. 26; for full list of rewards offered see below, ch. IV, note 54; for rewards claimed see *City Records*, III, December 1, 1825, 326; *ibid.*, XIX, September 13, 1841, 233; *ibid.*, XXIII, September 22, 1845, 391. These three were the only rewards listed as claimed in the period. It is possible that others were paid out, but the fact does not appear in the records.

38. St. 1838, ch. 123; *City Records*, XVI, May 21, 1838, 159; *ibid.*, XVI, July 18, 1838, 220.

CHAPTER FOUR

OPPORTUNITIES AND PROBLEMS, 1838-1845

1. Quotations in Eliot, *Inaugural Address* (1839), p. 236; expenditures in Charles P. Huse, *The Financial History of Boston from May 1, 1822, to January 31, 1909* (Cambridge, 1916), p. 348.

2. St. 1838, ch. 157.

3. A review of early Massachusetts legislation is contained in Robert C. Pitman, *Alcohol and the State: A Discussion of the Problem of Law as Applied to the Liquor Traffic* (New York, 1877), pp. 151-159; for a more general view, see Frederick A. Johnson and Ruth R. Kessler, "The Liquor License System: Its Origin and Constitutional Development," *New York University Law Quarterly Review*, vol. XV (1936), pp. 210-251, 380-424.

4. Pitman, *Alcohol and the State*, p. 159; st. 1786, ch. 68.

5. Adams quoted in Pitman, *Alcohol and the State*, p. 157; interest of grocers and others in "M.V.L.," *Licensed Houses: An Examination of the License Law of the Commonwealth of Massachusetts* (Boston, 1833), pp. 19, 22-26.

6. 1816 statute in *City Charter and Ordinances* (1827), pp. 200-203; for licenses see Massachusetts Temperance Society, *Plain Facts Addressed to the Inhabitants of Boston on the City Expenses for the Support of Pauperism, Vice, and Crime* (Boston, 1834), p. 21; Quincy statement in Josiah Quincy, *A Municipal History of the Town and City of Boston during Two Centuries* (Boston, 1852), p. 273; for power of grocers see, e.g., Boston *Advertiser*, December 3, December 17, 1831.

7. "M.V.L.," *Licensed Houses*, p. 34; st. 1832, ch. 166.

8. The names of the constables for 1822 are listed in *City Records*, I, July 29, 1822, 64; their former occupations are obtainable in *The Boston Directory* (Boston, 1800), and the editions of subsequent years; lack of prosecution in "M.V.L.," *Licensed Houses*, p. 27; attorney general's report *ibid.*, p. 18; antimonopoly sentiment in Arthur Burr Darling, *Political Changes in Massachusetts, 1824-1848: A Study in Liberal Movements in Politics* (New Haven, 1925), pp. 161-162.

9. Mass. Temp. Soc., *Plain Facts*, pp. 8-13.

10. Alice Felt Tyler, *Freedom's Ferment: Phases of American Social History to 1860* (Minneapolis, 1940), pp. 320-325; Mass. Temp. Soc., *Address . . . to the Friends of Temperance* (Boston, 1836), p. 5.

11. Tyler, *Freedom's Ferment*, pp. 327-346; House Doc. no. 62 (1837), *Report and Bill Concerning Licensed Houses and the Sale of Intoxicating Liquors*, p. 16.

12. *City Records*, XI, February 18, 1833, 35; *The Argument of Peleg Sprague, Esq., before the Committee of the Legislature upon the Memorial of Harrison Grey Otis*, 3rd ed. (Boston, 1843), p. 21.

13. B. F. Clark, *Prohibition of the Sale of Intoxicating Liquors Impracticable: The Maine Law a Failure* (Lowell, 1864), pp. 8-9.

14. For instability, see Oscar Handlin and Mary Flug Handlin, *Commonwealth: Massachusetts 1774-1861: A Study of the Role of Government in the American Economy* (New York, 1947), p. 216; for opposition, see *Argument of Peleg Sprague, passim*; for election and repeal, see Darling, *Political Changes,* p. 240.

15. House Doc. no. 37 (1839), *Reports and Bills Relating to the Sale of Spirituous Liquors, passim.*

16. Arguments in House Doc. no. 37 (1839), *Spirituous Liquors, passim;* testimony of mayor and marshal in *Argument of Peleg Sprague,* p. 16; figures in House Doc. no. 37 (1839), *Spirituous Liquors,* p. 38.

17. Statistics in *Argument of Peleg Sprague,* p. 21; dealers *ibid.;* prosecutions in House Doc. no. 37 (1839), *Spirituous Liquors,* p. 15; mayor in *Argument of Peleg Sprague,* p. 21.

18. Chapman, *Inaugural Address* (1842), p. 279.

19. *City Records,* XIX, March 29, 1841, 59.

20. Mass. Temp. Soc., *Plain Facts,* p. 21; *City Records,* XX, April 19, 1842, 89; Chapman, *Inaugural Address* (1842), p. 281.

21. Quotations in Chapman, *Inaugural Address* (1842), pp. 281, 280.

22. For Lyman's interest in reform see James McKellar Bugbee, "Boston under the Mayors, 1822-1880," *The Memorial History of Boston,* ed. Justin Winsor (Boston, 1881), vol. III, ch. II, p. 251; for Armstrong see, e.g., Mass. Temp. Soc., *Circular to the Members* (Boston, 1814); for Brimmer see Samuel Eliot, "Memoir of Martin Brimmer," MHS *Proceedings,* 2nd series, vol. X (1895-96), p. 587; for Eliot see Boston *Recorder,* June 1, 1838.

23. Brief biographies of marshals who were lawyers in William T. Davis, ed., *Professional and Industrial History of Suffolk County, Massachusetts,* vol. I: *History of Bench and Bar* (Boston, 1894), pp. 399, 418, 611; appointments in Edward H. Savage, *Police Records and Recollections: Or, Boston by Daylight and Gaslight* (Boston, 1873), pp. 76, 77, 79, 83, 84.

24. Bugbee, "Boston under the Mayors," pp. 247, 249, 250.

25. The officers of Boston in 1822, and their occupations, are contained in *The Boston Directory* (1822), p. 268 and *passim;* the aldermen of 1845 are listed in *Stimpson's Boston Directory* (Boston, 1845), p. 8 and *passim;* for the common council see *Members of the Common Council of the City of Boston for 1845, with Their Place of Birth, Occupation, Condition in Life, etc.* (Boston, 1845), *passim.*

26. For multiple tickets see, e.g., Boston *Traveller,* December 8, 1851.

27. For newspapers see Priscilla Hawthorne Fowle, "Boston Daily Newspapers: 1830-1850" (unpublished Ph.D. dissertation, Radcliffe College Archives, 1920).

28. *Ibid.,* pp. 72 ff., 172-173.

29. *Ibid., passim.*

30. Punditry in Fowle, "Boston Newspapers," pp. 108 ff.; Boston *Post,* April 17, April 24, 1833; and Boston *Daily Mail,* January 9, 1843; patrol in *Speech of Francis W. Emmons on Regulating the Sale of Alcohol* (Boston, 1848), pp. 6-7; Channing in Nathan Irving Huggins, "Private Charities in Boston, 1870-

1900: A Social History" (unpublished Ph.D. dissertation, Harvard University Archives, 1962), p. 7.

31. St. 1787, ch. 54; st. 1823, ch. 25.

32. Common drunkenness defined in *Commonwealth v. Whitney*, 5 Gray 85 (1855); history of legislation in *Commonwealth* v. *Miller*, 8 Gray 484 (1858); statistics of drunkenness in court in Mass. Temp. Soc., *Plain Facts*, p. 15; arrests in *Speech of Francis W. Emmons*, p. 7. See also Appendix I.

33. Tyler, *Freedom's Ferment*, pp. 278-281; *Revised Statutes* (1835), ch. 143, sec. 9; *The Collected Works of Theodore Parker*, ed. Frances Power Cobbe (14 vols.; 1863-1876), vol. VII: *Discourses on Social Science*, pp. 142, 137; *City Records*, XIX, May 24, 1841, 147.

34. Boston *Daily Mail*, June 20, 1845; John Augustus, *A Report on the Labors of John Augustus* (Boston, 1852), pp. 4, 5, 7, 13, 40-41.

35. Augustus, *A Report*, pp. 30-31.

36. *Ibid.*, pp. 37-38.

37. Lawrence Lader, *The Bold Brahmins: New England's War Against Slavery: 1831-1863* (New York, 1961), pp. 113-117; see also *Commonwealth* v. *Tracy*, 5 Metcalf 536 ff. (1843).

38. Fowle, "Boston Newspapers," p. 4; Oscar Handlin, *Boston's Immigrants: A Study in Acculturation*, rev. ed. (Cambridge, 1959), pp. 9, 18, 54-87.

39. Huse, *Financial History*, pp. 349, 348.

40. Sewer department in Huse, *Financial History*, p. 28.

41. Quincy, *Inaugural Address* (1848), p. 353.

42. For advantages of transport to criminals, see Senate Doc. no. 29 (1844), *Petition of Samuel D. Parker, The Attorney of the Commonwealth in and for the County of Suffolk*, p. 2.

43. For the use of the licensing authority see Handlin and Handlin, *Commonwealth*, pp. 3, 72-80, 82, 96, 102, 104, 223-225, 253-255.

44. For licenses issued by the municipality see *City Charter and Ordinances* (1827), pp. 35, 12, 134, 73, 213-216, 61-62, 80, 106; for list of later licenses see *ibid.* (1850), pp. 143, 175-180; for revenue from licensing see Huse, *Financial History*, p. 43.

45. St. 1839, ch. 53; *City Charter and Ordinances* (1850), pp. 350-353.

46. James Faxon, *The Record of Crimes in the United States* (Buffalo, 1833), pp. 68 and *passim*.

47. For descriptions of later criminality see Ch. Seven, pp. 142-150.

48. Howard O. Sprogle, *The Philadelphia Police, Past and Present* (Philadelphia, 1887), p. 69.

49. For extent of counterfeiting in this period, see George Rogers Taylor, *The Transportation Revolution: 1815-1860* (New York, 1951), p. 326.

50. MS "Report to the New England Association Against Counterfeiting, November 27, 1833," in collection of The Bostonian Society.

51. *Ibid.*

52. *Report of December 10, 1833, to the Member Banks*, in collection of The Bostonian Society.

53. Letter from William H. Blayney to Parker D. Pierce, March 4, 1835, in collection of The Bostonian Society, *Report of December 10, 1833*.

54. Letter from Gates in *City Records*, VII, February 9, 1829, 42; fear of burglary in House Doc. no. 15 (1845), *Abstract of District Attorney's Reports*; full list of rewards in *City Records*, as follows, with volume numbers omitted: November 11, 1822, p. 117; December 1, 1825, p. 386; September 17, 1827, p. 274; September 22, 1834, p. 266; January 26, 1836, p. 21; May 1, 1837, p. 50; September 2, 1839, p. 292; March 26, 1841, p. 52; September 13, 1841, p. 233; November 22, 1841, pp. 305-306; April 19, 1842, p. 86; May 5, 1843, p. 165; June 3, 1845, p. 230; July 28, 1845, p. 313; November 3, 1845, p. 46; November 6, 1845, p. 468.

55. English law in Patrick Pringle, *The Thief Takers* (London, 1958), pp. 38, 160-161; Massachusetts law in *Revised Statutes* (1835), ch. 128; see also *Commonwealth* v. *Pease*, 16 Mass. 91 ff. (1820).

56. Boston *Daily Mail*, March 26, March 27, April 1, 1841; *Bunker Hill Aurora*, April 3, 1841.

57. Boston *Daily Mail*, April 1, 1841; *City Records*, XIX, September 13, 1841, 233. The commonwealth also offered rewards, several of which went to Clapp. See st. 1843, ch. 13; st. 1844, ch. 55; st. 1846, ch. 71.

58. *City Records*, XXIII, July 14, 1845, 296-297; *ibid.*, XXI, March 6, 1843, 56.

CHAPTER FIVE

A VIGOROUS POLICE: MARSHAL TUKEY, 1845-1853

1. Bigelow, *Inaugural Address* (1849), pp. 368-369.

2. Charles P. Huse, *The Financial History of Boston from May 1, 1822 to January 31, 1909* (Cambridge, 1916), pp. 348, 82, 79, 70-72, 78, 62.

3. Political splintering in William Gleason Bean, "Party Transformation in Massachusetts, 1848-1860, with Special Reference to the Antecedents of Republicanism" (unpublished Ph.D. dissertation, Harvard University Archives, 1922), *passim.*

4. Boston *Advertiser*, December 8, 1845; James McKellar Bugbee, "Boston under the Mayors, 1822-1880," *The Memorial History of Boston*, ed. Justin Winsor (Boston, 1881), vol. III, ch. II, p. 251; Huse, *Financial History*, pp. 105-106.

5. Tukey biography in *Gleason's Pictorial Drawing Room Companion*, May 10, 1851, p. 75; appointments in Edward H. Savage, *Police Records and Recollections: Or, Boston by Daylight and Gaslight* (Boston, 1873), p. 84; detectives in City Doc. no. 8 (1871), *Annual Report of the Chief of Police*, p. 68. This and the reports for other years hereinafter referred to as *Annual Police Report*, with date issued.

6. Huse, *Financial History*, p. 354; *Annual Police Report* (1852), pp. 3-5.

7. Numbers of watchmen in *Auditor's Report* (1846), p. 58; *ibid.* (1852), p. 84; constables in *City Records*, XXVI, October 9, 1848, 439; Clapp and Eaton in Boston *Daily Mail*, February 3, 1848.

8. *Auditor's Report* (1847), p. 45; *ibid.* (1848), p. 41; *ibid.* (1851), p. 72.

9. St. 1848, ch. 270; *City Records*, XXVI, September 25, 1848, 426-427.

10. St. 1796, ch. 32; *City Records*, I, November 13, 1823, 476; st. 1847, ch. 247; *Annual Police Report* (1852), p. 4; *City Charter and Ordinances* (1850), pp. 61-76.

11. City Doc. no. 18 (1846), *Truancy*, p. 2; *Revised Statutes* (1835), ch. 23, sec. 19; st. 1850, ch. 294; City Doc. no. 18 (1846), *Truancy*, p. 3; *Annual Police Report* (1852), p. 10; City Doc. no. 58 (1852), *Officer's Report in Relation to Truant Children, passim.*

12. Estimates of the success of temperance before 1850 in, e.g., B. F. Clark, *Prohibition of the Sale of Intoxicating Liquors Impracticable: The Maine Law a Failure* (Lowell, 1864), p. 17, and House Doc. no. 415 (1867), *Reports on the Subject of a License Law: Appendix*, pp. 322 ff.; for earlier number of convicted nightwalkers see, e.g., City Doc. no. 21 (1838), *Report on Prisons*, pp. 11-12; views of elder Quincy in Josiah Quincy, *A Municipal History of the Town and City of Boston During Two Centuries* (Boston, 1852), p. 104. For record of arrests and other statistics, see Appendix I.

13. Bigelow, *Inaugural Address* (1849), p. 373; Bugbee, "Boston under the Mayors," pp. 253, 254.

14. *City Records*, XXVII, October 1, 1849, 459; *Annual Police Report* (1851), p. 10; *Annual Police Report* (1852), pp. 9, 10.

15. Arrest statistics in *Annual Police Report* (1851), p. 10.

16. Bugbee, "Boston under the Mayors," p. 253; *City Records*, XXV, May 21, 1847, 222.

17. Boston *Daily Mail*, March 10, 1851; *Annual Police Report* (1871), p. 77. The *Annual Report* for 1871, written by Chief E. H. Savage, includes considerable historical material omitted in his *Police Records*.

18. Boston *Semi-Weekly Atlas*, April 26, 1851; Savage, *Police Records*, pp. 254-262.

19. For "Bristol Bill" see Boston *Semi-Weekly Atlas*, September 17, 1851.

20. *Annual Police Report* (1858), p. 4; *Poole* v. *Boston*, 5 Cushing 219 ff. (1849); Quincy, *Inaugural Address* (1848), p. 356.

21. *Annual Police Report* (1851), pp. 13-15; *Auditor's Report* (1852), p. 66.

22. Boston *Daily Atlas*, June 20, 1846; Boston *Daily Mail*, January 31, 1853; *Auditor's Report* (1849), p. 46; *Annual Police Report* (1851), pp. 13-14.

23. James Spear Loring, *The One Hundred Boston Orators* (Boston, 1852), p. 367; Savage, *Police Records*, p. 86; Boston *Semi-Weekly Atlas*, September 17, 1851.

24. Internal Health expenditures in *Auditor's Report* (1852), p. 43; Tukey's power of appointment in Boston *Herald*, November 11, 1851; salaries in *Auditor's Report* (1848), p. 58.

25. Boston *Daily Mail*, May 3, 1848; *Gleason's Pictorial Drawing Room Companion*, May 10, 1851, p. 75; Savage, *Police Records*, p. 375; Bugbee, "Boston under the Mayors," p. 258.

26. Bugbee, "Boston under the Mayors," p. 253; *Bunker Hill Aurora*, July 17, 1852.

27. For omnibus owners' suit, see *Commonwealth v. Robertson*, 5 Cushing 438 ff. (1850); quotation, and arrest figures, in *Annual Police Report* (1871), pp. 77-78.

28. *Annual Police Report* (1851), pp. 5-6, 13-15; Ball Fenner, *Raising the Veil: Or, Scenes in the Courts* (Boston, 1856), pp. 68-70.

29. Officer George S. McWatters, *Knots Untied: Or, Ways and By-Ways in the Hidden Life of American Detectives* (Hartford, 1871), p. 648.

30. Boston Prison Discipline Society, *The Prisoner's Friend*, March 1851, p. 322.

31. *Annual Police Report* (1851), pp. 26-31; Prison Discipline Society, *The Prisoner's Friend*, March 1851, pp. 320-321.

32. Oscar Handlin, *Boston's Immigrants: A Study in Acculturation*, rev. ed. (Cambridge, 1959), pp. 52, 240, 114, 116.

33. Estimates of temperance success in, e.g., Clark, *Prohibition*, p. 17, and House Doc. no. 415 (1867), *Reports on License Law: Appendix*, pp. 322 ff.

34. Quincy complaint in *Inaugural Address* (1848), p. 357; Tukey complaints in *Annual Police Report* (1851), pp. 17 and *passim*, and *ibid.* (1852), pp. 13-14; fines *ibid.* (1852), pp. 13-14, and in Fenner, *Raising the Veil*, p. 88.

35. Bigelow, *Inaugural Address* (1849), pp. 373-374.

36. *Annual Police Report* (1852), pp. 13, 11-12.

37. *City Records*, XXVIII, November 25, 1850, 488; *ibid.*, XXVIII, December 16, 1850, 516; Bugbee, "Boston under the Mayors," pp. 256-257.

38. Lawrence Lader, *The Bold Brahmins: New England's War Against Slavery: 1831-1865* (New York, 1961), pp. 161-167.

39. *Ibid.*, pp. 174-175.

40. Lader, *The Bold Brahmins*, pp. 174-180; Senate Doc. no. 89 (1851), *Report on Whether the Freedom of any of the Inhabitants is Endangered*, pp. 4-25.

41. Boston *Daily Mail*, April 4, 1851; Senate Doc. no. 89 (1851), *Report on the Freedom of the Inhabitants*, p. 6; Lader, *The Bold Brahmins*, p. 175.

42. Account of case in Senate Doc. no. 89 (1851), *Report on the Freedom of the Inhabitants, passim*; chain in Lader, *The Bold Brahmins*, p. 176; quotation in James Freeman Clarke, "The Anti-Slavery Movement in Boston," *The Memorial History of Boston*, ed. Justin Winsor, vol. III, ch. VI, p. 398.

43. Praise in *Gleason's Pictorial Drawing Room Companion*, May 3, 1851, p. 5; account of case in Lader, *The Bold Brahmins*, pp. 177-179; quotation, and account of case, in Senate Doc. no. 89 (1851), *Report on the Freedom of the Inhabitants*, p. 27 and *passim*.

44. Coalition legislature in Handlin, *Boston's Immigrants*, pp. 194-195; Whig alliance with Irish, *ibid.*, pp. 196-197.

45. For biographies of marshals see earlier, Ch. Four, note 23; for appoint-

ment procedures see, e.g., *City Records,* XXXI, October 3, 1853, 608, *ibid.,* XXXIII, July 21, 1845, 301, *ibid.,* XX, March 14, 1842, 53; for applications see *Annual Police Report* (1851), p. 34; for petitions see, e.g., Boston *Post,* February 2, 1848.

46. Boston *Herald,* October 8, 1851.

47. *Ibid.*

48. Boston *Herald,* November 11, 1851; *Annual Police Report* (1851), pp. 20-21, 23; *ibid.* (1852), p. 19. It is notable that the Boston *Pilot,* the organ of the Irish Catholic population, voiced no complaints about either Tukey or the police during the McGinniskin affair, which it followed through the reports of other local papers.

49. Wages of common labor and of master masons in Handlin, *Boston's Immigrants,* p. 85, in chart reproduced from *Third Annual Report of the Bureau of Statistics of Labor* (1872), pp. 517-520.

50. Boston *Herald,* November 11, 1851.

51. Savage, *Police Records,* p. 91; Boston *Daily Mail,* December 14, 1853; Bugbee, "Boston under the Mayors," p. 258.

52. Savage, *Police Records,* p. 91.

53. *Annual Police Report* (1851), pp. 8-9.

54. Indictment of night policemen in *Bunker Hill Aurora,* July 17, 1852; attack on "show-up" in Boston *Daily Mail,* November 10, 1852.

55. *City Records,* XXX, April 12, 1852, 158; *Annual Police Report* (1851), p. 9; Boston *Herald,* November 11, 1851.

56. *City Records,* XXX, September 6, 1852, 431-434; *ibid.,* XXX, May 17, 1852, 248.

57. St. 1850, ch. 232; st. 1852, ch. 322.

58. St. 1852, ch. 322, sec. 7; *City Records,* XXX, July 19, 1852, 372.

59. *City Records,* XXX, June 19, 1852, 292; Boston *Daily Mail,* June 24, 1852; *City Records,* XXX, September 6, 1852, 432.

60. Boston *Daily Mail,* June 29, 1852; *Congregationalist* quoted *ibid.,* July 17, 1852; *Journal* quoted *ibid.,* July 15, 1852; *Bunker Hill Aurora,* June 26, 1852, and July 17, 1852; Boston *Post,* July 16, 1852.

61. Smith nomination in Boston *Daily Mail,* December 4, 1852; character of support *ibid.,* December 11, 1852, and in Boston *Semi-Weekly Atlas,* December 11, 1852; earlier appeal to Native Americans in Boston *Daily Mail,* December 11, 1848; condemnation of Tukey in Boston *Semi-Weekly Atlas,* December 11, 1852.

62. *City Records,* XXX, August 16, 1852, 409; City Doc. no. 63 (1852), *Report on the Watch and Police Departments;* Boston *Semi-Weekly Atlas,* December 11, 1852.

63. Boston *Semi-Weekly Atlas,* December 15, 1852.

64. City Doc. no. 63 (1852), *Report on the Police, passim.*

65. *Ibid.,* p. 8 and *passim.*

66. Boston *Semi-Weekly Atlas,* December 15, 1852; *ibid.,* December 18, 1852; *ibid.,* January 19, 1853; Boston *Daily Mail,* January 31, 1853.

67. The description of this occasion, here and in the following paragraphs, is taken from two slightly different freehand accounts in the Boston *Daily Mail,* January 31, 1853, and Boston *Herald,* January 31, 1853.

68. Boston *Daily Mail,* February 1, 1853; Boston *Herald,* December 29, 1853. News of Tukey's death reached the East on November 23, 1867. There were no obituaries. See Savage, *Police Records,* p. 106.

69. Rising expenditures in Huse, *Financial History,* p. 354.

CHAPTER SIX

ADJUSTMENT AND DEFINITION, 1853-1860

1. Growth of immigrants in Oscar Handlin, *Boston's Immigrants: A Study in Acculturation,* rev. ed. (Cambridge, 1959), p. 52; population and real estate valuation in Charles P. Huse, *The Financial History of Boston from May 1, 1822 to January 31, 1909* (Cambridge, 1916), p. 376.

2. Factory industry in Handlin, *Boston's Immigrants,* pp. 74-83.

3. Boston *Daily Mail,* December 16, 1840; *ibid.,* December 4, 1852; Boston *Traveller,* December 10, 1853; Boston *Herald,* December 9, 1851.

4. *City Charter and Ordinances* (1856), pp. 1-32; Boston *Herald,* December 9, 1851; Boston *Herald,* December 5 and December 26, 1853; *ibid.,* January 10, 1854; Boston *Traveller,* December 11, 1854; Boston *Advertiser,* December 5 and December 11, 1855; *ibid.,* December 8 and December 9, 1856; *ibid.,* December 15, 1857; Boston *Herald,* December 14, 1858; *ibid.,* December 13, 1859.

5. For joint conventions see Boston *Advertiser,* December 8, 1857; for later candidates see James McKellar Bugbee, "Boston under the Mayors," *The Memorial History of Boston,* ed. Justin Winsor (Boston, 1881), vol. III, ch. II, pp. 262-263. This arrangement produced some strange situations. Nathaniel Shurtleff, who headed the American ticket in 1855, had earlier tried for the Citizens' nomination (Boston *Advertiser,* December 6 and December 11, 1855). In national politics he was a lifelong Democrat (Bugbee, "Boston under the Mayors," p. 276). Mayor Lincoln, who ran against a Republican in his first bid for office, later emerged as a member of that party (Boston *Advertiser,* December 14, 1857, November 27, 1860). T. C. Amory, an avowed Breckenridge Democrat, was the only alderman elected in 1860 on the straight Republican ticket (Boston *Advertiser,* November 7, December 11, 1860).

6. Occupations of mayors in State Street Trust Company, *The Mayors of Boston* (Boston, 1914), pp. 23-25; for Lincoln see also Boston *Herald,* December 11, 1857; for workings of charter see Bugbee, "Boston under the Mayors," pp. 260-261.

7. For prohibitionist vote at height see Boston *Advertiser,* December 14, 1853. The Young Men's League, representing the prohibitionist party, won 2,010 votes out of 12,984.

8. Boston *Daily Mail,* January 26, 1853; Boston *Semi-Weekly Atlas,* July 21, 1852; *Modification or Absolute Prohibition, Which? . . . An Address by Francis W. Bird* (Boston, 1869), p. 5.

9. For legal problems involved in prohibition see Frederick A. Johnson and Ruth R. Kessler, "The Liquor License System, Its Origin and Constitutional Development," New York University *Law Quarterly Review,* vol. XV (1937-38), pp. 233-238; for chicken salad, see Boston *Herald,* November 4, 1854.

10. Seaver, *Inaugural Address* (1853), pp. 49-50.

11. Smith comment in *Inaugural Address* (1855), pp. 86-88; Lincoln comment in *Inaugural Address* (1859), pp. 209-210; Seaver comment in *Inaugural Address* (1853), p. 50; licenses sent to court in Boston *Semi-Weekly Atlas,* July 24, 1852; instructions to police in Seaver, *Inaugural Address* (1853), p. 48.

12. First sentence in Boston *Traveller,* December 16, 1853; for some of the dozens of liquor cases heard during the 1850's see, e.g., *Commonwealth* v. *Edwards,* 12 Cushing 185; *Commonwealth* v. *Kendall,* 12 Cushing 414; *Commonwealth* v. *Tuttle,* 12 Cushing 502; *Commonwealth* v. *Burding,* 12 Cushing 506; all heard in 1853 and all decided against the dealers; *Fisher* v. *McGirr,* 1 Gray 1 ff. (1854).

13. Taylor appointment in *City Records,* XXXII, May 8, 1854, 321; police prosecutions of liquor cases in House Doc. no. 415 (1867), *Reports on the Subject of a License Law: Appendix* (Boston, 1867), p. 238; Coburn appointment in *City Records,* XXXIV, April 9, 1856, 148.

14. William Gleason Bean, "Party Transformation in Massachusetts, 1848-1860, with Special Reference to the Antecedents of Republicanism" (unpublished Ph.D. dissertation, Harvard University Archives, 1922), p. 263; st. 1855, ch. 215, sec. 13, sec. 22, sec. 15.

15. Character of legislature in Bean, "Party Transformation in Massachusetts," p. 288; debate in *Massachusetts State Convention Debates and Proceedings* (Boston, 1853), vol. III, p. 442; juries in st. 1855, ch. 408; reaction to liquor law in House Doc. no. 415 (1867), *Reports on a License Law: Appendix,* p. 238.

16. Firing of Butman in *City Records,* XXXI, October 3, 1853, 608.

17. Lawrence Lader, *The Bold Brahmins: New England's War Against Slavery: 1831-1865* (New York, 1961), p. 204; Boston *Herald,* December 14, 1853.

18. Lader, *The Bold Brahmins,* pp. 205-209; *Ela* v. *Smith,* 5 Gray 121 ff. (1855).

19. Objections of federal officials in *Ela* v. *Smith,* p. 121; political contest in Lader, *The Bold Brahmins,* p. 210; operations of police in *Ela* v. *Smith* and Boston *Herald,* June 3, 1854.

20. Rewards in *City Records,* XXXII, June 6, 1854, 412; reluctance of police in Boston *Herald,* June 3, 1854, and Edward H. Savage, *Police Records and Recollections: Or, Boston by Daylight and Gaslight* (Boston, 1873), p. 96; orders to soldiers in *Ela* v. *Smith,* p. 122; opinion of Smith in Lader, *The Bold Brahmins,* p. 212; abolitionists' mood in Harold Schwartz, "Fugitive Slave Days in Boston," *New England Quarterly,* vol. XXVII, no. 2 (June 1954), pp. 207-208.

21. Lader, *The Bold Brahmins*, pp. 215-216; Boston *Traveller,* December 11, 1854; st. 1855, ch. 152; st. 1855, ch. 116.

22. Character and fortunes of Know-Nothing party in Massachusetts in Bean, "Party Transformation in Massachusetts," *passim.*

23. Irish weakness in Boston in George Potter, *To the Golden Door: The Story of the Irish in America* (Boston, 1960), pp. 280-281; nationalist leadership *ibid.,* pp. 389-390.

24. For Henshaw see Arthur Burr Darling, *Political Changes in Massachusetts, 1824-1848* (New Haven, 1925), pp. 7, 59, 71 ff.; for effect of poll taxes see Handlin, *Boston's Immigrants,* pp. 191, 260. Of a population of over 160,000, some 24,272 were legal voters, 4,564 of them naturalized citizens.

25. *Ibid.,* pp. 190-199.

26. Action of Know-Nothing administrations *ibid.,* pp. 202-203; McGinniskin was not listed as a policeman in the annually published *Municipal Register of the City of Boston* after 1854.

27. Blunders of Know-Nothing legislature in Bean, "Party Transformation in Massachusetts," pp. 265-267; political decline *ibid.,* p. 295; 1854 campaign in Boston *Traveller,* December 11, 1854, January 10, 1855; 1855 campaign in Boston *Advertiser,* December 11, 1855.

28. Potter, *To the Golden Door,* p. 562; Howard O. Sprogle, *The Philadelphia Police, Past and Present* (Philadelphia, 1887), pp. 77-86, 89-93, 96, 102, 128-129; Augustine E. Costello, *Our Police Protectors: History of the New York Police from the Earliest Period to the Present Time* (New York, 1885), pp. 83-84, 106, 115, 117-119, 137-143.

29. Fire department improvements in Huse, *Financial History,* pp. 65-66.

30. Holiday appointments in, e.g., *City Records,* XXIV, June 29, 1846, 367; specials for riot in, e.g., *Auditor's Report* (1835), p. 36; st. 1850, ch. 186.

31. Attitude toward Burns affair in Boston *Herald,* June 3, 1854, and Savage, *Police Records,* p. 96.

32. Handlin, *Boston's Immigrants,* p. 199; William Byrne, "The Roman Catholic Church in Boston," *The Memorial History of Boston,* ed. Justin Winsor (Boston, 1881), vol. III, ch. XIV, p. 532.

33. City Doc. no. 43 (1850), *Report on the Watch and Police Departments,* pp. 21-22; Boston *Post,* November 3, 1846; City Doc. no. 66 (1851), *Report Relating to the Watch and Police Departments,* pp. 4-6.

34. City Doc. no. 43 (1850), *Report on the Watch,* pp. 15-18; City Doc. no. 47 (1853), *Report on the Reorganization of the Police and Watch Departments,* pp. 1-10; City Doc. no. 63 (1852), *Report on the Watch and Police Departments,* pp. 4-5.

35. Boston *Herald,* January 11, January 15, January 18, January 24, January 25, 1853.

36. Watch rules in *City Records,* XXX, February 9, 1852, 42-43; operations in City Doc. no. 43 (1850), *Report on the Watch, passim.*

37. In these and the following paragraphs, the figures are from the quarterly watch report printed in the Boston *Herald,* July 7, 1853.

38. Other watch reports, including number held for trial, in Boston *Herald,* January 12, April 5, October 3, 1853; legal question *ibid.,* January 20, 1853.

39. *Ibid.,* January 25, 1853.

40. Boston *Herald,* January 24, 1853; *City Records,* XXXI, February 21, 1853, 90; C. W. Ernst, *The Constitutional History of Boston, Massachusetts* (Boston, 1894), pp. 125-126; st. 1853, ch. 354.

41. For difference between aldermen and common council see City Doc. no. 28 (1853), *An Ordinance Providing for the Organization of the Police Department of the City of Boston,* the common councillors' version.

42. *Annual Police Report* (1871), pp. 71-72.

43. Boston *Herald,* May 27, 1854.

44. *Ibid.*

45. In this and the succeeding four paragraphs the number of men in each division is taken from the Boston *Herald,* May 27, 1854, and the divisional boundaries from the *Annual Police Report* (1871), pp. 1-8. See also Appendix II for maps.

46. Establishment of harbor division in *City Records,* XXXI, July 25, 1853; Tukey suggestion in *Annual Police Report* (1851), p. 14; pirates in *Annual Police Report* (1854), p. 7, and *ibid.* (1871), p. 69; routine work *ibid.* (1861), pp. 7-8.

47. City Doc. no. 78 (1853), *An Ordinance Providing for the Police,* sec. 11; *City Records,* XXXII, March 22, 1854, 167-173; *ibid.,* XXXII, March 27, 1854, 195; *City Charter and Ordinances* (1856), pp. 385-393.

48. Boston *Herald,* December 24, 1853; *Annual Police Report* (1871), p. 72.

49. Information about special police in City Doc. no. 73 (1856), *Report on Appointment of Special Police Officers;* Nurse appointment in Boston *Daily Mail,* June 29, 1852. The undefined legal status of these officers makes it impossible to determine their effective number. It is not clear whether all appointments were recorded in the *City Records.* Nor is it clear whether their warrants were good for one year only or until canceled. Policy in granting them often varied. Most of the recipients would find it possible to work, as watchmen or otherwise, without the extra authority conferred. On the other hand, a decrease in their number might impel some places to substitute regular policemen, hired in their off-duty hours.

50. *Annual Police Report* (1857), pp. 14-15.

51. *City Records,* XXXIV, July 21, 1856, 386-387; *ibid.,* September 15, 1856, 470; *Commonwealth* v. *Hastings,* 9 Metcalf 259 ff. (1838); City Doc. no. 73 (1856), *Report on Appointment of Special Police Officers;* Rice, *Inaugural Address* (1857), p. 146.

52. The police rules and regulations were not codified or published between 1855 and 1863; the rules regarding specials, published in the latter year but operative before that, are contained in *A Supplement to the Laws and Ordinances of the City of Boston* (Boston, 1866), p. 95.

53. *Annual Police Report* (1858), p. 6.

54. Complaints about applicants and discipline in, e.g., Rice, *Inaugural Address* (1857), p. 145, and *Annual Police Report* (1858), pp. 22-24; lines of

authority in City Doc. no. 31 (1854), *Rules and Regulations of the Police Department*, p. 10.

55. Taylor's comment in *Annual Police Report* (1855), p. 13; primacy of New York in eliminating watch in Costello, *Our Police Protectors*, pp. 104-106; in uniforming force, *ibid.*, p. 127; primacy of Philadelphia in police telegraph in Sprogle, *Philadelphia Police*, p. 112; for primacy of Boston in establishing harbor police, cf. Costello, *Our Police Protectors*, p. 448, and Sprogle, *Philadelphia Police*, pp. 123 ff.

56. A history of the police stations is included in the *Annual Report* (1871), pp. 1-8; description of station five *ibid.* (1858), pp. 17-18.

57. *Annual Police Report* (1855), pp. 11-12; City Records, XXXIII, September 4, 1855, 577; *Annual Police Report* (1859), p. 20.

58. *Annual Police Report* (1855), pp. 10-11; st. 1855, ch. 118.

59. Murders of peace officers in Savage, *Police Records*, pp. 65, 87, 98.

60. St. 1850, ch. 194; st. 1859, ch. 199. Cf. also *Commonwealth* v. *O'Connor*, 7 Allen 583 (1863).

61. Boston *Daily Mail*, April 28, 1848; Boston *Herald*, October 19, 1857. The murder of Watchman Jonathan Houghton, in December of 1825, prompted the city government to continue his salary for twelve months, for the benefit of the widow (*City Records*, III, December 19, 1825, 401). Sheriff Sumner, in an even more unusual move, donated his thirty-dollar executioner's fee to the same good cause (*Bowen's Boston News-letter and City Record*, I, April 8, 1826).

62. *Annual Police Report* (1854), p. 7; *ibid.* (1871), p. 69.

63. *Annual Police Report* (1857); *City Records*, XXXVI, June 8, 1858, 341-342; Lincoln, *Inaugural Address* (1859), pp. 181-182; *City Records*, XXXVI, September 27, 1858, 330-332; City Doc. no. 38 (1858), *Report Concerning Uniforms for the Police.*

64. Common councillors' regret in City Doc. no. 38 (1858), *Uniforms*, p. 1; letters to press in Boston *Herald*, September 25, September 28, 1858; troubles in New York in Costello, *Our Police Protectors*, pp. 127-129; in Philadelphia in Sprogle, *Philadelphia Police*, pp. 103, 122-123; voluntary uniforms in Boston *Herald*, September 28, 1858; design in *City Records*, XXXVI, September 20, 1858, 515-519; allowance in *City Records*, XXXVI, October 11, 1858, 562-563.

65. St. 1851, ch. 162.

66. The history of search warrants in the commonwealth is summarized in *Commonwealth* v. *Hinds*, M.R. 145, 184 ff. (1887).

67. *Commonwealth* v. *Dana*, 2 Metcalf 329 (1841); *Banks* v. *Farwell*, 21 Pick. 156 ff. (1838); *City Records*, XXX, September 6, 1852, 432.

68. Pre-1845 cases are *Commonwealth* v. *Dana* and *Banks* v. *Farwell*, above; cases between 1845 and 1861 include *Commonwealth* v. *Hastings*, 9 Metcalf 259 (1845), *Commonwealth* v. *Dugan*, 12 Metcalf 233 (1847), *Tubbs* v. *Tukey*, 3 Cushing 438 (1849), *Rohan* v. *Sawin*, 5 Cushing 281 (1850), *Barnard* v. *Bartlett*, 10 Cushing 50 (1852), *Commonwealth* v. *Carey*, 12 Cushing 246 (1853), *Commonwealth* v. *McLaughlin*, 12 Cushing 615 (1853), *Commonwealth* v. *Cooley*, 6 Gray 350 (1856), *Mason* v. *Lathrop*, 7 Gray 364 (1856),

Commonwealth v. *Presby,* 14 Gray 65 (1859), *McLennon* v. *Richardson,* 15 Gray 74 (1860), *Commonwealth* v. *Irwin,* 1 Allen 587 (1861).

69. *Rohan* v. *Sawin,* p. 285.

70. *Commonwealth* v. *Carey,* pp. 251-254; *Commonwealth* v. *McLaughlin,* pp. 616-619; *Commonwealth* v. *Presby,* pp. 65-69.

71. *Mason* v. *Lathrop,* p. 354; *Kennedy* v. *Favor,* p. 202.

72. *Barnard* v. *Bartlett,* pp. 502-503; *Commonwealth* v. *Irwin,* p. 588; *McLennon* v. *Richardson,* pp. 77-78.

73. City Doc. no. 31 (1854), *Police Rules and Regulations,* pp. 20-25.

74. *City Charter and Ordinances* (1856), p. 393; City Doc. no. 63 (1852), *Report on the Watch and Police Departments,* p. 8.

75. Stolen property report for 1850 in *Annual Police Report* (1851), p. 9; those for later years summaried *ibid.* (1871), p. 37.

76. City Doc. no. 31 (1854), *Police Rules and Regulations,* pp. 17-20.

77. Responsibility of street superintendent in *City Charter and Ordinances* (1856), p. 321; of police *ibid.,* p. 391; fire department *ibid.,* p. 81; building permits *ibid.,* p. 82-83; buildings survey in *Annual Police Report* (1861), pp. 24-25; Coburn comment *ibid.* (1859), pp. 27-28.

78. For early traffic regulations see earlier, Ch. Five, note 10; for transportation in mid-1850's see Handlin, *Boston's Immigrants,* pp. 94-100.

79. *City Charter and Ordinances* (1856), pp. 90-107.

80. *Annual Police Report* (1852), p. 10; *ibid.* (1854), p. 6; *ibid.* (1857), p. 9; Boston *Herald,* May 21, 1853.

81. *Annual Police Report* (1857), p. 18.

82. For earlier figure, in 1830, when an estimated 300 unlicensed and 690 licensed places served a population of less than 62,000, see "M.V.L.," *Licensed Houses: An Examination of the License Law of the Commonwealth of Massachusetts* (Boston, 1833), p. 18; figures for the 1850's summarized in *Annual Police Report* (1871), p. 37.

83. Effect of prohibition on beer in *Annual Police Report* (1859), p. 25; quality of liquor in Ball Fenner, *Raising the Veil; Or, Scenes in the Courts* (Boston, 1856), pp. 179-180.

84. For attempts to coordinate charity, see Nathan Irving Huggins, "Private Charities in Boston, 1870-1900: A Social History" (unpublished Ph.D. dissertation, Harvard University Archives, 1962), pp. 53-67, 70.

85. *Commonwealth* v. *Miller,* 8 Gray 484 (1858).

86. Difficulties of institutions and establishment of board of directors in Huse, *Financial History,* pp. 67-70; distrust of outdoor relief in Bugbee, "Boston under the Mayors," pp. 271-272.

87. Criticism of drunk arrests in Boston *Herald,* January 25, 1853; prosecutions in 1849, in City Doc. no. 94 (1849), *Report of City Marshal;* watch statistics in Boston *Herald, January* 12, 1853; statistics of drunkenness after 1853 summarized in *Annual Police Report* (1871), p. 37.

88. *The Annual Police Report* for 1857, pp. 17-19, gives the following statistics: total arrests, 17,538; drunk arrests, 6,780; total committed, 8,979;

females arrested, 3,888; foreigners arrested, 14,067; nonresidents arrested, 3,507; for "helped home drunk" see *ibid.* (1859), p. 25.

89. Senate Doc. no. 155 (1859), *An Act to Prohibit the Punishment of Drunkenness as a Crime;* st. 1860, ch. 166; *Annual Police Report* (1861), p. 21.

90. *Annual Police Report* (1851), pp. 20, 18; *ibid.* (1852), p. 19; *Auditor's Report* (1851), p. 73; *Annual Police Report* (1859), p. 16.

91. Permission for lodgers in *City Records,* XXXII, December 26, 1854, 821; statistics summarized in House Doc. no. 415 (1867), *Reports on a License Law: Appendix,* p. 238.

92. Cholera in Savage, *Police Records,* pp. 263-273; hospital movement in Huse, *Financial History,* p. 70; station physicians in *City Records,* XXXIII, April 23, 1855, 231; call for hospital in, e.g., *Annual Police Report* (1855), p. 9.

93. *Annual Police Report* (1851), pp. 20-21, 23, 26-31; *ibid.* (1857), p. 18.

94. *Address of the State Temperance Alliance to the People of Massachusetts* (Boston, 1864), p. 11; Fenner, *Raising the Veil,* pp. 88, 93.

95. City Doc. no. 58 (1856), *Reports of the Inspector of Prisons,* p. 5, reports 36 persons jailed that year for keeping houses of ill fame. For difficulty in prosecuting liquor and gambling shops, see, e.g., House Doc. no. 415 (1867), *Reports on a License Law: Appendix,* pp. 72, 194-195.

96. *Annual Police Report* (1861), p. 11; Boston *Advertiser,* April 17, 1855. For upper New England background of prostitutes, see Handlin, *Boston's Immigrants,* p. 20.

97. Savage biography in Boston *Evening Transcript,* February 1, 1893; "idle and dissolute persons" in, e.g., *Annual Police Report* (1857), p. 11; trial in Boston *Herald,* October 2, 1858.

98. Accusations in *Address of the State Temperance Alliance* (1864), p. 11; nightwalking statistics summarized in *Annual Police Report* (1871), p. 37; Ann Street Descent in Savage, *Police Records,* pp. 259-262.

99. House Doc. no. 90 (1859), *Annual Report of the Attorney General,* p. 11; Fenner, *Raising the Veil,* p. 53.

CHAPTER SEVEN

THE VIOLENT YEARS, 1860-1869

1. Formation of American systems in Raymond B. Fosdick, *American Police Systems* (New York, 1920), pp. 62-67.

2. Charles Tempest Clarkson and J. Hall Richardson, *Police!* (London, 1889), p. 73; Raymond B. Fosdick, *European Police Systems* (New York, 1915), pp. 201-204; George Dilnot, *The Story of Scotland Yard* (New York, 1927), p. 88; W. L. Melville Lee, *A History of Police in England* (London, 1901), p. 377.

3. Fosdick, *American Police Systems*, pp. 82-94.

4. *Ibid.; People v. Draper*, 15 N.Y. 556 (1857).

5. Edward H. Savage, *Police Records and Recollections: Or, Boston by Daylight and Gaslight* (Boston, 1873), pp. 160-166; House Doc. no. 415 (1867), *Reports on the Subject of a License Law: Appendix* (Boston, 1867), p. 216; *Annual Police Report* (1863), p. 30; Senate Doc. no. 171 (1865), *Report on a Metropolitan Police*, p. 4; Wendell Phillips, *Speech at the Melodeon, April 5, 1863* (Boston, 1863), p. 4.

6. *People v. Draper*, p. 574.

7. City Doc. no. 51 (1860), *Report of the Committee on Police on the Recent Criminalities in the Department;* Boston *Herald*, May 23, 1860.

8. *Annual Police Report* (1861), p. 5; Boston *Herald*, June 12, 1860.

9. Boston *Advertiser*, November 7, 1860; Boston *Herald*, November 21, 1860; James McKellar Bugbee, "Boston under the Mayors, 1822-1880," *The Memorial History of Boston*, ed. Justin Winsor (Boston, 1881), vol. III, ch. II, p. 265.

10. Boston *Herald*, November 14, 1860; Boston *Advertiser*, December 11, 1860.

11. *City Records*, XXXIX, February 4, 1861, 50; Savage, *Police Records*, p. 110.

12. *City Records*, XXXIX, January 14, 1861, 16; *ibid.*, January 21, 1861, 27.

13. Lawrence Lader, *The Bold Brahmins: New England's War Against Slavery: 1831-1863* (New York, 1961), pp. 256-258; *Buttrick v. Lowell*, 1 Allen 172 (1861).

14. Boston *Herald*, January 22, 1861; Bugbee, "Boston under the Mayors," p. 266; Boston *Herald*, February 8, 1861.

15. Senate Doc. no. 149 (1861), *An Act to Establish a Metropolitan Police for the City of Boston.*

16. Boston *Herald*, February 8, 1861; Senate Doc. no. 149 (1861), *Joint Special Committee on a Metropolitan Police*, pp. 7, 8, 9; Boston *Herald*, February 13, February 15, 1861.

17. *Ibid.*, March 12, 1861; February 8, 1861.

18. *Ibid.*, February 13, 1861.

19. *Ibid.*, February 15, 1861; February 13, 1861.

20. *Ibid.*, March 10, March 13, 1861.

21. Senate Doc. no. 149 (1861), *A Metropolitan Police*, pp. 1, 2, 3.

22. Boston *Advertiser*, April 9, 1861; Lader, *The Bold Brahmins*, pp. 258, 259.

23. Bugbee, "Boston under the Mayors," pp. 265-266.

24. Charles P. Huse, *The Financial History of Boston from May 1, 1822 to January 31, 1909* (Cambridge, 1916), p. 143; *ibid.*, pp. 172-173; *Annual Police Report* (1861), p. 3; *ibid.* (1866), p. 7.

25. *Annual Police Report* (1863), pp. 3, 4; *ibid.* (1862), pp. 18-19; *ibid.* (1863), pp. 32-33.

26. Amee quotation *ibid.*, p. 5; aldermen quoted in City Doc. no. 68 (1862),

Report of the Police Committee on Special Police Officers and Street Stands, pp. 9-10.

27. *Ibid.,* p. 12; st. 1846, ch. 244; *Annual Police Report* (1863), pp. 32-35; City Doc. no. 68 (1863), *Report of Police Committee,* p. 15; *City Records,* XLVI, January 27, 1868, 66-68.

28. City Doc. no. 68 (1862), p. 17.

29. *A Supplement to the Laws and Ordinances of the City of Boston* (Boston, 1868), pp. 73, 77, 89-93, 82, 88, 90-91; pp. 71-98.

30. *City Records,* XL, November 24, 1862, 730; December 1, 1862, 749; December 4, 1862, 762; December 8, 1862, 764, 769; December 22, 1862, 811; December 31, 1862, 859; Boston *Herald,* December 2, 1862; February 25, 1863.

31. Character of mayors in Bugbee, "Boston under the Mayors," pp. 265, 273; naturalized voters in City Doc. no. 68 (1865), *Report on a New Division of the City into Wards;* names of councillors, 1861-1870, in *Municipal Register* (1875), pp. 295-300; tax-dodging in Huse, *Financial History,* pp. 87, 147, and Lincoln, *Inaugural Address* (1865), p. 329.

32. Boston *Herald,* April 15, 1863.

33. *Ibid.,* March 7 and 13, 1863.

34. Description of Amory in *The Argument of Charles M. Ellis, Esq., in Favor of the Metropolitan Police Bill* (Boston, 1863), p. 21; qualifications in *The Argument of Thomas C. Amory Against the Proposed Metropolitan Police Bill* (Boston, 1863), p. 5; quotations *ibid.,* pp. 9, 11, 13, 14.

35. *Ibid.,* p. 13.

36. *Ibid.,* pp. 14, 15.

37. *Ibid.,* pp. 17, 19, 20.

38. *Ibid.,* p. 22.

39. *Ibid.,* pp. 26, 25, 27.

40. *Ibid.,* pp. 28, 29.

41. *Argument of Ellis,* pp. 32-33, 26, 3-4.

42. *Ibid.,* pp. 1 5.

43. *Ibid.,* pp. 6, 7.

44. *Ibid.,* pp. 13, 21, 31.

45. *Ibid.,* pp. 25, 32-35, 34, 35.

46. *Ibid.,* pp. 10, 13, 16.

47. Boston *Advertiser,* April 6, 1843; Boston *Herald,* March 13, 1863; *City Records,* XLI, April 17, 1863, 166.

48. Senate Doc. no. 129 (1863), *Report of the Joint Special Committee on a Metropolitan Police,* pp. 2, 3; Boston *Advertiser,* April 18, 1863.

49. Boston *Herald,* March 9, 1863; *Annual Police Report* (1864), p. 28.

50. Bugbee, "Boston under the Mayors," pp. 268-269.

51. This riot is described in Bugbee, "Boston under the Mayors," pp. 269-270, and in Savage, *Police Records,* pp. 347-348.

52. *Annual Police Report* (1871), p. 43; st. 1864, ch. 110.

53. Praise of individual policemen in Wendell Phillips, *Speeches, Lectures, and Letters* (Boston, 1863), p. 497.

54. St. 1861, ch. 136; st. 1862, ch. 189; st. 1860, ch. 58; st. 1869, ch. 55; st. 1864, ch. 258; st. 1864, ch. 225.

55. Statistics of drunkenness in *Annual Police Report* (1871), p. 37; reclassification *ibid.*, p. 38; temperance work *ibid.* (1865), p. 20; probation report *ibid.* (1866), pp. 25-28; "dipsomania" *ibid.* (1865), p. 19.

56. Hospital in Huse, *Financial History*, p. 124; overseers in Bugbee, "Boston under the Mayors," pp. 271-272; temporary home and other plans in City Doc. no. 91 (1864), *Report of Committee on the Overseers of the Poor Recommending a Relief Building*, and City Doc. no. 95 (1864), *Report on a Building for the Overseers of the Poor*.

57. House Doc. no. 415 (1867), *Reports on License Law: Appendix*, p. 216.

58. Testimony of ministers *ibid.*, pp. 72-73, 89, 92, 106, 111, 113, 156, 165, 168.

59. *Ibid.*, pp. 865-866.

60. *Modification or Absolute Prohibition, Which? . . . an Address by F. W. Bird* (Boston, 1869), pp. 5-6; Senate Doc. no. 224 (1864), *An Act to Establish a Metropolitan Police;* Boston *Herald*, May 4, May 11, 1865.

61. St. 1865, ch. 249; Boston *Herald*, May 12, 1865.

62. House Doc. no. 20 (1868), *Annual Report of the Constables of the Commonwealth*, p. 3; Boston *Herald*, April 29, 1871. The annual report of the chief constable and his successors is hereinafter referred to as *Annual State Police Report*, with date issued.

63. *Annual State Police Report* (1868), pp. 3, 4-5.

64. *Ibid.*, pp. 3, 8.

65. *Ibid.* (1869), pp. 6-7.

66. Arrests in 41 different categories are recorded *ibid.* (1868), p. 50; a total of $31,675.85 in recovered property is listed *ibid;* arrests in 141 different categories are recorded in the *Annual Police Report* (1868), pp. 8-11; a total of $124,020.00 in recovered property is listed *ibid.*, p. 21; military terms in *Annual State Police Report* (1872), p. 24.

67. A total of 131 constables is listed in *Annual State Police Report* (1868), p. 3; 1865 population of Massachusetts, 1, 267,031, in *Abstract of the Census of Massachusetts: 1865* (Boston, 1867), pp. 2-3; a total of 521 state police is listed in *Massachusetts Department of Public Safety, Report of Commissioner; Division of State Police* (Boston, 1963), p. 55; 1960 population of Massachusetts, 5,148,758 in *The American Annual: 1961* (New York, 1961), p. 451; raids and arrests summarized in *Annual State Police Report* (1868), p. 39; claim *ibid.*, p. 14.

68. Boston *Herald*, April 29, 1871; *Annual State Police Report* (1868), p. 20; *ibid.* (1869), p. 35; House Doc. no. 415 (1867), *Reports on a License Law: Appendix*, pp. 240-241; *Address by F. W. Bird*, p. 9.

69. Boston *Herald*, October 2, 1867; *Annual State Police Report* (1869), pp. 9-10; *Worcester* v. *Walker*, 9 Gray 78 (1857); *Annual State Police Report* (1868), p. 17.

70. *Address of F. W. Bird*, p. 7; House Doc. no. 415 (1867), *Reports on a*

License Law, p. 5; *Reports on a License Law: Appendix,* pp. 280, 195, and *passim.*

71. *Reports on a License Law* (1867), pp. 5-22, 9.

72. *Ibid.,* pp. 22, 44, 63, 69; Boston *Herald,* November 6, 1867.

73. *Annual State Police Report* (1868), pp. 10, 3, 4.

74. Senate Doc. no. 2 (1868), *An Act to Abolish the State Constabulary; Journal of the Massachusetts Senate* (1868), p. 233.

75. St. 1868, ch. 141.

76. *Annual State Police Report* (1869), pp. 17-18, 21-22, 9, 2.

77. *Address by F. W. Bird,* pp. 7-9; *Annual State Police Report* (1869), p. 15; Boston *Herald,* September 19, 1868 and November 5, 1868.

78. St. 1869, ch. 191; st. 1869, ch. 452.

79. *Annual State Police Report* (1869), p. 25.

80. Finances in Huse, *Financial History,* p. 351; birthplaces of members of police force in *Annual Police Report* (1872), pp. 1-24; annexations in Bugbee, "Boston under the Mayors," pp. 275-278; opening of police hearings in Boston *Herald,* March 23, 1869.

CHAPTER EIGHT

CRIME AND SCANDAL, 1869-1870

1. For materials on criminal fraternity in general see Notes on Sources, and notes below; for English slang in period see "Thieves and Thieving," *Cornhill,* vol. II (June 1860), pp. 334-335; for American see *Langdon W. Moore: His Own Story of His Eventful Life* (Boston, 1893), *passim,* and Josiah Flynt (Willard), *Tramping with Tramps* (New York, 1901), pp. 385 ff.

2. Specialization in, e.g., William P. Watts and Benjamin P. Eldridge, *Our Rival the Rascal* (Boston, 1897), pp. 36, 65, 73; decline of "panel thievery" in Howard O. Sprogle, *The Philadelphia Police, Past and Present* (Philadelphia, 1887), p. 331, and Boston *Herald,* February 21, 1875; decline of pickpocketing *ibid.;* changing techniques of burglary in Watts and Eldridge, *The Rascal,* pp. 34-92, 391-420; interchangeability in *Langdon W. Moore, passim.*

3. Edwin Crapsey, "Our Criminal Population," *Galaxy,* vol. VIII (October 1869), p. 346. The estimate of Josiah Flynt, for the 1880's and 1890's, is one thousand top criminals all over the United States; see *The World of Graft* (New York, 1901), p. 174. The same author counts some thirty to fifty thousand professionals all told, in *Notes of an Itinerant Policeman* (Boston, 1900), p. 58.

4. Crapsey, "Criminal Population," pp. 349, 351, 352, 353.

5. *Ibid.,* p. 351; for "bank sneaking" see also Boston *Herald,* May 7, 1864.

6. Crapsey, "Criminal Population," p. 350.

7. *Ibid.,* pp. 347-349.

8. Record of major robberies in 1860's and 1870's in Thomas J. Byrnes,

Professional Criminals of America (New York, 1886), pp. 337-340; see also Watts and Eldridge, *The Rascal,* pp. 60-62; for fame of burglars see, e.g., Boston *Herald,* January 6, 1875, January 9, 1876, March 29, 1880, September 19, 1891.

9. Safe and lock history in Watts and Eldridge, *The Rascal,* pp. 391-420; burglar's tools in Boston *Herald,* April 24, 1869.

10. Million-dollar robberies in Boston *Herald,* April 26, 1869; Watts and Eldridge, *The Rascal,* p. 43; Sprogle, *Philadelphia Police,* pp. 348-349; and Byrnes, *Professional Criminals,* pp. 337-340.

11. Record of detective work in 1850's and 1860's summarized in *Annual Police Report* (1871), p. 37.

12. Detective salaries in *Annual Police Report* (1863), p. 38; character of men in Hill, *Argument Against a State Police,* pp. 13, 14.

13. Chapman story in Boston *Herald,* September 21, 1891, and February 5, 1879; see also *Langdon W. Moore,* pp. 566, 600.

14. Private detectives in Edwin Crapsey, "The Nether Side of New York, I: Private Detectives," *Galaxy,* vol. XL (February 1872), pp. 188-199; for subsidy see, e.g., st. 1860, ch. 26, st. 1869, ch. 31; "Boston detectives" in *Langdon W. Moore,* pp. 58-59, 102, 152; "John Bull" in Boston *Herald,* April 13, 1871.

15. Respect for Pinkertons in *Langdon W. Moore,* p. 249, and Flynt, *The World of Graft,* pp. 182-183; insecurity of criminals *ibid.,* p. 150. Flynt's estimate is that professional criminals spent roughly one-half of their lives in prisons.

16. Moore's description of detective-criminal relationship in Boston *Herald,* October 7, 1891.

17. *Ibid.,* May 7, 1869.

18. Lord Bond Robbery *ibid.;* compounding practices in Crapsey, "Criminal Population," p. 346, and Flynt, *The World of Graft,* p. 158; Philadelphia robbery in Boston *Herald,* April 26, 1869.

19. *Ibid.,* May 7, 1869; *Annual Police Report* (1866), p. 12.

20. Parkman murder in "Crime and Its Detection," *Dublin Review,* 2d series, vol. 50 (May 1861), pp. 180 ff.; homicides before 1850, in Lemuel Shattuck, *Bills of Mortality, 1810-1849* (Boston, 1893), pp. 3-79, a total of thirty; homicides thereafter are listed in Table IX of *Registry of Births, Marriages, and Deaths in Massachusetts for the Year Ending December 31, 1850,* and its successor volumes, except for the years 1852 to 1856 inclusive, where they are listed in Table VIII: the total is fifty-nine in the 1850's and seventy in the 1860's; homicide arrests are summarized in *Annual Police Report* (1871), p. 37; indictments and convictions are listed in *Annual Report of the Attorney General for the Year Ending December 31, 1860* and its successor volumes through 1870. See also Appendix I.

21. "Aids of Science in the Detection of Crime," *Chambers's Edinborough Journal,* vol. 53 (February 5, 1876), pp. 101-103; *General Statutes* (1860), ch. 17, secs. 74-80.

22. "Sweat Box" in *Langdon W. Moore,* p. 125.

23. Boston *Herald*, February 15, 1870; "The Criminal Law and the Detection of Crime," *Cornhill*, vol. II (December 1860), p. 898; Boston *Herald*, February 16, 1870.

24. Boston *Herald*, May 7, 1869 and May 13, 1869.

25. *Ibid.*, April 1, 3, and 6, 1869.

26. *Ibid.*, April 14, 22, and 29, 1869.

27. *Ibid.*, May 7, 1869; Clement Hugh Hill, *Argument Against a State Police* (Boston, 1869), p. 31; Boston *Herald*, May 1, 1869.

28. Frank Wadleigh Chandler, *The Literature of Roguery* (Boston, 1907), vol. II, pp. 527-533.

29. William E. S. Fales, *Brooklyn's Guardians: A Record of the Faithful and Heroic Men Who Protect the Peace in the City of Homes* (Brooklyn, 1887), p. 51; Boston *Daily Mail*, March 27, 1841; Chandler, *Literature of Roguery*, pp. 533-534.

30. Hill, *Argument Against a State Police*, pp. 6-7, 10, 16, 17, 19.

31. Boston *Herald*, May 7, 1878; Hill, *Argument Against a State Police*, pp. 4-5, 31-32; Boston *Herald*, April 14 and 22, 1869.

32. Senate Doc. no. 378 (1869), *Report of the Joint Special Committee on a Metropolitan Police*, p. 16 and *passim*; Boston *Herald*, June 8, 1869.

33. Boston *Transcript*, November 9, 1864 and November 4, 1868; Boston *Herald*, December 14, 1869; Bugbee, "Boston under the Mayors," pp. 273, 276.

34. Boston *Herald*, March 23, 1869; City Doc. no. 13 (1867), *Police Rules and Regulations;* City Doc. no. 39 (1860), *Report on Establishing a Fund for Aged and Invalid Policemen.*

35. Boston *Herald*, February 10, 1870.

36. *Ibid.*, November 23, 24, 26, and 29, 1869.

37. *City Council Minutes,* February 14, 1870, p. 35; Boston *Herald*, February 15, 1870. *The City Council Minutes,* which have no other title for the early volumes, replace the *City Records* as the official record of the proceedings of both aldermen and common councillors, beginning in 1869.

38. Hill, *Argument Against a State Police*, p. 11.

CHAPTER NINE

CHIEF SAVAGE AND READJUSTMENT, 1870-1878

1. Charles P. Huse, *The Financial History of Boston from May 1, 1822 to January 31, 1909* (Cambridge, 1916), pp. 225-226; Oscar Handlin, *Boston's Immigrants: A Study in Acculturation,* rev. ed. (Cambridge, 1959), p. 214; James McKellar Bugbee, "Boston under the Mayors, 1822-1880," *The Memorial History of Boston,* ed. Justin Winsor (Boston, 1881), vol. III, p. 284.

2. Boston *Herald*, February 16, 1870.

3. *Ibid.*, February 17, 1870; *City Council Minutes,* March 14, 1870, p. 60; Boston *Evening Transcript,* February 1, 1893.

4. *City Council Minutes,* February 21, 1870, p. 39; March 14, 1870, p. 60.

5. *Annual Police Report* (1873), p. 57; *ibid.* (1871), p. 52; Boston *Evening Transcript,* February 1, 1893; *Annual Police Report* (1872), p. 68.

6. Boston *Herald,* November 14, 1875; *Annual Police Report* (1873), p. 61; Boston *Herald,* February 5, 1878.

7. *Annual Police Report* (1872), p. 68.

8. *Ibid.* (1871), p. 63; *ibid.* (1872), pp. 68, 78; Boston *Herald,* March 18, 1873, and February 21, 1875. For "show-up" system see also *Langdon W. Moore: His Own Story of His Eventful Life* (Boston, 1893), pp. 649 ff.

9. Table of stolen property in *Annual Police Report* (1877), p. 36; contributions *ibid.* (1873), p. 35.

10. Ellis case summed up in Boston *Herald,* November 10, 1872; its importance in history of detective work in Thomas M. McDade, ed., *The Annals of Murder: A Bibliography of Books and Pamphlets on American Murders from Colonial Times to 1900* (Norman, Oklahoma, 1961), p. 5; Savage claim in *Annual Police Report* (1875), p. 37; homicides in Table IX of *Registry of Births, Marriages, and Deaths in Massachusetts for the Year Ending December 31, 1870,* and its successor volumes through 1879; indictments in *Annual Report of the Attorney General for the Year Ending December 31, 1870,* p. 17, and in Waldo L. Cook, "Murders in Massachusetts," *American Statistical Association Publications,* new series, vol. III (1892-1893), p. 360. The Cook article covers the years 1871-1891. See also Appendix I.

11. Last reference to Cluer in *Annual Police Report* (1866), pp. 25-28; last gift to Washingtonians in st. 1872, ch. 39; treatment of drunkenness in Public Doc. no. 17 (1870), *Annual Report of the Secretary of the Board of State Charities,* pp. 17-18.

12. Table of arrests for 1870's in *Annual Police Report* (1880), p. 16.

13. Population in City Doc. no. 104 (1885), *An Analysis of the Population of the City of Boston,* pp. 4-5; immigrant population in Handlin, *Boston's Immigrants,* p. 213.

14. Economic growth in Handlin, *Boston's Immigrants,* pp. 214-215.

15. Boston *Herald,* November 3, 1869; st. 1870, ch. 389; Boston *Herald,* November 11, 1870.

16. St. 1871, ch. 334; Boston *Herald,* March 21, 1871 and April 5, 1871.

17. St. 1871, ch. 394; *Annual State Police Report* (1873), pp. 10-12, 6.

18. House Doc. no. 91 (1874), *Veto Message;* Boston *Herald,* October 8, 1874 and November 4, 1874.

19. St. 1875, ch. 15; st. 1875, ch. 99. The history of the state police after 1875 was at first erratic. They were used increasingly to enforce the commonwealth's early industrial legislation; see *Annual State Police Report* (1878), pp. 5-9. Reorganized and reduced again by st. 1878, ch. 242, they were renamed "District Police" by st. 1879, ch. 305, and a portion assigned to the offices of the various district attorneys. Into the twentieth century they developed in two different directions, as detectives and as factory inspectors, coming together as a force during such emergencies as strikes. See *Annual State Police Report* (1880), *passim,* and *ibid.* (1905), *passim,* Their existence enabled

Massachusetts to outlaw the use of out-of-state private police in industrial disputes, by st. 1893, ch. 413.

20. *Annual Police Report* (1876), p. 36; City Doc. no. 37 (1878), *Annual Report of the Board of License Commissioners,* p. 10.

21. Occupations of common councillors in Boston *Herald,* January 5, 1877; votes in 1870's in *Municipal Register* (1890), pp. 27-28; wholesalers' power in Boston *Herald,* April 3, 1885; liquor industry in politics *ibid.,* October 15, 1876.

22. St. 1875, ch. 99; *City Council Minutes,* April 12, 1875, p. 208; City Doc. no. 18 (1877), *Annual Report of the Board of License Commissioners,* pp. 3-5; *City Council Minutes,* July 8, 1875, pp. 400-402.

23. City Doc. no. 118 (1875), *Report of the Board of License Commissioners,* pp. 3-5; *City Council Minutes,* July 8, 1875, pp. 400-402.

24. *Annual Police Report* (1876), p. 36; City Doc. no. 18 (1877), *Annual Report of the Board of License Commissioners,* p. 2; *Annual Police Report* (1877), p. 22. The discrepancies between licenses granted and licensed places result from the large number of simple business failures unconnected with the activity of commissioners or police.

25. Number of unlicensed places in *Annual Police Report* (1876), p. 36, and *ibid.* (1877), p. 22; complaints in *City Council Minutes,* July 8, 1875, pp. 400-402; liquor prosecutions summarized in Public Doc. no. 15 (1880), *Annual Report of The Bureau of Statistics of Labor,* pp. 130-169.

26. Boston *Herald,* November 13 and 25, 1876, and December 13, 1876.

27. City Doc. no. 37 (1878), *Annual Report of the Board of License Commissioners,* pp. 4-5, 6-7.

28. *Ibid.,* pp. 1, 6.

29. *Ibid.,* pp. 7, 13-25.

30. *Ibid.,* p. 4.

31. *Annual Police Report* (1878), p. 16; Pierce, *Inaugural Address* (1878), pp. 24-25. The inaugural addresses of the mayors were published individually after 1867, and the page numbers cited hereinafter refer to the individual rather than the collected addresses.

32. Birthplace of members of the force in *Annual Police Report* (1872), pp. 1-24; Savage obituary in Boston *Evening Transcript,* February 1, 1893. Portrait in Savage, *Police Records,* frontispiece.

33. Charles K. Smith, "Memoir of the Honorable Nathaniel B. Shurtleff, M.D.," MHS *Proceedings,* vol. 13 (1873-1875), pp. 389-395; Edward Stanton, "Memoir of James McKellar Bugbee," MHS *Proceedings,* vol. 46 (1912-1913), pp. 372-378; Boston *Evening Transcript,* February 1, 1893.

34. *Annual Police Report* (1873), pp. 46-57; Boston *Herald,* May 9, 1870 and October 17, 1875.

35. Edward Hartwell Savage, *Police Records and Recollections: Or, Boston by Daylight and Gaslight* (Boston, 1873), pp. 184-187; *Annual Police Report* (1874), pp. 49, 50; *ibid.* (1873), pp. 29, 43.

36. *Annual Report of the Secretary of the Board of State Charities* (1870), p. 38; *Annual Police Report* (1872), p. 62.

37. Leonhard Felix Fuld, *Police Administration: A Critical Study of Police Organizations in the United States and Abroad* (New York, 1909), pp. 397-400; Boston *Herald,* March 12, 1872; *Annual Police Report* (1872), p. 64.

38. *Annual Police Report* (1872), pp. 89, 62; ibid. (1871), p. 60; *ibid.* (1872), p. 64; *ibid.* (1873), p. 46.

39. Boston *Herald,* May 9, 1870; *Annual Police Report* (1871), pp. 57-58.

40. Boston *Herald,* May 9, May 10, and May 13, 1870; *Annual Police Report* (1872), pp. 62-63.

41. *Municipal Register* (1865), p. 100 and *ibid.* (1866), p. 141; City Doc. no. 53 (1867), *Report on the Subject of Truants and Absentees from School;* City Doc. no. 83 (1867), *Report of the Committee on Minor's Licenses; Annual Police Report* (1872), p. 42.

42. First report of police superintendent of buildings in *Annual Police Report* (1871), p. 28; survey, e.g., *ibid.* (1872), p. 54; building inspector in Bugbee, "Boston under the Mayors," p. 281; transfer in City Doc. no. 28 (1878), *Report of Inspector of Buildings,* pp. 6-7.

43. *Annual Police Report* (1871), pp. 3-4.

44. *Ibid.,* pp. 25-26, 33-35.

45. *Ibid.,* pp. 27-28.

46. *Ibid.,* p. 27.

47. *Ibid.,* pp. 28-29; City Doc. no. 102 (1866), *Report on Free Bathing Facilities; Annual Police Report* (1871), p. 29.

48. *City Council Minutes,* June 20, 1870, pp. 163-164.

49. *Annual Police Report* (1871), p. 11; *ibid.* (1873), p. 34; Savage, *Police Records,* p. 161; *Annual Police Report* (1880), p. 31.

50. Number of police in 1854 in Boston *Herald,* May 27, 1854; number of police in 1870 in *Annual Police Report* (1871), p. 12; population figures in City. Doc. no. 104 (1885), *An Analysis of the Population of the City of Boston,* pp. 4-5; st. 1878, ch. 181.

51. Establishment of police stations in *Annual Police Report* (1875), pp. 8-9.

52. In this and succeeding paragraphs the number of men in 1854 is taken from the Boston *Herald,* May 27, 1854. The number of men, length of beats, and characteristics of each division in 1870 is taken from the *Annual Police Report* (1871), pp. 1-8, 12-13, 36; the number of men in 1875 is taken from the 1876 *Report,* pp. 1-10; the number of men in 1878 is taken from the 1879 *Report,* p. 4; the number of men in 1880 is taken from the 1880 *Report,* p. 3; and arrests in 1878 are taken from the 1879 *Report,* pp. 5-6. All population figures are taken from City Doc. no. 104 (1885), *An Analysis of the Population of the City of Boston.* See also Appendix II for maps of police divisions.

The harbor division, number eight, is not included in the detailed analysis; although the most obvious example of police protection for property, its work and functions are not easily compared with those of other stations. The number of men assigned to it, twenty-two in 1870, is included, however, in all figures relating to the total number of divisional policemen in the central peninsula.

53. *City Council Minutes,* April 4, 1870, p. 78; *ibid.,* June 20, 1870, pp. 163-164.

54. *The Municipal Register of Roxbury* (1867), pp. 55-58.

55. *Thirty-First Annual Report of the Receipts and Expenditures of the Town of Dorchester* (1869), p. 36; Shurtleff, *Inaugural Address,* p. 45; *Annual Police Report* (1874), p. 46.

56. *Report of the Chief of Police,* in *Official Reports of the Town of West Roxbury* (1872-73), p. 1.

57. Charlestown City Doc. no. 38 (1873), *Inaugural Address of Mayor Johnathan Stone,* p. 10; *Official Reports of the Town of Brighton for the Year Ending January 31, 1873,* p. 145.

CHAPTER TEN

POLITICAL UNCERTAINTY: THE COMMISSION MOVEMENT, 1870-1878

1. The need to rebuild the districts devastated by the Great Fire jumped expenditures nearly four million in 1873, to $18,841,414.94. By 1878 they were back to $12,420,853.49, less than in 1870, despite the assumption of the debts and populations of the new areas. See Charles P. Huse, *The Financial History of Boston from May 1, 1822 to January 31, 1909* (Cambridge, 1916), pp. 169, 351.

2. Pay scales in *Journal of the Common Council,* November 5, 1868, p. 323; per capita spending in Huse, *Financial History,* p. 366. *The Journal of the Common Council* was published only in the single year 1868.

3. *City Council Minutes,* March 21, 1872, p. 80; March 11, 1872, p. 72.

4. *Ibid.*

5. 1877 pay cut *ibid.,* July 18, 1878, p. 475. The effective number of policemen varied from year to year as positions remained unfilled. The authorized strength, however, was not cut.

6. *City Council Minutes,* April 25, 1872, p. 118; March 11, 1872, p. 72; March 21, 1872, p. 82; April 29, 1872, p. 129; May 20, 1872, p. 155.

7. Age of men, and witness fee receipts, in *Annual Police Report* (1871), p. 41; policy to retain older men in *City Council Minutes,* February 18, 1875, p. 66; illegality of pensions and similar payments in City Doc. no. 71 (1868), *Report of the Special Committee on Police;* payment to incapacitated in *City Council Minutes,* May 15, 1871, p. 151; May 8, 1871, p. 136; December 26, 1878, p. 747.

8. Cobb, *Inaugural Address* (1875), p. 20; Prince, *Inaugural Address* (1877), pp. 25-28; Pierce, *Inaugural Address* (1878), pp. 20-23; opinion of Savage in *City Council Minutes,* February 11, 1878, p. 50.

9. Names of aldermen and prior years of service in *Municipal Register*

(1890), pp. 305-310, 325-327; police committee members *ibid.* (1870), p. 64; (1871), p. 84; (1872), p. 66; (1873), p. 66; (1874), p. 67; (1875), p. 69. In 1872 all three members were freshmen.

10. *City Council Minutes,* February 11, 1878, p. 50; December 6, 1875, p. 706; July 18, 1878, p. 475; July 18, 1878, p. 471; June 13, 1870, p. 164; July 28, 1873, p. 205.

11. Selection procedure in *Annual Police Report* (1874), p. 5; physical standard in *City Council Minutes,* April 20, 1875, p. 226; veto, e.g., *ibid.,* September 24, 1877, p. 613.

12. "Three-headed control" problems in Boston *Herald,* October 19, 1878; license superintendents in *Annual Police Report* (1878), p. 3; transfers in Boston *Herald,* November 14, 1875, and *City Council Minutes,* February 11, 1878, p. 51; jealousies in Boston *Herald,* November 14, 1875.

13. Street commission in James McKellar Bugbee, "Boston under the Mayors, 1822-1880," *The Memorial History of Boston,* ed. Justin Winsor (Boston, 1881), vol. III, ch. II, p. 278; health commission *ibid.,* pp. 279-280; fire commission *ibid.,* p. 282; park commission *ibid.,* pp. 284-285; water board *ibid.,* p. 285.

14. St. 1875, ch. 209; Huse, *Financial History,* p. 222.

15. Bugbee, "Boston under the Mayors," pp. 282, 283.

16. City Doc. no. 50 (1875), *New City Charter as Amended by the Board of Aldermen,* pp. 35-38.

17. Bugbee, "Boston under the Mayors," p. 283; *City Council Minutes,* October 18, 1875, p. 563 and December 30, 1875, p. 768.

18. St. 1865, ch. 31; st. 1869, ch. 344; st. 1869, ch. 334; st. 1876, ch. 181; st. 1866, ch. 344; st. 1876, ch. 180; st. 1879, ch. 159.

19. Activities of M.S.P.C.A. in *Our Dumb Animals,* vol. I (June 2, 1868), pp. 1-8; market scandals in Bugbee, "Boston under the Mayors," p. 279; abortionists in Boston *Herald,* October 10, 1873.

20. Cases involving the rights and powers of peace officers include *Morris* v. *Chase,* 100 M.R. 79 (1868), *Conway* v. *Perkins,* 100 M.R. 316 (1868), *Commonwealth* v. *Martin,* 105 M.R. 178 (1870), *Brock* v. *Stimson,* 108 M.R. 520 (1871), *Mitchell* v. *Wall,* 111 M.R. 492 (1872), *Commonwealth* v. *Reynolds,* 120 M.R. 191 (1876), *Commonwealth* v. *Coughlin,* 122 M.R. 436 (1877), *Phillips* v. *Fadden,* 125 M.R. 198 (1878), *Commonwealth* v. *Ducey,* 126 M.R. 269 (1879).

21. *Conway* v. *Perkins,* 100 M.R. 316 (1868); *Commonwealth* v. *Reynolds,* 120 M.R. 191 (1876).

22. City Doc. no. 13 (1867), *Police Rules and Regulations,* p. 30; Boston *Herald,* February 15, 1870 and February 9, 1883; Edward Hartwell Savage, *Police Records and Recollections: Or, Boston by Daylight and Gaslight* (Boston, 1873), p. 344. Savage, in the *Annual Police Report* (1871), p. 48, admitted that no one really understood the legal powers of police.

23. Routine violations of law in Boston *Herald,* February 9, 1883.

24. Accounts of case in Boston *Herald,* April 5, 1871, and Boston *Advertiser,* April 5, 1871.

25. Boston *Herald,* April 7 and April 10, 1871.

26. Boston *Advertiser,* April 8, 1871; Boston *Herald,* April 10, 1871.

27. Boston *Herald,* April 12, 1871.

28. Boston *Herald,* April 12 and April 19, 1871.

29. Boston *Advertiser,* April 23 and April 29, 1871; Boston *Herald,* May 3, 1871.

30. Investigations in *City Council Minutes,* August 12, 1870, pp. 211-212; June 27, 1872, p. 199; December 31, 1874, p. 761; suits in Boston *Herald,* November 16, 1871 and December 19, 1871; criticism of brutality *ibid.,* May 3, 1874, August 1, 1874, and November 7, 1870.

31. The shooting of the children is described in the Boston *Advertiser,* August 8, 1870; the publicity given the matter in council was simply the printing of official depositions without any real debate; see *City Council Minutes,* August 12, 1870, pp. 211-212; for attitude of courts see *City Council Minutes,* May 2, 1889, p. 504.

32. The council's reticence was also illustrated by its total silence regarding another shooting of innocent bystanders, recorded in the Boston *Herald,* August 1, 1874. Once the members were relieved of direct control, however, they did not hesitate to name individuals in negligence or brutality. See *City Council Minutes,* May 26, 1881, p. 351; January 12, 1882, pp. 18-19; January 26, 1882, p. 51.

33. Chardon Street offices in Nathan Irving Huggins, "Private Charities in Boston, 1870-1900: A Social History" (unpublished Ph.D. dissertation, Harvard University Archives, 1962), pp. 72-73; soup in Boston *Herald,* February 6, 1870.

34. City Doc. no. 48 (1875), *Report of the Chief of Police on the Cost of the Distribution of Soup; City Council Minutes,* April 7, 1873, p. 150.

35. *City Council Minutes,* November 24, 1873, p. 489.

36. *Ibid.,* November 24, 1873, p. 491; December 18, 1873, p. 531; November 20, 1873, p. 486.

37. *Ibid.,* December 11, 1873, p. 521; December 15, 1873, p. 538; December 26, 1873, p. 554; December 26, 1873, p. 567; for objections to Benthamism, see also City Doc. no. 28 (1874), *Reports on Elections of Overseers of the Poor,* which records Councillor Shaw's attempt to place some more liberal members on the board.

38. *City Council Minutes,* December 22, 1873, pp. 553, 555; December 15, 1873, pp. 536, 538.

39. St. 1874, ch. 374; *City Council Minutes,* November 16, 1874, p. 623; City Doc. no. 48 (1875), *Report of the Chief of Police on the Cost of the Distribution of Soup.*

40. *City Council Minutes,* December 15, 1873, p. 536 and November 27, 1874, p. 654.

41. Figures on lodgers, 1860-1875, in City Doc. no. 36 (1878), *Report of Commission on the Treatment of the Poor: Appendix,* p. xvii, indicate that 13,316 of the total of 17,362 in 1860 were foreign and 12,776 nonresident; in 1875, 38,778 of 62,740 were foreign, and 48,657 nonresident; antivagrant

provisions in st. 1866, ch. 235; failure of legislation in *Annual Report of the Secretary of the Board of State Charities* (1871), pp. 26-29.

42. Josiah Flynt, *Tramping with Tramps* (New York, 1901), pp. 6, 10, 67, and *passim;* Boston *Herald,* February 21, 1875; *Annual Report of the Secretary of the Board of State Charities* (1871), pp. 20-21.

43. Official view in *Annual Report of the Secretary of the Board of State Charities* (1871), pp. 21, 26-29; Savage view in *Annual Police Report* (1876), pp. 37-38; *Herald* view in Boston *Herald,* February 21, 1875; Langmaid hysteria, in, e.g., Boston *Globe,* October 2, 1875; *Annual Police Report* (1878), pp. 17-24. The Langmaid murder has a dual interest. On the one hand it represented the height of antitramp hysteria in New England, with police called in from as far away as Boston, and vagrants arrested as far away as Pittsfield—see Boston *Globe,* October 16, 1875. On the other, the trial of the man finally indicted, a local woodcutter, was one of the first to involve scientific identification of human blood. The experts, from Canada and Boston, were in sharp disagreement—see Boston *Herald,* January 12 and January 17, 1876.

44. *Annual Police Report* (1877), p. 32; *City Council Minutes,* December 4, 1876, pp. 663-664; City Doc. no. 36 (1877), *Report of Commission on the Treatment of the Poor,* pp. 38-39.

45. *Annual Police Report* (1878), p. 34; (1879), pp. 19-20. The work test was already a common practice among state and private institutions; see *Annual Report of the Secretary of the Board of State Charities* (1871), pp. 29-30.

46. Cobb, *Inaugural Address* (1875), p. 20; Prince, *Inaugural Address* (1877), pp. 25-28; Pierce, *Inaugural Address* (1878), pp. 20-23; *City Council Minutes,* February 21, 1878, p. 77. Prince's inaugural did not directly advocate a commission, but he later joined the movement; see *City Council Minutes,* May 31, 1878, p. 333.

47. *City Council Minutes,* February 14, 1878, p. 59; Boston *Herald,* March 16, 1878 and May 8, 1878.

48. Mayors in Bugbee, "Boston under the Mayors," pp. 276, 279, 281-282, 284. See also Charles C. Smith, "Memoir of Hon. Nathaniel B. Shurtleff, M.D.," MHS *Proceedings,* vol. 13 (1873-1875), pp. 389-395; James M. Bugbee, "Memoir of Hon. Samuel Crocker Cobb," *ibid.,* 2nd series, vol. 6 (1891-1892), pp. 318-330; James M. Bugbee, "Memoir of Henry Lille Pierce," *ibid.,* 2nd series, vol. 11 (1896-1897), pp. 386-410.

49. Wealth of aldermen in Boston *Herald,* December 18, 1874; for tickets see Boston *Transcript,* December 14, 1869, December 12, 1871, and December 11, 1874; Boston *Advertiser,* December 16, 1873; Boston *Transcript,* December 16, 1873, December 15, 1875, December 13, 1876, and December 12, 1877.

50. Occupations of common councillors in Boston *Herald,* January 5, 1877; for tickets see note 49, above.

51. Boston *Herald,* December 3, December 5, and December 15, 1875; Boston *Evening Transcript,* December 13, 1875.

52. George Potter, *To the Golden Door: The Story of the Irish in America*

(Boston, 1960), p. 281; Boston *Herald,* December 9, 1877; Boston *Evening Transcript,* December 11, 1872; Boston *Herald,* October 10, 1875.

53. Wirepullers in Boston *Herald,* November 19, 1881; Democratic gains *ibid.,* November 13, 1876; Irish policemen in *Annual Police Report* (1872), pp. 1-24, and (1880), p. 3; resentment of police appointments in Boston *Herald,* November 25, 1877.

54. Boston *Herald,* December 12, 1877; Bugbee, "Boston under the Mayors," pp. 288-289; Pierce, *Inaugural Address* (1878), pp. 20-23.

55. St. 1878, ch. 224, secs. 1, 3, 4, 6, 7, 8.

56. *Ibid.,* secs. 1, 3.

57. *Ibid.,* sec. 9.

CHAPTER ELEVEN

POLITICAL BREAKDOWN: CHARTER REFORM, 1878-1885

1. Boston *Herald,* June 21, 1878.

2. *Annual Police Report* (1879), pp. 3-4, 22-23, 62-65. The mayor was free to choose any citizen as probation officer, but for the next several years always appointed a member of the police department.

3. *Annual Police Report* (1879), pp. 101, 3-4, 5, 105.

4. *Ibid.,* pp. 48-49; Boston *Herald,* October 19, 1878; *Annual Police Report* (1879), pp. 2, 3.

5. *Ibid.,* pp. 48-49, 50, 57.

6. *Ibid.* (1880), pp. 13-14, 32, 3; *City Council Minutes,* March 15, 1881, p. 155.

7. *Annual Police Report* (1880), p. 37; (1879), p. 106; (1887), pp. 20-21; (1884), p. 30; st. 1884, ch. 320; House Doc. no. 24 (1886), *Second Annual Report of the Civil Service Commissioners of Massachusetts,* pp. 123-127; *Annual Police Report* (1885), p. 2.

8. Charles Phillips Huse, *The Financial History of Boston from May 1, 1822 to January 31, 1909* (Cambridge, 1916), p. 350; *Annual Police Report* (1883), p. 19; Boston *Herald,* February 10, 1883 and March 14, 1883; *Annual Police Report* (1880), p. 22 and (1885), p. 18.

9. City Doc. no. 166 (1881), *Reports of the Special Committee Appointed to Investigate the Official Conduct of the Members of the Board of Police Commissioners,* p. 5; *Annual Police Report* (1879), pp. 72-73 and (1881), pp. 32-33.

10. *Annual Police Report* (1882), pp. 26-27; (1883), p. 26; (1880), pp. 29-30; (1885), pp. 28-30. The aesthetic standards of the commissioners may be judged at the corner of Boylston and Hereford Streets, where stands the building once occupied by station sixteen.

11. *Annual Police Report* (1871), p. 44 and (1885), p. 29.

12. City Doc. no. 50 (1883), *Report in Relation to a Police Signal System.* For working of signal system when later adopted, see Boston *Herald,* October 15, 1905.

13. City Doc. no. 50 (1883), *Police Signal System,* pp. 3, 2; *City Council Minutes,* December 17, 1883, p. 592.

14. City Doc. no. 50 (1883), *Police Signal System,* p. 3.

15. Exemption from requirements in *Annual Police Report* (1879), p. 48; inspectors in Boston *Herald,* October 19, 1878; former jobs in *Annual Police Report* (1878), p. 2; new rule *ibid.* (1879), p. 68.

16. Boston *Herald,* October 19, 1878; *Langdon W. Moore: His Own Story of His Eventful Life* (Boston, 1893), pp. 26-30; *City Records,* XXV, October 12, 1857, 588; November 9, 1857, 639; Boston *Herald,* October 19, 1878.

17. *Annual Police Report* (1882), p. 11 and (1885), p. 11.

18. Homicides in Table IX of *Registry of Births, Marriages, and Deaths in Massachusetts for the Year Ending December 31, 1879* and its successor volumes through 1885; examiners in st. 1877, ch. 200; admiration in Boston *Herald,* June 11, 1899. See also Appendix I.

19. *City Council Minutes,* October 23, 1884, p. 463; October 23, 1884, p. 484; November 28, 1884, p. 551.

20. *Annual Police Report* (1879), pp. 19-20 and (1880), p. 17; *City Council Minutes,* January 14, 1884, pp. 13-14; *Annual Police Report* (1885), p. 11.

21. *City Council Minutes,* December 23, 1878, p. 716; City Doc. no. 29 (1860), *Report on the Powers and Duties of the Police in Relation to the Suppression of Tumults in Suburban Towns or Cities; City Records,* XXXVIII, March 12, 1860, 148-151; *Annual State Police Report* (1877), p. 6.

22. *City Council Minutes,* December 23, 1878, p. 717, and December 26, 1878, p. 730.

23. *Ibid.,* December 23, 1878, p. 716; Boston *Herald,* December 14, 1869; Boston *Evening Transcript,* December 11, 1872; *City Council Minutes,* January 2, 1879, pp. 773, 774, and December 23, 1878, p. 716.

24. *City Charter and Ordinances* (1882), p. 64.

25. For badges see, e.g., *City Council Minutes,* February 2, 1871, p. 31; for junkets and picnics see *ibid.,* November 3, 1879, p. 627 and November 10, 1879, p. 642.

26. *Ibid.,* October 20, 1879, p. 600; *ibid.,* November 3, 1879, p. 627; *ibid.,* November 10, 1879, p. 642.

27. *Ibid.,* March 10, 1881, p. 122; City Doc. no. 22 (1882), *Report of the Joint Standing Committee on Ordinances; City Council Minutes,* January 18, 1883, pp. 27-28; City Doc. no. 48 (1883), *An Ordinance to Amend Chapter 24 of the Revised Ordinances.*

28. Elections of mayors in Boston *Evening Transcript,* December 11, 1878, December 12, 1879, December 13, 1880, and December 14, 1881; Boston *Advertiser,* December 13, 1882 and December 12, 1883; police commissioners in *A Catalogue of the City Councils of Boston . . . Also of Various Other Town and Municipal Officers* (Boston, 1909), pp. 388-389; their other city jobs *ibid.,* pp. 371, 375, 376, 388, 394.

29. The Russell confirmation in *City Council Minutes,* June 27, 1878, pp. 408-411; later jobs by members of the commission in *A Catalogue of the City Councils of Boston,* pp. 378, 373, 838.

30. City Doc. no. 50 (1883), *Police Signal System,* p. 2; *City Council Minutes,* December 17, 1885, p. 850; City Doc. no. 50 (1883), *Police Signal System,* p. 4; *City Council Minutes,* December 17, 1885, p. 850.

31. Council members in *Municipal Register* (1890), p. 318; their party affiliations in Boston *Advertiser,* December 13, 1882; refusal of signals in *City Council Minutes,* May 8, 1884, p. 276; Martin's difficulty *ibid.,* May 1, 1884, p. 259, and October 20, 1884, p. 477.

32. *City Council Minutes,* June 28, 1883, p. 366; September 11, 1882, p. 403; June 5, 1879, pp. 398-400.

33. State-wide arrest totals in Frederick G. Pettigrove, "Statistics of Crime in Massachusetts," American Statistical Association *Publications,* new series, vol. 3 (March 1892), p. 9; Boston arrests through 1882 in *Annual Police Report* (1885), p. 16; other Boston arrests *ibid.* (1883), p. 7, (1884), p. 7, and (1885), p. 7.

34. St. 1880, ch. 221; *Annual Report of the Secretary of the Board of State Charities* (1880), pp. 27-31; *Annual Police Report,* pp. 28-29; st. 1881, ch. 276.

35. *Annual Police Report* (1879), p. 32, (1884), p. 26, (1881), pp. 27-28, (1879), p. 31, (1880), p. 26, (1881), p. 27, (1882), p. 23, (1883), p. 23, (1884), p. 25, and (1885), p. 25; doubling of fees *ibid.* (1884), p. 26.

36. Local option votes in Louis Epple, ed., *The Liquor Laws of Massachusetts and Digest of Cases Thereon* (Boston, 1912), p. 9.

37. *City Council Minutes,* May 19, 1881, p. 330.

38. City Doc. no. 166 (1881), *Reports of the Special Committee Appointed to Investigate the Official Conduct of the Members of the Board of Police Commissioners,* pp. 14, 1-2, 53.

39. *City Council Minutes,* December 29, 1881; Boston *Evening Transcript,* December 14, 1881; City Doc. no. 166 (1881), *Investigation of the Police Commissioners,* pp. 4, 8, 12.

40. City Doc. no. 166 (1881), *Investigation of the Police Commissioners,* pp. 14-23; *City Council Minutes,* April 3, 1882, pp. 194, 205; Boston *Herald,* April 4, 1882.

41. *City Council Minutes,* April 3, 1882, p. 206.

42. Formation of society, and sponsorship, in *New England Society for the Suppression of Vice, Annual Report for the Year 1879-1880* (Boston, 1880); help of police in Boston *Herald,* January 24, 1883; gambling interest in *Annual Report of the Society for the Suppression of Vice* (1883). The first few reports of the society are unpaginated; all hereinafter cited by date of issuance.

43. Liveried servants in Boston *Herald,* October 4, 1883; lottery in *Annual Report of the New England Society for the Suppression of Vice* (1884), p. 8; pools and warnings to businessmen *ibid.* (1885), pp. 9-10; *Herald* comment in Boston *Herald,* January 29, 1878.

44. History of Law and Order League in Boston *Herald,* July 19, 1885; liquor cases summarized in Public Doc. no. 15 (1880), *Annual Report of the Bureau*

of Statistics of Labor, pp. 130-189; difficulties of police prosecution in Boston *Herald,* January 19, 1877; figures for 1881-1882 *ibid.,* November 16, 1882. The district attorney had no investigating staff of his own until the twentieth century; see Boston *Herald,* March 9, 1906.

45. *Proceedings of the First Annual Meeting of the Citizens' Law and Order League of Massachusetts* (Boston, 1883), p. 7; *Annual Report of the Society for the Suppression of Vice* (1883).

46. *Ibid.* (1884), pp. 3-4, 9-11; *Proceedings of the Citizens' Law and Order League* (1884), p. 13; Boston *Herald,* July 19, 1885; *Proceedings of the Citizens' Law and Order League* (1885), pp. 8-11.

47. Boston *Herald,* November 8, 1882 and December 13, 1882; *City Council Minutes,* April 26, 1883, p. 240; Boston *Evening Transcript,* November 7, 1883; Boston *Herald,* December 12, 1883 and March 27, 1885. Martin's failure to appoint Col. Arnold A. Rand, an authority on etiquette and member of the Law and Order League, offers an ironic insight into the problems of reform. The city councillors righteously pointed out that some of his property was let to gamblers, a discovery he did not make until his name was up for the commission. See *City Council Minutes,* May 21, 1885, pp. 352, 355.

48. St. 1884, ch. 320; Boston *Herald,* November 7, 1884.

49. Boston *Herald,* December 9, 1877; February 7, 1885; December 12, 1883; December 10, 1884; January 16, 1885; February 7, 1885; March 16, 1885.

50. Huse, *Financial History,* p. 209; st. 1885, ch. 178; C. W. Ernst, *Constitutional History of Boston, Massachusetts* (Boston, 1891), p. 163.

51. St. 1885, ch. 226.

52. Boston *Herald,* April 14, April 16, and March 11, 1885.

53. Petition *ibid.,* January 16, 1885; newspapers in *Annual Report of the Society for the Suppression of Vice* (1885), pp. 12-13; Gove petition in Boston *Herald,* May 8, 1885; city council position in *City Council Minutes,* May 21, 1885, p. 357.

54. *Testimony of Hon. Augustus P. Martin . . . for a Metropolitan Police Commission* (Boston, 1885), pp. 4, 12; Boston *Herald,* March 19, 1885; *Testimony of Hon. Augustus P. Martin,* p. 14.

55. Boston *Herald,* March 19, 1885; April 17, 1885; March 22, 1885; March 18, 1885.

56. *Ibid.,* April 3, 1885 and March 25, 1885; *City Council Minutes,* February 24, 1885, p. 151; Boston *Herald,* April 17, 1885.

57. Boston *Herald,* March 14, 1885, June 10 and 12, 1885; st. 1885, ch. 338.

58. Workings of charter in Ernst, *Constitutional History,* pp. 164-165; rising expenditures in Huse, *Financial History,* pp. 332-339; quotation in Ernst, *Constitutional History,* p. 164.

CHAPTER TWELVE

EPILOGUE AND CONCLUSION

1. The Boston police were brought under state control later than in most other major cities where the experiment was tried; see Raymond B. Fosdick, *American Police Systems* (New York, 1920), p. 95. The fact that the transition was made only after most outstanding issues had been settled accounts for the relatively quiet way in which it was accepted; in New York City, in contrast, the municipal police, encouraged by the local authorities, conducted an armed battle with the metropolitan force which replaced them in 1857; see Augustine E. Costello, *Our Police Protectors: History of the New York Police from the Earliest Period to the Present Time* (New York, 1885), p. 102. In general, state control proved satisfactory enough that the acknowledged authority, in 1920, noted that for thirty years the force had "stood well in the lead of police organizations throughout the nation" (Fosdick, *American Police Systems*, p. 122). The lack of any deeply rooted differences contributed also to the long continuance of state control; the department was given back to the city only recently, by st. 1962, ch. 322.

2. Butler quote in Senate Doc. no. 1 (1883), *Address of His Excellency Benjamin F. Butler*, p. 45.

3. Last soup distribution in *Annual Police Report* (1890), p. 17; strike protection in *City Council Minutes*, February 17, 1887, pp. 179-180; signals in *Annual Police Report* (1886), p. 26.

4. Licenses in *Annual Police Report* (1886), p. 23. The men appointed by the state were subject, also, to the same temptations which had beset their predecessors. In 1888 the new head of detectives was fired for moral turpitude. In 1891, the commissioners were investigated for misconduct in the enforcement of the vice laws and other offenses, and the superintendent resigned after revelations of an unsavory association. See Boston *Herald,* July 6, 1888, February 8 and October 7, 1891.

Index

Abolitionists, 47, 58, 71-72, 85, 90, 132, 134; riots, 122, 123, 129, 130. *See also* Slavery

Abortion, 186

Adams, John, 40

Adams, Samuel, 201

Agassiz, Louis, 139

Aldermen, 13, 15, 18, 46; and police appointments, 75-86, 184; and police reform, 79-80, 98; and metropolitan commission controversy, 132; average experience of, 183; as "amateur politicians," 196; and amusement licenses, 207-208

Ambulances, police, 203

Amee, General L. C., 122, 126, 127, 130, 131-132

American Society for the Promotion of Temperance, 42, 43

Amory, Thomas Coffin, 129-130, 131-132

Andrew, John Albion, 123, 125, 154; and liquor law, 136, 138, 139, 140; and supralocal "constables of the Commonwealth," 137

Ann Street, 24, 27, 48, 93; and Tukey's raids, 65; and McGinniskin, 77; and poverty, 114; and prostitution, 116; Descent of *1851*, 116

Antimonopolists, 41, 45, 63

Anti-Slavery movement, *see* Abolitionists

Anti-Slavery Society, 123

Arms, 18, 103-104, 187-188, 223; and harbor police, 104, 134; and state police, 139; provided to patrol force (1884), 203

Armstrong, Samuel Turrell, 32, 45

Arrest, 7, 8, 16, 36, 187, 224; rise in (1840's), 49-50; mass, 68; by watchmen (1850's), 97; without warrant, 106-107, 186; statistics, 131-132, 225-229; and reasonable grounds, 107-108; for drunkenness, 113, 135; figures by divisions, 174-176

Arson, 56

Assault and battery, 6, 7

Association of New England Bankers, 160

Augustus, John, 50-51, 65, 168

Autonomy, 125

Back Bay, 99, 175-176; station sixteen, 203, 236

Badges, 100-101, 104, 108, 208

Baltimore, Maryland, 1; metropolitan commission, 119

"Bank sneaking," 144

Banking, 55-56

Banks v. *Farwell,* 106

Barnard v. *Bartlett,* 108

Barry, David, 206

Barry, James, 96

Batchelder, James, 91

Beacon Hill, 6, 175

Beacon Street, 99, 175

Beecher, Reverend Lyman, 42

"Beehive, The," 24, 30

Benevolence, police, 190-195. *See also* Charity

Bigelow, John Prescott, 59, 64, 71-72, 85, 86; on first Irish policeman, 76-77

Bill of Rights, 104

"Black Sea" (Negro vice district), 99

Blackmail, 57

Blake, James, 46

Board of Health, 5-6; enforcement of regulations, 6; abolition of, 13, 17

Boardman, Halsey J., 196

Boston, 1-2; incorporation controversy, 3, 13, 14; and town meeting, 4; constable in, 9-10; charter, 15, 216-219; appointment of policemen, 37; metropolitan police commission hearings (1861), 123-127, (1863), 128-133; war expenditures, 125-126; Great Fire of *1872,* 157, 172, 185; during 1870's, 161-162; School Committee, 170, 200; downtown district, 174, 176, 177, 178; per capita spending for government, 181

Boston *Advertiser,* 28; and police court reportage, 48

352.2
L26

Date Due
